UFOs
TODAY

*70 Years of Lies, Misinformation
and Government Cover-Up*

Irena McCammon Scott, Ph.D.

UFOs TODAY

By Irena McCammon Scott, Ph.D.

Edited by Philip Mantle

First edition published in 2017 by FLYING DISK PRESS

FLYING DISK PRESS
4 St Michaels Avenue
Pontefract
West Yorkshire
England
WF8 4QX

Published by
FLYING DISK PRESS

Designed and typeset by: Bob Tibbitts (iSET)

Cover artwork by Sebastian Woszczyk

ISBN: 978-0-9934928-4-6

CONTENTS

ACKNOWLEDGEMENTS

I AM greatly indebted to many people who made this work possible:

Special thanks to the initial UFOlogists I met: Bill Jones, J.D., former Senior Contracting Officer for Federal Projects at Battelle Memorial Institute (Battelle) and Ohio director of the Mutual UFO Network; Pete Hartinger, director of the Roundtown UFO Society; and Jennie Zeidman, who worked with Dr. Hynek, at Battelle, in Wright-Patterson AFB's Project Blue Book and in many similar positions. Additional investigators who originally brought me into UFOlogy include members of the MidOhio Research Associates: Frank Reams, pilot; Joe Stets, Battelle scientist; Rebecca Minshall; and Barbara Spellerberg, as did Warren Nicholson, Battelle scientist; Jean and Richard Siefried; Paul Burrell; and Paul Althouse.

Many others helped me in numerous ways including: Phyllis Budinger, MS, former Research Scientist from BP/Amoco and head of Frontier Analysis, Ltd.; writer, publisher and investigator Rick Hilberg; Budd Hopkins, artist, abduction authority and author of many seminal UFO books; and J. Allen Hynek, Ph.D., noted astronomer, writer, founder the Center for UFO Studies and Father of UFOlogy.

Others have included Walt Andrus, former head of MUFON, with whom I edited a number of MUFON Symposium Proceedings; and Leonard H. Stringfield, who told me about his intensive investigation of the UFO phenomena including Wright Patterson AFB. Julia Shuster, daughter of Walter Haut, who was the public information officer at Roswell Air Base who put out its press release about the UFO, told me a lot about the Roswell AFB and its UFO involvement.

Additional people who were of immense help included William Allen, Ohio State University professor emeritus who had published his own experience;

Dr J. Allen Hynek –
courtesy Rick Hilberg

Ray Palmer – courtesy Rick Hilberg

Robert Dixon, Ph.D., former director of the Ohio State University Radio Observatory "Big Ear," director of the Argus and SETI projects; and Walt Mitchell, Ph.D., former Astronomy Department professor at OSU. Also, State of Ohio seismologist Mike Hansen, Ph.D. Mr. Reams, William Carlisle and Rick Shackelford, with whom I worked at the Defense Intelligence Agency, were very helpful. French UFOlogist Jean Sider and I wrote several articles and the Cordell Hull family members helped with other stories. Kathleen Marden; Art Sill, Ph.D.; Brian Thompson, Ph.D.; Jan Aldrich; fire chief Virgil Newell and many others have provided great help. My family including John and Rosa Scott and Sue Postle, who tolerated and aided this work, were also very helpful.

Harley D. Rutledge, Ph.D., in his Project Identification study and discussions greatly aided my understanding of the phenomena. I wish to thank writers Lee Jansen, John and Jan Brinkerhoff and Randall Silvis, who helped me with the writing, Daniel Ramirez for the illustrations and Rick Hilberg, Phyllis Budinger and Jennie Zeidman for the photographs.

Still others who I have met or corresponded with include: Timothy Good, author and investigator; James Spangler; Jerry Ehman, Ph.D., discoverer of the "Big Ear" telescope WOW signal; Stanton Friedman, nuclear physicist and UFOlogist; Bruce Maccabee, Ph.D.; and Leo Sprinkle, Ph.D. Others include Beverly Trout, Robert Orndoff, Ph.D., Linda Wallace, John Carpenter, Stan Gordon, Diana DeSimone, John Timmerman, Bruce Widaman and Terry Hamilton. Bob Collins, who was operative "Condor" of the Aviary; and Donald Schmitt, Tom Carey and Anthony Bragalia, UFO authors, have spent much time exploring the field. Especial thanks also to the many very helpful and insightful witnesses and experiencers that I interviewed.

And many thanks to Bruce Ash-croft, Ph.D., Wright-Patterson AFB historian and archivist, who invited me to meetings, discussed UFOs with me, showed me around the AFB and helped me to understand much about UFOlogy.

WESTERN UNION

1206

Send the following telegram, subject to the terms on back hereof, which are hereby agreed to

To- Commanding General
Wright Field
Dayton, Ohio

Dear Sir:

You have my permission to quote, give out, or reprint my written account and report of nine strange aircraft I observed on June 24th, in the Cascade Mountains in the State of Washington. This report was sent to you at request some days ago. It is with considerable disappointment you cannot give the explanation of these aircraft as I felt certain they belonged to our government. They have apparently meant no harm, but used as an instrument of destruction in combination with our atomic bomb the effects could destroy life on our planet. Capt. Smith, co-pilot, Stevens of United Air Lines, and myself have compared our observations in as much detail as possible, and agreed we had observed the same type of Aircraft as to size, shape and form.

We have not taken this lightly. It is to us of very serious concern, as we are as interested in the welfare of our country as you are.

Boise, Idaho
Pilots License 333487
Kenneth Arnold

Kenneth Arnold telegram

Kenneth Arnold

PAGE 2   THE CHICAGO SUN. THURSDAY, JUNE 26, 1947

In These United States

Supersonic Flying Saucers Sighted by Idaho Pilot

Speed Estimated at 1,200 Miles an Hour When Seen 10,000 Feet Up Near Mt. Rainier

PENDLETON, Ore., June 25.—

NINE bright, saucer-like objects flying at "incredible" speed at 10,000 feet altitude were reported here today by Kenneth Arnold, Boise, Idaho, pilot, who said he could not hazard a guess as to what they were.

Arnold, a U.S. Forest Service employee searching for a missing plane, said he sighted the mystery craft yesterday at 3 p.m. They were flying between Mount Rainier and Mount Adams, in Washington state, he said, and appeared to weave in and out of formation. Arnold said he clocked them and estimated their speed at 1,200 miles an hour.

Inquiries at Yakima last night brought only blank stares, he said, but he added he talked today with an unidentified man from Utah, south of here, who said he had seen similar objects over the mountains near Utah yesterday.

"It seems impossible," Arnold said, "but there it is."
• • •

Chicago Sun newspaper detailing Kenneth Arnold sighting

vii

I wish to extend very special thanks to Philip Mantle, director of Flying Disc Press the publisher of this book, whose effort has very greatly improved all aspects of this work.

Cover design by Sebastian Woszczyk.

Artwork by Daniel Ramirez, Sebatian Woszczyk, Jason Chapman and Modo.

INTRODUCTION

U FOs are one of the most talked about—and least understood—phenomena of this century. However, the meaning of the acronym "UFO" is simple: the universal definition and the one used in this book, is "unidentified flying object." If it's flying and unidentified, it's a UFO. If it's flying and identified, then it's an "identified flying object" or IFO.

For example, if you see an unusual balloon and don't recognize it, it's an unidentified flying object, a UFO. As soon as you do recognize it, it becomes an IFO. UFOs can, in actuality, be many things: balloons, airplanes, lightning balls, snowballs, unusual atmospheric events, unusual people, spotlights and planets—anything that's in the sky. Often they are ordinary but unexpected.

A strange example of a UFO involved an ordinary truck driver in California named Larry Walters—a man who had long had a dream of flying. On July 2, 1982, Walters inflated 45 weather balloons with helium, rigged them to a lawn chair,

1

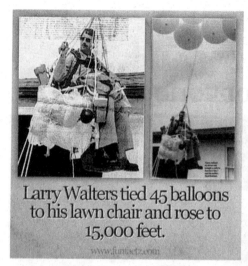

Larry Walters tied 45 balloons to his lawn chair and rose to 15,000 feet.

www.funfactz.com

Larry Walters' home-made balloon chair

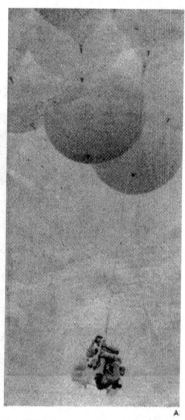

A

Up And Away

Larry Walters, sitting in his lawn chair appears a bit concerned as he watches hi last tether line break, shooting him skyward over California. Walters and his 45 weathe balloons soared 16,000 feet high, excitin two jetliner pilots.

Wright Patterson Air Force Base

UNITED STATES AIR FORCE
WRIGHT - PATTERSON AIR FORCE BASE
GATE 12-A
AFMC

Battelle

Battelle Memorial Institute

Hot Air Balloon. Japan's Project Fugo

asked some friends to help and took off into the sky. To everyone's amazement, he quickly ascended to 16,000 feet, a height where people generally need oxygen masks. Approaching TWA and Delta pilots saw him and didn't know what to make of what they saw. For a while, therefore, Walters was not only the first lawn-chair pilot, he was also a UFO. But after witnesses understood this unexpected sight, he became an IFO.

When Walters descended, he became entangled in a power line and briefly caused an outage in Long Beach—in effect, a UFO-related blackout. Walters could have won an altitude record for gas-filled clustered balloons, but he was unlicensed. After he finally landed, his friends said he was not the same man, possibly due to oxygen deprivation and the extreme cold at the high altitude.

What is intriguing about UFOs is that while many, such as the one above, are easily explained when the facts are known, some are difficult to identify and some have never been identified.

This work is unique because, until now nearly all UFO inquiries have focused on the witnesses and the sites of UFO sightings, with little research into our government's UFO investigations. This book deals with the history of UFO studies, but more importantly, it also investigates government UFO research and cover-up from the very first sightings to today. In these studies, my colleagues and I found much new material and significant "smoking guns."

Unlike other investigators, we not only probed, but worked in some of the most crucial organizations and facilities that conducted government UFO research. I have worked at Battelle Memorial Institute, the world's largest private scientific research and development organization located in Columbus, Ohio, that made the

A National Oceanic and Atmospheric Administration weather balloon after launching

best-known scientific investigation of UFO phenomena. I have also worked at the Defense Intelligence Agency (DIA), a manager of military intelligence for the US Department of Defense in Washington, D. C and UFO investigative agency, where I had top security clearances and worked with satellite photography in an Air Order of Battle section to identify all flying craft over a specific area. I have been stationed at Wright-Patterson Air Force Base (WPAFB), a government military installation near Dayton, Ohio and a chief government agency for UFO investigation. I have had top security clearances and unlike many who have used faked documents, I have been able to obtain authentic documents from the agencies themselves. I have also been acquainted with some of the leading government researchers, which resulted in a privileged track to understanding the organizations, the scientists and the research results. In addition, John Scott, my husband, worked at Area 51 and on the Nevada Test Site. I have visited and interviewed people at Roswell, White Sands Missile Range (WSMR) and similar places.

My UFO background consists of serving on the Mutual UFO Network (MUFON) Board of Directors, serving as a consultant in physiology and astronomy and serving as a field investigator for both MUFON and the Center for UFO Studies (CUFOS). My UFO publications include books, articles in the journals for both organizations and papers on UFOs in peer reviewed scientific journals. My work has been referenced and excerpted in several publications.

This work also includes some of the best classic and freshly investigated reports of UFOs from around the world. The variety of content involves cases I've personally investigated or re-investigated–either independently or with regional UFO research groups. Other reports include interviews with witnesses or their associates, Freedom of Information Act (FOIA) searches, information collected via site visits and experiences with government cover-up and UFO hoaxers. Some material comes from individual studies, published sources and database documents of the leading international UFO investigation groups—the Mutual UFO Network, Inc. (MUFON) and the Center for UFO Studies (CUFOS) or their local affiliates and from a local group MidOhio Research Associates (MORA).

This research has included smoking gun discoveries, such as our making the first report of possible UFO material having been analyzed by Battelle Memorial Institute and our new discoveries and unpublished information about other institutions. It incorporates new material about the Roswell event and the scientific analysis of other material such as an unexplained October 1973, sound that covered a large area of the Eastern US. It includes many first-hand, interviews and correspondence with some of the key original UFO investigators. Because many of these individuals are deceased and others quite old, it's vital to publish these accounts–for a historical record of the thought-processes of those who have made initial and continuing impact in the field of UFO studies.

I have tried to put my scientific training–including a Ph.D. from the University of Missouri Veterinary Medicine Department, post-doctoral work at Cornell, professorship at St. Bonaventure and much published research–to use in researching the phenomena based on scientific principles.

Moreover, UFO phenomenon is extremely complex. Although the phenomenon is generally associated with the idea of interplanetary visitation, it may actually consist of a variety of objects and activities that today's science does not yet encompass. In addition, the term UFO carries a lot of baggage–people associate it with Loch Ness monster, séances and similar activities. This book takes into account the inherent difficulties and controversies of UFO research.

Even if the phenomena in question were not extraterrestrial, is it is still vital to record this material because of the tremendous impact of UFO phenomena upon our civilization and psychology. As evidenced in popular songs, TV series and specials, best-selling books, films such as Stephen Spielberg's epics and concepts of the nations around the world uniting—not to mention the launching of the Space Age itself—the subject of UFOs has influenced our culture. Not only have most people heard of aliens and flying saucers, but the concepts of other worlds, of mysterious lights in the sky and of government cover-ups are part of the fabric of our current world-view.

UFOlogy, the study of UFO phenomena, is typically presented as being done by "true believers," and these believers are often viewed as different from scientists and other "rational thinkers." The reality is that UFOlogists, many of whom are well-trained scientists, collect information for various reasons and are interested in the information for numerous reasons. Some UFOlogists may work toward a goal of proving that extraterrestrials are real, but this is not my aim here. The material in this book is presented as empirical data, with some speculation about its meaning, but my intention is not to instill belief or disbelief, but to encourage examination.

And the subject is simply fascinating—not just because the exploration itself, with secret documents and Capitol Building sub-basements, carries the high adventure of a J. K. Rowlings or Dan Brown novel, but also because contact with other life forms is a real possibility in the future.

Perhaps collectively, the data herein with similar information from other sources may eventually yield some unifying threads or rational conclusions that will help to put the UFO mystery to rest.

CHAPTER ONE

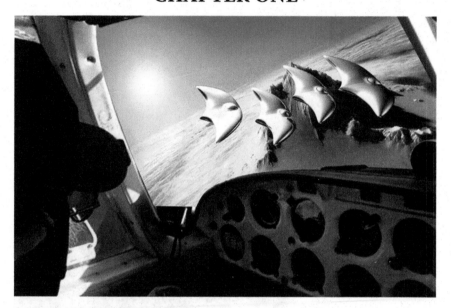

The Mystery Begins

ALTHOUGH UFOlogy is often viewed as beginning with a simple sighting, it actually began with events that could make the *Star Wars* movies seem dull by comparison. This complex series of events included an extremely good observation by a highly skilled aviator, similar observations by other credible witnesses and a reported crash—possibly with space-alien bodies.

Kenneth Arnold's June 1947 sighting inaugurated the public's idea of UFOs. Although this is normally viewed as a straightforward sighting of flying discs, this observation and the events surrounding it were complex and bizarre: plane crashes, intimidation by "Men in Black," and peculiar activities by representatives of government agencies. Other occurrences included poltergeist-like activity, large and small UFOs, magnetic and radiation effects, abduction phenomena and mind control.

Kenneth Arnold holding a drawing of the UFOs he observed

I've investigated Arnold's sighting by interviewing some of the principals and their family members, by searching WPAFB for documentation and hidden reports, by interviewing informants and by examining technical information about aircraft at the time of Arnold's sighting to determine whether he had viewed a secret government aircraft. Our group also interviewed a member of Arnold's family. She said that for many years no one in her family wanted to discuss flying saucers and that only recently had they taken any steps in this direction; she added that the family felt they'd been ridiculed and taken advantage of financially. They did not profit from Arnold's experiences.[1]

My research showed that although most UFOlogists view Arnold's sighting as the event that precipitated UFO study, the government actually might have begun to study the phenomena as early as January 1947. This claim is supported by a government document given to me by Dr. Bruce Ashcroft, who was then the official base historian at WPAFB, titled "Technical Report No. F-TR-2274-IA Unidentified Aerial Objects Project 'Sign' AMC Wright-Patterson Air Force Base (B1 UFO 1947)." This document describes the Arnold sighting and includes additional sighting information dating back to January 1947. In addition, the book Arnold co-wrote with Raymond Palmer, *The Coming of the Saucers*, reports that the government had been investigating discs for six months before Arnold's sighting.

These sources with Roswell and some even earlier 1930s material that we present later, suggest that a cover-up already might have been developing when Arnold's observation was reported. This information could help to legitimately explain some of the complex (but generally hidden and likely suppressed) events surrounding this initial observation and the UFO phenomena itself. (Additional information about Arnold's sighting, the evidence of collaborating sightings and reports of associated events were reviewed by Walter Andrus and myself in editing *The Fiftieth Anniversary of UFOlogy*, the proceedings of the MUFON 1997 International UFO Symposium.[2])

* * *

On June 24, 1947, Kenneth Arnold—an experienced, highly skilled pilot with more than 9,000 hours of flying time—made a detour to search for a transport airplane that had crashed near Mount Rainer in Washington State. Arnold did not find the transport plane. But what he did find was so astounding, it was described as "the most significant phenomenon discovered in this century, or even in the history of humanity" (100).[3]

Arnold's observation was precise, very credible and his assumptions were scientific and logical. His credentials, experience and credibility were impeccable. As founder of the Great Western Fire Control Supply Company of Boise, Idaho (which sold and installed fire suppression systems), Arnold routinely flew throughout the Pacific Northwest. He had devoted many of his flying hours to Search and Rescue Mercy Flyer efforts; these were demanding missions requiring expert knowledge. He flew a CallAir A-2, an advanced and difficult-to-fly airplane in those days. He was serious and even-handed, was not self-important about his later fame and publicity and retained a good reputation among those who knew him personally. Arnold's precise observations have withstood the test of time, but the Air Force's official analysis of his observations has not.

After Arnold, completed his search for the marine transport that had reportedly gone down on or around the southwest side of Mount Rainier, he flew directly toward the mountain. At approximately 9,500 feet, he reported that the air was as clear as crystal. He saw a DC-4 to his left and rear at approximately 14,000 feet.

Page 9

I have received lots of requests from people who told me
to make a lot of wild guesses. I have based what I have
written here in this article on positive facts and as far as
guessing what it was I observed, it is just as much a mystery
to me as it is to the rest of the world.

My pilot's license is 333487. I fly a Callair airplane;
it is a three-place single engine land ship that is designed and
manufactured at Afton, Wyoming as an extremely high performance,
high altitude airplane that was made for mountain work. The
national certificate of my plane is 33355.

Kenneth Arnold's report complete with a drawing of the objects he observed

10

After two or three minutes, he noticed a bright flash reflected on his airplane. Then to the left and north of Mount Rainier, he saw a chain of nine unusual objects flying from north to south at approximately 9,500 feet. They approached Mount Rainier rapidly and he assumed they were jet aircraft. Every few seconds two or three of them would dip or change course slightly, enough for the sun to strike them at an angle and reflect brightly. At first he was unable to discern their shapes or formation, but as they approached Mount Rainier he saw their outlines quite clearly.

The objects passed the southern edge of Mount Rainier, flying directly south to southwest down the hog's back of a mountain range. Arnold later stated that he estimated that their elevation had varied by approximately 1,000 feet one way or another but that they remained close to the horizon, which indicated to him that they were nearly at the same elevation as he was. He described them as flying like geese, in a diagonal chain-like line as if they were linked together. They appeared to hold a definite direction but swerved in and out of the area's high mountain peaks. He saw the objects pass a high, snow-covered ridge between Mount Rainier and Mount Adams; he noticed that as the first object passed the southern crest of this ridge, the last entered the northern crest about five miles away, so he estimated the chain of objects was five miles long. He timed the objects between Mount Rainier and Mount Adams and determined they covered 47 miles in 1 minute and 42 seconds. This was the equivalent of a speed of 1,657 miles per hour, significantly faster than any aircraft known at that time. Arnold described these events in *The Coming of the Saucers,* a book he co-wrote in 1952 with Ray Palmer:

> I observed . . . a formation of very bright objects . . . traveling at tremendous speed. . . . I watched as these objects rapidly neared the snow border of Mount Rainier, all the time thinking to myself that I was observing a whole formation of jets. . . . What startled me most . . . was the fact that I could not find any tails on them. I felt sure that, being jets, they had tails, but figured they must be camouflaged in some way so that my eyesight could not perceive them. . . . I observed the objects' outlines plainly as they flipped and flashed along against the snow and also against the sky. . . . The giant bulks of both Mount Rainier and Mount Adams made perfect markers. . . . They flew like a saucer would if you skipped it across the water. . . I knew where I was and they revealed their true position by disappearing from my sight momentarily behind a jagged peak that juts out from the base of Mount Rainier. (10-12)

* * *

Watch Out for Japanese Balloons, Sheriff Warns

"There is no assurance that Japanese balloons or bombs cannot reach this territory," L. P. Deuel, Nobles county sheriff, declared today. Deuel has been kept informed of the situation through the federal bureau of investigation and the seventh army service command, U. S. army.

News of the actual location of balloon bombings cannot be published at this time, Deuel emphasized, since such information might aid the Japanese.

However, it has been revealed that the bombs are of two types. One is filled with explosives which will start fires. The other is designed to explode and kill any persons nearby.

The balloons are equipped with devices intended to destroy the balloon in the air after it has dropped its bombs. Because of this, there may be no balloons to be found. The bombs sometimes are in the shape of a box about 18 inches square, Deuel said, and these are extremely dangerous.

Damage has been slight so far, but individuals finding strange objects are urged to keep away from them as they may be dangerous.

This advice is given to anyone finding a bomb or balloon:

Don't touch it.

Stay at least 100 yards away and keep others that distance away.

Leave a guard to keep people away from the balloon or bomb.

Report the location of the balloon or bomb to nearest sheriff or police officer.

Arizona Republic newspaper 1947

Several additional sightings occurred at about the same time as Arnold's. These were: the viewing of nine objects by a United Airlines pilot and crew; the photography of an object similar to Arnold's; an independent observation by a prospector; the Roswell incident; and a UFO report from near Maury Island. Together these incidents make up a complex web of story lines.

On July 4, Arnold's report was corroborated by a sighting of nine objects, very similar to the ones Arnold saw, flying over Idaho in a formation. These were witnessed by United Airlines pilot Captain E. J. Smith, his copilot, his flight attendant and the entire crew. According to the United Airlines witnesses, the objects were flat and circular. The first group of five appeared to open and close in formation before veering to the left. After the first group of discs disappeared, observers saw a second group of three together and a fourth by itself. These were flat on the bottom and circular and they seemed rough on top. They were larger than the observers' aircraft.

An independent observation of what is also thought to be the same objects as Arnold saw had been made in the same area at the same time. A Mount Adams prospector named Fred Johnson reported that on June 24, 1947, he had observed

Arizona Republic newspaper July 9th 1947

discs proceeding through the sky in a southeasterly direction and he watched one through his telescope. He noted that immediately before the sighting, his compass hand had begun to wave, but it corrected itself after the discs disappeared. He was in the right area at the right time to see Arnold's objects. Because his compass was affected as has also been noted in later sightings, it is unlikely these were conventional aircraft. Johnson's sighting holds a unique place in the history of the Air Force's UFO investigations, for it is listed as the first unexplained sighting.

On July 7, 1947, an Arizona man named William Rhodes had taken photos during his sighting of a disc-shaped object in the sky over Phoenix. This object circled a house, made a sideways turn and shot straight up. Rhodes felt the object maneuvered better and accelerated faster than any aircraft he knew of. Individuals who saw the photographs later thought the object resembled one of the objects Arnold had described.[4]

The Maury Island Incident of June 21, 1947 involved a Harold Dahl and his colleague, Fred Crisman, who claimed to be Tacoma, Washington, harbor patrol officers. They reported a disabled doughnut-shaped UFO that dropped rock-like material over Maury Island in Puget Sound near Tacoma. This event is now generally considered a hoax; however, aspects remain unexplained, such as that this hoax seemed to be associated with much more involved activities.

13

Arizona Republic newspaper 1947

14

A few days after Arnold's sighting, something reportedly crashed near Roswell, New Mexico. The first report from Roswell Army Air Field announced that a flying saucer had been captured. This news was broadcast around the world according to what Julia Shuster told me in an interview. She is daughter of Walter Haut who was the public information officer at Roswell Air Base who put out its press release about the UFO.[5] Under orders from superiors, officials at the air field quickly changed their story and from then on authorities denied not only that there was a UFO, but that there had been a crash at all

That report, however, is highly significant because if any group in the world were trained to identify a UFO, it would have been the officers and scientists in the vicinity of Roswell. The Roswell base was a highly sensitive area from the standpoint of security: in 1947 it was the home of the elite 509 Operations Group, the only military unit in the world able to drop nuclear weapons. The 509th Composite Group was created by the United States Army Air Forces during World War II and tasked with the deployment of nuclear weapons. In August 1945, it conducted the atomic bombings of Hiroshima and Nagasaki, Japan.

In addition, it was near the Army's White Sands Proving Ground (now WSMR) and the Alamogordo Bombing Range, where new weapons, balloons and rocket systems were being developed and where the first atomic bomb had been detonated two years earlier.

Arnold's sighting has been common knowledge among UFOlogists for many years, but today Roswell is probably better known to the public in general. Although representatives from the military and intelligence communities appeared oblivious to such incidents at the time, subsequent investigations suggest they were concerned when numerous civilians reported sightings of unidentified aircraft over America's well-protected air space. For example, Jan Aldrich, Bruce Maccabee and others many years later, reported that investigators searching through local newspapers discovered thousands of sightings throughout the US during that time. Contrary to what members of the intelligence community have claimed, FOIA documents prove that they were, alarmed.

* * *

The UFOs reported by Arnold, Smith and Rhodes share several important characteristics that were not found in aircraft of the time: high speed, large size, great maneuverability, disc- or crescent-shaped design, possible magnetic effects and soundlessness. These unique features are important because they refute the claim that the observers saw some kind of known aircraft and mistook them for UFOs.

Roswell Daily Record 1947

Based on descriptions given by Kenneth Arnold and William Rhodes, the discs were much faster than airplanes of that time. Arnold later said that even if he had misjudged the distance and therefore the speed of his objects, his margin of error was small. Even adjusting for a margin of error, he said, the objects were a good deal faster than any of that day's known aircraft.

The objects were also quite large. For example, the Rhodes photographs were taken with an upward-facing box camera at an estimated distance of about 1,000 feet and the object must have been large to have shown up in the photo as well as it did. The objects were highly maneuverable: Arnold said they swerved in and out among mountain peaks. The crescent-shaped design reported for some UFOs in these sightings is somewhat similar to today's stealth aircraft (stealth technology interferes with radar and this may explain why many UFOs evade radar detection). This crescent shape also does not match known aircraft of that era, although some German aircraft and some aircraft later flown in the US had a boomerang shape. The UFOs in these sightings were able to operate soundlessly or nearly so—a quality lacking in aircraft of that time and even in aircraft today.

Thus, these objects had performance characteristics beyond that day's and even today's aircraft. The UFOs that Arnold saw appeared horseshoe, or crescent-shaped. They didn't match the shape of any aircraft known at the time.[6]

* * *

Dayton's Wright-Patterson Air Force Base (WPAFB) inaugurated UFOlogy during the Roswell events and when the base's commanding officer asked Arnold

Rhodes photo – Air Force Analysis

to report his observations. Thus, its importance in the history of UFOs was established at the outset.

No one knew exactly what Arnold's flying objects were, but authorities wondered if they might be a new type of guided missile. By July 15, 1947, the commanding officer of WPAFB requested a full report from Arnold. Arnold, who was quite logical, wondered why the government had taken so long to contact him about something so potentially important. This by itself suggests that a cover-up was already in place, as also shown by Roswell. Later, two Air Force intelligence officers, Lieutenant Frank Brown and Captain William Davidson, visited Arnold from Hamilton Army Air Field in California. By now, Arnold had described the objects as looking like saucers skipping on water (this description was shortened to "flying saucers" by the media and led to the popular use of this expression). The two officers openly admitted they didn't know what flying saucers were and said they had never seen one, but were practically bug-eyed from watching for them.

This information indicates that although the government likely had been aware of UFO phenomena, these two initial investigators were not yet part of the cover-up. They were open, interactive and showed as much intrigue and enthusiasm as members of the public.

Arnold had received much correspondence and felt incapable of evaluating it. The officers were interested in this and, with his permission, collected mailings that concerned them. Arnold noticed the mail they selected was primarily from societies or organizations that were then starting investigations. It is unknown why the military was more interested in gathering information about civilian agencies than about UFO sightings and also unknown what they did with the information about the societies–could they have been interested in influencing them.

The officers impressed upon him that if anything unusual happened; he was immediately to contact them in care of A-2, Fourth Air Force, Hamilton Field, California. Arnold was impressed with the officers and described them as courteous and considerate. He particularly commented that they were not rude to him (though his report was sometimes ridiculed by others).

Meanwhile Arnold had received correspondence about other sightings including a letter from Raymond Palmer, who he didn't know. He later said that had he known Palmer was a science fiction editor and publisher, which were then looked down upon, he wouldn't have answered his letter. However, science fiction is a respectable and very profitable genre today and Palmer made important contributions. He was editor of *Amazing Stories*, the world's first science fiction magazine and he was a founder of the first ever serious magazine devoted to the paranormal, *FATE* which still exists today. Palmer asked Arnold to investigate the Maury Island Incident of June 21, 1947, which involved Harold Dahl and Fred Crisman. In response, on the spur of the moment, on July 29, although reluctant to go, Arnold readied his plane and at 5:30 a.m., he left for Washington State. He did not file a flight plan, tell anyone about the flight, or have a radio.

During this flight, he had a second UFO encounter. He observed a group of about twenty to twenty-five brass-colored objects that came to within 400 yards of him, appeared to be twenty-four to thirty inches in diameter, flipped as they went and seemed to have a terrific rate of speed. He attempted to photograph them. He noted that they had the same flight characteristics as the larger objects that he had seen. They were round, rough on top and had a dark or light spot on the top of each one.

Later he learned of simultaneous local reports about small flying disks. This initial sighting is highly significant, but little known, because among other factors it is not compatible with the general idea that UFOs were space ships.

On arrival in Tacoma, Arnold couldn't find a room, but finally as a lark called the most expensive hotel in town. To his amazement, he discovered that a hotel room had mysteriously been reserved in his name, but he hadn't made the reservation and had told no one about his flight there.

In the room's phone book, he found Dahl's name and called him. During his initial telephone conversation, Dahl seemed hesitant to talk to Arnold and it took Arnold about a half hour to convince him. Dahl told him to go back home and forget about the whole business.

When they met, Dahl reported elements that had not generally been associated with UFO phenomena until years later. For example, Dahl described what would today be called a "Men in Black" (MIB) encounter. He told Arnold that the day after his sighting, a stranger in a black suit called at his home and related his experience in great detail. He was puzzled because there were no other observers to this sighting. The man also told Dahl that if he wanted his family to stay healthy, he would shut up about his sighting. This initial UFO event also included radiation effects, such as when Dahl said he tried to photograph the objects there were spots on the negatives such as could be found on film exposed to x-rays and electromagnetic effects such as static on his radio. (Arnold later tested for radiation, by laying his camera near the debris, but did not detect anything unusual on the film.)

American Airlines pilot E. J. Smith joined Arnold in Tacoma, but because the two felt incapable of adequately investigating the incident (and probably suspected a hoax), they enlisted the aid of the Air Force's Lieutenant Brown and Captain Davidson. To do this, Arnold telephoned Brown at Hamilton Army Air Field and gave his name as requested. However, Brown refused to take the call on the military line and called Arnold back from an off-base pay phone. Brown and Davidson immediately flew to Tacoma.

During this July 31 visit to Arnold, Davidson drew a picture of the Rhodes object. Davidson said it was a drawing of one of several photographs his organization considered authentic. Davidson and Brown said the photograph had been received at the airfield in California where they were stationed. Brown said it came from Phoenix, Arizona and that there were prints of it at Hamilton, but that the original negatives had been sent to Washington, DC. Arnold found it to be nearly identical to one of the UFOs he'd seen that he thought differed slightly from the others, but which he had not specifically reported earlier.

The officers left Tacoma to fly back to California, although they were tired from the trip they needed to return for an airshow. They did not particularly want the debris that Dahl and Crisman claimed a UFO had dropped on Maury Island, but Crisman had insisted that they take a box of fragments. Arnold, who lifted the box into the plane, thought these fragments were heavier and differed in appearance from the ones Dahl and Crisman had shown him earlier (and later might have wondered if the box also contained a bomb). Arnold also thought that the officers suspected a hoax.

Early the next morning Crisman called Arnold to report that the officer's military B-25, which Arnold had heard had been under armed guard (for unknown reasons), exploded soon after takeoff. When Arnold and Smith checked they were told that both Davidson and Brown had been killed (although others on the plane parachuted to safety). Arnold reported that the next day the *Tacoma Times* carried a news story saying the plane was sabotaged to destroy the debris from Dahl's UFO.

Meanwhile Arnold had begun to wonder whether his Tacoma hotel room, the one mysteriously reserved for him, might have been bugged, because someone was passing almost verbatim information from discussions in his room, even when all four, Arnold, Smith, Dahl and Crisman were there–the *Times* reporter had them count noses while listening to the informant give information. Thus, more were involved in this activity than Dahl and Crisman. Arnold and Smith searched everywhere for a bug, which they called a Dictaphone and which may have been larger and wired in those days, but they couldn't find anything. This bug sounds as if it were beyond Palmer's capabilities, but if this activity were being carried out by the government it might have had much smaller and more sophisticated listening devices. In addition, the informant seemed very involved in the events. For example, it appeared the informant had given Davidson and Brown's names to the newspaper, twelve hours before the army released their identification, which also suggests that several people were involved in these activities.

Arnold and Smith later met with an intelligence officer, a Major Sanders, who took the position that the government commonly takes today—he attempted to "debunk" or discredit their ideas. For example, he insisted the B-25 crash was an accident, a stance Arnold and Smith considered odd because the crash was still under investigation. He also told them that the debris was slag, but he none-the-less collected every piece of it.

* * *

UFOlogy not only explores UFO events themselves; it attempts to discover what various government entities know about UFOs and whether and how they are covering up information. One investigative method involves researching simultaneous events, comparing them and examining behaviors of government representatives, for example, reactions of intelligence officers who had contact with Kenneth Arnold. It's possible to do this for the Arnold, Smith and Johnson sightings, the Maury Island incident and additional events mentioned in this chapter. Because of the early nature of these incidents, it's also possible to determine government attitudes about UFOs when the phenomena first came to the public's attention, their cover-up strategy and perhaps some of the motives for this. And because some evidence of early government study now exists, the events that had been attributed to mere happenstance might be interpreted as possible cover-up activity, as discussed below.

The COMING
of the SAUCERS

By Kenneth Arnold & Ray Palmer

Ray Palmer & Kenneth Arnold book –
'The Coming of the Saucers'

The request by WPAFB's commanding officer for a full report from Arnold and the subsequent interaction with him by two Air Force intelligence officers, is evidence that the US government was interested in UFOs from the beginning. In addition, the fact that prints of the Rhodes photograph had been sent to Hamilton Army Air Field in California while the original negatives had been sent to Washington, DC., shows that a higher level, but unknown, agency in Washington was also investigating UFOs early on. But by as soon as July 1947, authorities had begun a debunking campaign—as evidenced by the WPAFB's delay when asking Arnold for a report, by Captain Brown not taking Arnold's phone call on-base and by Major Sanders' behavior.

During their first meeting with Arnold, officers Brown and Davidson cautioned him to be quiet about UFOs. By July, without even knowing why Arnold was phoning him, Brown refused to take Arnold's call on a military telephone line and returned the call from an off-base pay phone. The previously very enthusiastic, Brown by then appeared to want to hide his UFO investigation from someone in the government. This suggests Brown's office phone may have been monitored, or there may have been an internal change (or dissent) in military intelligence involving the monitoring of personnel or involving UFO investigations, or Brown knew more than he should. By the time Sanders came into the picture, the attitude of government representatives seems to have changed from interest in UFOs (however guarded) to debunking. Indeed, after meeting Sanders, Arnold described him as a phony dressed up in a lot of sheer intelligence on how psychologically to handle men.[7]

* * *

These events contain many complex elements that suggest a high level sophisticated cover-up may have already been developing. (Although Maury Island is now generally considered a simple hoax by Dahl and Crisman, for example it appeared that they didn't even have a seaworthy boat, some of their activities might suggest it to have been associated with a larger event with more people involved.)

For example, how did someone know to reserve a room for Arnold, when he told no one he was coming and its being in the most expensive hotel might suggest the cover-up was well financed. Was there a bug in Arnold's room that appeared to be above that day's technology? How did the MIB idea enter this story, when it did not officially enter UFOlogy until 1955? Why were radiation and electromagnetic effects among the first reported characteristics and why would Dahl know about this—would someone have told Dahl to include these elements in his story.

Arnold initially contacted Dahl because he found Dahl's name in his hotel room phone directory, but when he tried to contact Dahl soon afterward, he was told there was no such name in the directory. Did someone manufacture a fake phone directory for his room only? Was Dahl really a local resident and harbor patrol officer? Were the "crew members" that Crisman and Dahl introduced Arnold and Smith to, actually their workers or plants? Also, Dahl and Crisman seemed to disappear quickly after the events, an activity that is sometimes associated with government cover-up.

Dahl also showed Arnold the UFO fragments in his "secretary's" house. She was there at the time doing bookwork, with receipts and other paper work covering the kitchen. The house furniture included a piano, large radio and other items. Why didn't Dahl have the fragments in his own house? Could she have also been a plant? If these people and the newspaper informant were plants, then a number of people took part in the hoax and it wasn't just Crisman and Dahl's simple hoax.

In addition, the UFO descriptions contained many strange elements besides their soundlessness and speed. Although the discs that Arnold witnessed have classically been described as smooth, sometimes domed, saucer-shaped objects, this is not what he saw. His were crescent shaped or somewhat oval and they appeared rough on top, as were the small UFOs he saw and the objects Smith observed. This topside roughness is not an aircraft characteristic (it is almost essential to have an aerodynamic upper surface to provide the lift that keeps the craft in the air). Smith also reported that the objects seemed to merge, disappear and then reappear. Their ability to seem to flip in unison and careen around mountaintops also seemed strange.

Arnold's sighting of the small discs probably would be impossible to hoax and it was odd that they so closely resembled the larger ones.

Why were mind control and poltergeist aspects included in this story? For example when Arnold took off after a refueling stop on his way home, his engine died at a low altitude. He had been very careful and even had others check his plane, because of the recent crashes. Only because he was a good flier did he survive. He thought the only way this could have happened would be for him to have turned off the gas himself, thus, he might have been subject to mind control, although his comments indicate he had not heard of this. He thought his mind in some peculiar way was being controlled or dictated to and that the idea it could have caused this to happen would seem perfectly preposterous to anyone who had not experienced what he had just experienced. He had no idea from where such mind control would have come. Likewise, it is unknown why such mind control (that was very significant because it could have killed Arnold) was used and how it could have been implemented.

Arnold expressed the idea of hypnosis and other forms of mind control several times. For example, Dahl had shown Arnold the UFO fragments in "his secretary's" house. But when Arnold made a return visit the next day, the house was completely empty, even the door was filed with cobwebs and it looked as if no one had been there for years. He was totally baffled. Could Arnold's original visit have represented some early form of abduction activity?

Arnold, who was very concerned about whether people believed him, said that he saved all evidence such as hotel receipts and others to show that his reports were true. His accounts of such activities as possible mind control and small discs might also support this, because he reported them even though they might make the accounts difficult to believe and thus it would not serve him to make them up.

The second plane crash (or maybe third if the transport airplane is counted) was another oddity. Arnold was given a United Press message that carried a story about Dick Rankin, one of the most celebrated stunt pilots in the US. Rankin had had his own UFO encounter a few weeks before (Arnold knew the Rankin family). In the message, he claimed that two intelligence officers named Brown and Davidson had interviewed him about his encounter and that in his opinion they were very close to learning the truth about the UFO mystery. Thus, he said that he was sure that they were in danger–he had even warned Brown and Davidson to get to a safe place. Nobody seems to have known why Rankin thought this (it appeared obvious

Roswell UFO crash site

that Brown's office was being monitored). Reports said that somebody was trying to kill them because they knew too much about UFOs. Why had their plane been under guard? It was also unclear why the two officers died, rather than parachuting.

Why was so much murder and danger, such as that of Brown and Davidson and Arnold in this story? And if this were a hoax why did so many people warn Arnold off, for example, Dahl warned Arnold several times that the saucer business is the most complicated thing you have ever got mixed up in and told him to go home (which would be odd for a hoaxer wanting to make money). This was good advice because Arnold almost did get killed. Arnold said that he and Smith both had a feeling of being watched or in danger. Many others thought that Arnold, Davidson and Brown and others were in danger. Ted Morello, from the *Tacoma Times* who had talked to the informant, said that the newspaper had tried everything to trace the informant's calls, but drew a blank. This was highly unusual because he was in the news business and thoroughly family with the territory. He told Arnold and Smith that they were involved in something beyond the newspaper's power to find out about. He told them to get out of town as fast as possible. Arnold had such a strong sense of danger, that he had called his family to tell them he might not make it home and worried that his house was bugged. Arnold and Smith had waited for the government to contact them after Brown and Davidson's crash because they were the last people who saw them, but were never contacted. Since it is routine to contact the last people involved, it suggests that the government already knew much about the crash. I did some further research on Crisman and found that portions of his background were also mysterious.[8]

How did Dahl know so much about UFOs then that wasn't known by others until many years later? Could someone have used him to plant these ideas?

Although Crisman and Dahl were obviously a part of a hoax and some think Palmer was in on it also, some aspects appeared to have been much more complex than done by simple hoaxers. It was obvious that others were involved. Who were they and what was their motive? UFO investigations were full time work for Brown and Davidson. Were they killed because they knew too much about UFOs or because they knew too much about the government? Why was the government monitoring Brown, why was his airplane under guard and why did people think they were in danger? Since it appeared that the only thing that entered the guarded airplane was the box of slag that Arnold lifted in (that they didn't want), could this have contained an incendiary device? Could these deaths have frightened other government workers, or made them cautious about examining UFO phenomena?

Information from other sources differs about when the cover-up began. Concerning government investigation, several sources report that studies started at the beginning of 1947. These were scientific studies, done by such people as Col. Howard M. McCoy, who later was heavily involved with Project Sign. Dr. Michael Swords reported that in the summer of 1947, UFO accounts were coming from everywhere but investigation, which involved WPAFB, the Pentagon and the FBI, was disorganized. In addition, little interest came from the higher echelons. The Pentagon first involved WPAFB about mid-July (this is when they contacted Arnold although someone already had appeared to cover-up Roswell). About July 28-29, McCoy was ordered to send a top-level assessment to eventually go to the Pentagon (this was around the time Brown and Davidson traveled to Tacoma). In September 1947 an investigation setup was ordered. This evolved into Project Sign, which became official in January 1948. At that time (and maybe now) the government agencies did not act in unison—the WPAFB group took a pro–extraterrestrial position, whereas the Pentagon took the opposing side and the Washington DC group eventually won out.

However, others noted cover-up activities began much earlier. England's Harold Wilkins wrote that although Arnold's sighting spread like wild fire, soon afterward censorship began and overnight saucer stories stopped appearing in the newspapers. He thought this censorship came from Washington, DC. Capt. Edward Ruppelt reported that by the end of July 1947, the UFO security lid was down tight. Donald Keyhoe said that UFO investigation had begun in January 1947, and that on July 4 the Air Force stated that no further investigation was needed; it was all hallucination. Obviously, the cover-up involved the Roswell events, including any related secret craft that were being tested at that time.

However, it is most likely that the UFO work was born classified. For example at Battelle, the Stork projects were not initially tied to UFO work. UFOs were originally investigated by the organization already studying foreign technology in Battelle.

It is also likely that the same type of organization existed in the ATIC/FTD divisions of WPAFB. Projects, such as the studies of foreign technology, were already

USAF crash test dummies

highly classified, before UFO information arrived (as discussed in Chapter Ten). Although such cover-ups receive the generic label of government cover-up, it appeared likely that most components of the government were not in on what was going on. It is also evident that the Arnold cover-up was very sophisticated, for not even experienced news organizations found out anything or even traced the calls. Even today, it is unknown what agency was involved.

These many elements of the story have caused several, such as Jenny Randles in *The Truth Behind Men in Black: Government Agents – or Visitors from Beyond*, to wonder if a complex cover-up existed around the time of Arnold's sighting, although this idea has generally been discounted. However, because some evidence exists that there was time to prepare a cover-up, one can legitimately speculate that an intelligence operation could have been in place. Perhaps it was set up specifically to discredit Arnold, who was then the world's most important UFO witness. It would diminish his credibility and dispel the idea that UFOs were real. It addition, it made it appear very dangerous to investigate the subject–the crash of Brown and Davidson and Arnold's near crash. Thus, it appeared some form of very complex cover-up could have been in place from UFOlogy's beginning, although it was unknown whose cover-up it was. The evidence also suggests that the phenomena itself might be much more complex and difficult to investigate than most even today would suspect.

These initial events have provided the framework for viewing UFO phenomena all through its history, including the impression that it is composed of physical space ships from other planets. However much evidence from the beginning shows that it is much more complex than this. Thus, even today this picture has a defining influence on public perception and obstructs investigation.

* * *

Many Air Force intelligence officers who investigated the initial saucer reports from the summer of 1947 through 1948 treated all of the sightings, including Arnold's, seriously. Arnold's sighting was included as unexplained in a top-secret intelligence memorandum compiled by Air Force intelligence during the late fall of 1948. However, in 1948 General Hoyt Vandenberg rejected the Air Force's conclusion, presented in an "Estimate of the Situation" report. This report had concluded that saucers were interplanetary vehicles (all traces of this report seem to have disappeared). In so doing, he established an Air Force policy that the "interplanetary hypothesis" was to be rejected, but many knowledgeable investigators hotly contested this rejection. Although people viewed a generic government cover-up, there was division among government agencies–possibly resulting in the deaths of Brown and Davidson. There seemed to be a hidden Washington agency in control that possibly acted because it had prior knowledge about UFO phenomena, as will be discussed in Chapter Four, or that wanted a cover-up for other reasons. In addition, the UFO phenomena became the providence of the military, rather than of the scientific sphere, which resulted in its being given security classifications, such that information was withheld from and false information given to the public.

During the early years of UFOlogy, explanations for Arnold's sighting were proposed by two scientists with close connections to the Air Force project: J. Allen Hynek, Ph.D. and Donald Menzel, Ph.D. Hynek based his analysis on assumptions about the visual capabilities of the human eye; because of these assumptions, the Air Force eventually settled on "mirage" as the explanation for Arnold's sighting. These assumptions are now thought to be incorrect.[9] Indeed, if Hynek had accepted as accurate Arnold's estimates of distance and velocity, the early history of the UFO subject would likely differ from what actually occurred and the government might have been less likely to reject the interplanetary theory. (Hynek later reversed his skeptical stance toward UFO reports and, in 1973, he founded the Center for UFO Studies, CUFOS, formerly a leading international UFO investigation group.)

Despite the evidence of cover-up, the cultural effects of the sightings by Arnold, Smith, Johnson and Rhodes were abrupt, extreme, intense and world-changing. Within days, Arnold's sighting made world news. And almost immediately, whether extraterrestrial phenomena existed or not, the human paradigm began to change. We began to view ourselves as possibly having contact with beings from another world. We began to entertain the idea that we might travel from our own world to meet these beings. And within 10 years of the Arnold sighting, we sent rockets into space.

* * *

This information could change the entire field of UFOlogy, because even modern ideas have always been based upon these initial events. However, these events might have been much different than thought. This also suggests that the phenomena itself might be much more complex and difficult to investigate than most suspect even today.

CHAPTER TWO

Crucial Facilities – Wright Patterson Air Force Base and Battelle Memorial Institute

AS lightning from a raging storm lit tumbleweeds whipping across the desert, an object soared overhead. It crossed the sky emitting a blue light with the intensity of an arc welder; then its trajectory changed and it slammed into the ground near Roswell, New Mexico.

Today the Roswell and WPAFB story are so deeply embedded in our culture that almost everyone has heard of the Roswell UFO crash, secret WPAFB vaults, a "Blue Room," and associated accounts, such as WPAFB's Hangar 18–the unloading point for Roswell debris. As a result, a Roswell television series debuted in 1999. Moreover, Hangar 18 stories have flourished and many of these are reflected in a film called *Hangar 18* and many additional TV shows, books and magazine articles. My colleague William (Bill) Jones, J.D. and I have been fortunate enough to actually examine some of the secret areas involved in this, as follows:

WPAFB became a part of the UFO picture immediately, not only because of Arnold's experience, but also because the first UFO reports stated that some Roswell debris was sent to WPAFB. Some evidence exists that some may have later been sent from there to Battelle Memorial Institute in Columbus. Although today Roswell may be the best-known event associated with UFO phenomena, it was generally unknown to the public until Berlitz and Moore's 1980, *The Roswell Incident,* was published. This chapter examines the evidence behind these accounts.

Even today, Roswell, WPAFB, Battelle Memorial Institute and some Washington DC agencies are the most crucial government organizations known to be associated with UFO study. They were the initial government organizations doing the investigations, the ones to receive the original information and possible materials and they continue to show activity in relation to the subject. They are the main institutions showing smoking gun evidence of serious government involvement with UFO phenomenon. Such smoking-gun results are vital in UFO studies because ultimately they can support the reality of UFO phenomena.

Aerial view of Wright Patterson Air Force Base

Moreover, even if Roswell turns out to not be an extraterrestrial event, it still appears that some kind of debris was studied and that Roswell debris was sent to WPAFB. Thus, this investigation into material artifacts is relevant, whether or not it concerns Roswell debris.

In these investigations, I discovered some smoking gun evidence that debris existed and it was sent to WPAFB, although the Roswell story is considered legend. We also discovered suggestive evidence for the underground crypts at WPAFB, where some say aliens have been stored. We have entered the highly secured area where UFO study was and still may be conducted.

Jones and I have unique backgrounds for investigations of both these stories and these facilities. Although very few UFOlogists have visited WPAFB or Battelle, we have worked in them. I was stationed as a civilian at WPAFB several times for work-related activities and was employed by Battelle. Bill Jones, an attorney and decades-long Battelle executive, was Senior Contracting Officer for Federal Projects at the Institute and the Ohio director of the Mutual UFO Network (MUFON). We've been invited to WPAFB for meetings with researchers working with UFO data and we've entered some of the base's most highly secured areas. We've also conducted interviews with WPAFB employees, families of former Project Blue Book personnel and we've listened to taped interviews with directors and others involved with that project. I have visited Roswell also and interviewed several researchers there, such as Julia Shuster, who helped me greatly to understand the events.

Although most researchers have been unable to gain even a toehold of information from such government agencies, several additional people went to great trouble to help us. One, Dr. Bruce Ashcroft, was chief historian at the National Air Intelligence Center (now NASIC), at WPAFB. Dr. Ashcroft had excellent credentials, numerous publications, was an assistant professor and had expertise in historical research. We met him through his interest in UFOs–once at a meeting I saw someone

Bill Jones on the left and Bruce Ashcroft on the right

in front intensively taking notes. Curiosity made me move up beside him to observe him and this is how we met. He gave freely of his official and personal time to assist us and unfortunately died at the young age of 56. It would be very difficult to find another government authority like him.

Bruce Ashcroft

* * *

Although it is often viewed as legend, I discovered hard, smoking gun, evidence that Roswell debris was sent to WPAFB. This is based on a discovery I made in Roswell museum archives. I found the original radio broadcast from the Roswell Army Air Field, which reported that

31

William Brazel, who turned the debris over to the Air Force, found crash artifacts. The broadcast said artifacts were sent to Fort Worth, Texas and from there, according to Brigadier General Roger Ramey, they were to be flown to the Army Air Force Research Center at Wright Field (today called Wright Patterson Air Force Base) near Dayton, Ohio.

The initial radio broadcast about the debris provided this smoking gun. During his broadcast, radio announcer Joe Wilson said on-air that a few minutes ago, he had just spoken to the officials at Wright Field and they were expecting a delivery but it had not yet arrived. It was shipped to the AAF research center at Wright Field Ohio. Wilson noted that Colonel William Blanchard refused to give details of what the disc (the Roswell UFO) looked like.[10]

The announcer's statement on-air that he had just talked to WPAFB about the delivery provides definite hard evidence that the debris was flown to WPAFB.

The Roswell newspaper then published a headline article about the event stating that after the intelligence office had inspected the instrument it was flown to higher headquarters.

And on July 8, 1947, Walter Haut was ordered by the base commander, Colonel William Blanchard, to draft a press release to the public, that announced that the United States Army Air Forces had recovered a crashed "flying disc" from a nearby ranch.

These events instantly associated WPAFB with UFO phenomena. WPAFB is one of the agencies where the first publicized reports of UFO phenomena were collected and investigated and it once housed Project Blue Book, the Air Force's chief investigatory unit for UFO matters. (Walter Andrus and I reviewed additional information about the Roswell event in editing *UFOs in the New Millennium,* the proceedings of the MUFON 2000 International UFO Symposium.)[11]

* * *

Although Hangar 18 may be mythical, Roswell debris was likely unloaded into an actual hangar. A long time Dayton resident told us that the Roswell hangar is the second from the left in a group of connected hangars near the runway in Area B.[12] These hangars can be seen from the public area of the Air Force Museum (they are the buildings that resemble drums cut in half and laid down in a series.). On current maps, this group of hangars is collectively identified as Building 4 A-E; thus, if what the Dayton informant said were true, the so-called Hangar 18 would be Building 4, B Hangar.

This informant said that the airplane carrying the Roswell artifacts landed and parked by the northeast end of the runway in front of the Hangars (Building 4 A-E); the Roswell debris was then unloaded into the second, or B, Hangar. This would seem logical, because in 1947, this runway was active and the military did indeed unload aircraft into these hangars. Perhaps the second Hangar from the left, B Hangar, is where authorities initially unloaded the Roswell debris.

When I looked over this secured area from on-base, a runway still existed to this area, in fact, I accidently drove onto it and think it is still active.

Another possible cause of the Hangar 18 rumors might be that Roswell artifacts were taken to Building 18-A, a large, nondescript brick structure centrally located in Area B several blocks north of the hangars. In addition, debris may have been taken to the Air Technical Intelligence Center (ATIC) and to many other places as well. Any alien bodies might have been taken to the Aero Medical Laboratory.

According to many reports, a B-29 bomber with four armed MPs aboard carried one or more crates of debris from Roswell to Fort Worth, Texas and subsequently to WPAFB. Reports claimed that at least one of those crates was approximately 12 feet long, 5 feet wide and 4 feet high and that the loading consumed eight hours prior to take-off for Fort Worth Army Air Field (later Carswell Air Force Base and now Naval Air Station Joint Reserve Base, Fort Worth). Some reports said that the crates were specially made and unmarked, that each crate had to be checked for size and that the crew had to know how to position the crates in the relatively small aircraft. Because a B-29 is a bomber that does not typically carry cargo, it is possible the crates were built on the spot to fit into the plane.

At the National Museum of the US Air Force at WPAFB, Bill Jones and I measured a modified B-29s on display, which had been cut open so people can walk through it. Our measurements confirmed that a crate of the reported size could fit—albeit snugly—in a B-29. Two crates could fit as well, because the aircraft has two bomb bays, one fore and one aft, which could accommodate them.

The plane reportedly flew at a very low altitude and this suggests the crates might have carried something other than inanimate debris. However, the plane might have flown at this altitude because the four MPs may have been riding in the unpressurized areas where the crates were stowed. Some reports say additional crates were loaded in larger C-54 transport planes that could easily have carried crates of the reported size.

* * *

As further smoking gun activities, Jones and I may have actually viewed a part of the area where the Roswell and possibly other debris is said to have been stored at WPAFB. A classic UFO legend is that alien debris is allegedly kept in huge underground tunnels, hangar-sized underground areas, cryogenic chambers and vaults.

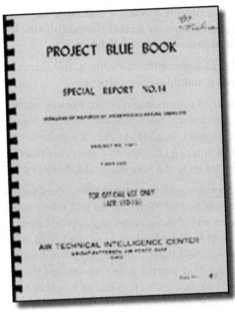

PROJECT BLUE BOOK

SPECIAL REPORT NO.14

Project Blue Book

According to several WP employees that we interviewed, the vaults were supposedly built for storage and evacuation. They were designed to protect sensitive material against earthquakes, missiles, explosions, radiation, tornados and other disasters, as will be described in Chapter Nine. Some of these vaults were built during World War II. Some were reportedly constructed to preserve photographic materials and these or similar vaults allegedly later housed alien artifacts and bodies. Tim Shawcross reports in *The Roswell Files* (1997) that alien artifacts and bodies were stored in cryogenic suspension at a secret WPAFB hangar in a location known as the Blue Room. Author Robert M. Collins and others have told me that one cryogenic vault is north of and connected to Building 620 (the Avionics Laboratories) and to Building 739.

As examples of smoking evidence, on March 18, 1994, Bill Jones and I were able to go into and observe this restricted area. We saw that Building 620 has doors wide enough to accommodate trucks.

We've also seen this location at a time when extensive digging was being done and a portion of this digging was in the area of these buildings and

seemed to follow the underground tunnels that several informants have reported. Because of the high dirt piles and heavy digging equipment, it appeared that deep areas were being dug, as I was able to photograph. I've also seen work-related materials about underground chambers to be described later.

One source reported that while working at WPAFB for a private contractor, he'd seen workers open a cement manhole-like cover on the floor of one of the Wright Field buildings.[13] The opening was the entrance to a huge vault or tunnel. He added that WPAFB had trouble with flooding in its tunnels and that several were full of water.

An informant raised in the Dayton area told Jones and me that it's common knowledge among residents that WPAFB houses alien artifacts. He recalled that people in his neighborhood, where many WPAFB personnel lived, openly talked about this. Another informant observed that people who work on the base still talk about this subject but do so informally because such information is classified.

* * *

Ohio UFO researcher Leonard String-field (1920-1994) has spent much time examining WPAFB. From 1953 to 1957, he investigated UFO activity in cooperation with the Air Force. His books include *Inside Saucer Post, 3-O Blue* and *Situation Red. The UFO Siege!* He published a series of six status reports to update information on this subject and served as the Director of Civilian Research, Interplanetary Flying Objects (CRIFO—one of the world's largest research groups during the mid-1950s).[14]

Stringfield told me that the existence of underground tunnels and facilities at WPAFB is a well-established fact. He noted

The late Leonard Stringfield – UFO crash retrieval researcher

that although these were not constructed for the storage of alien artifacts and bodies, some have been put to that use. He maintained records of a number of accounts involving people who viewed alien bodies at WPAFB and elsewhere and thought that some of these visits included tests to see how people would react to the sudden revelation that space aliens are real. He was probably the first expert on UFO crashes and retrievals. Much of his information came from informants at WPAFB.

Stringfield has also recounted a number of informant stories about alien bodies at WPAFB. In one account, a dying Cincinnati woman told UFO researcher Charles Wilhelm she had top security clearances at WPAFB and had seen two saucer-shaped spacecraft—one intact and one damaged—in a secret hangar. She said she'd personally handled the autopsy report paperwork for the bodies of two small

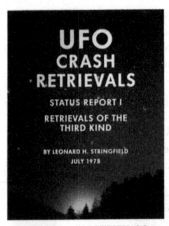

UFO
CRASH
·RETRIEVALS

STATUS REPORT I

RETRIEVALS OF THE
THIRD KIND

BY LEONARD H. STRINGFIELD
JULY 1978

UFO CRASH RETRIEVALS
publication by Leonard Stringfield

creatures preserved in another secret building. Stringfield said Wilhelm heard a similar story from a friend in the Army Reserve whose father worked with Project Blue Book at WPAFB and held high security clearances. On his deathbed, the father told his son he'd seen two disc-shaped spacecraft, one intact and one damaged and four small dead space alien bodies preserved in chemicals. These two anecdotes might refer to events inside Building 18-A in area B at WPAFB and such accounts may be the origin of the Hangar 18 stories.

One thing I especially remember about Stringfield is that when I visited him in his house, he had us go outdoors when he talked about certain things. He said that his house might be bugged. I wasn't very experienced in UFOlogy then and didn't pay attention to what particular subjects he discussed when we went outside.

Pete Hartinger, another Ohio UFOlogist, told me that one of the last stories he heard from Stringfield involved a woman taken to WPAFB and shown an alien body. She reportedly noticed a camera pointed at her, as if her reactions were being monitored. Hartinger added that he'd heard similar stories about the Defense Construction Supply Center (now the Defense Supply Center, Columbus, or DSCC)

This photo shows the building that a long-time Dayton, Ohio, resident said was once Hanger 18, the hanger where the Roswell debris was unloaded at WPAFB. This hangar is the second from the left in a group of connected hangars near the runway in Area B

in Columbus and about the National Aeronautics and Space Administration (NASA) in Cleveland. He said other people reported being shown films of UFOs.

Stringfield was also involved in a key report on government-connected UFO informants according to Hartinger, Jones and some other investigators.[15]

Astronaut Neil Armstrong, the first person to walk on the moon and astronomy professor J. Allen Hynek were a part of this. Stringfield knew of more than 50 government-connected informants who'd divulged information about UFO events. However, he refused to release their names and his critics insisted that without the identities of the sources, the stories lacked credibility. Stringfield recognized this problem, but he had promised to protect the identities of his informants and felt that if he didn't he'd get no further information from them or anyone else. Stringfield said that a number of years ago when retired astronaut Neil Armstrong was on the board of directors of a Cincinnati bank, Armstrong and Hynek approached Stringfield with a proposal to protect the names of the government-connected informants. Armstrong said Stringfield could put his list of names in a safety deposit box at Armstrong's bank, to which it was assumed Armstrong would also have access. The intention was that in the event of Stringfield's death, the names wouldn't be lost, but Stringfield rejected the idea.

There is no proof that this happened; however, Armstrong and Hynek did communicate, as shown by a letter from Armstrong to Hynek now in the possession of CUFOS. In addition, Stringfield, Hynek, Jacques Vallée, Ted Phillips and astronaut Gordon Cooper had made two public visits to the UN in 1994. Moreover, investigator Jenny Zeidman has reported that Hynek and Stringfield met and discussed UFOs. These accounts also support rumors of Armstrong's interest in UFOs.

* * *

UFO documents are also reportedly housed at WPAFB, including those of studies of the Roswell bodies and debris. Kevin Randle and Donald Schmitt, in their 1994 book *The Truth about the UFO Crash at Roswell,* report that Brigadier-General Arthur Exon, who became commander of WPAFB in August 1964, told them that he was sure that at least some Roswell material was still housed at WPAFB. Exon thought that photographs of the Roswell debris field, of the crash site, of the alien bodies and of the autopsies of those bodies existed at WPAFB and that reports filed in the Foreign Technology Division (FTD) building described what the military learned about the crash in the ensuing years. Exon also said all but one of the bodies was taken to WPAFB immediately after the crash.

* * *

Jones and I found additional WPAFB smoking gun evidence on-base. During one visit, we were privileged to have Ashcroft invite us to the last of the briefings he had arranged for NAIC (now NASIC) employees on the history of this organization. The subject of this briefing was Project Blue Book. Ashcroft's presentation included a video, *NAIC Alumni Days Operation Blue Book V-7512*, which showed a reunion of former Blue Book employees, including three former Blue Book directors: Robert Friend, George Gregory and Hector Quintanilla. About 30 officers, enlisted people and civilians attended the reunion. (This event was even more historic because he held it in the main conference room of the National Air and Space Intelligence Center, NASIC, headquarters building 856, which appears to be the most highly secured of any base building and is the complex that has historically housed the WPAFB UFO research).

Ashcroft also played a tape of an interview between Carl Day (a veteran Dayton broadcaster and Emmy-winning television news anchor who worked with WDTN-TV Channel 2) and Hector Quintanilla (the last Project Blue Book director). In this interview, Quintanilla said Project Blue Book was completely separate from the Central Intelligence Agency (CIA) and, later, from the Defense Intelligence Agency (DIA). Quintanilla noted that he lacked the required security clearances for intelligence work. He added that authorities at the time thought UFOs were Soviet in origin; thus, they were taken quite seriously.

During the question-and-answer session following Ashcroft's presentation, we might have gained additional smoking gun information. It appeared that classified UFO information may have existed and it was clear there was no unanimity of opinion about UFOs among the Air Force members and employees in the audience. One officer doubted Ashcroft's claim that all reports about UFOs in Air Force custody had been declassified and he mentioned a secret message he'd once seen about the pursuit of a UFO by an Air Force pilot. This officer asked Ashcroft if he thought that message would now be declassified. Ashcroft replied, "Yes," and he reminded everyone that the audience included people (Jones and I) who lacked security clearances. To me this suggested that UFO information had continued to be classified and the discussion might have been different if the audience had included only those having proper security clearances.

Ashcroft's assertion that all UFO reports were now declassified solidified my belief that UFO information had been covered up by the American military. For example, I would certainly think that some information would be classified because it would show our country's technological expertise. Also, in several interviews with government workers I'd heard of films showing Air Force pilots pursuing UFOs; thus, the officer's remark about the pursuit was in line with my own experience.

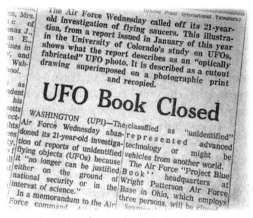

Newspaper clipping discussing the closure of Project Blue Book

UFOlogist Donald Schmitt, after a Columbus, Ohio, talk about the Roswell crash (January 13, 1994, at Battelle Memorial Institute), told me he'd heard that the American military sometimes showed UFO photographs and films to selected people as part of a US government study of witness reactions to such material.

Thus, I thought it suspicious that Ashcroft answered affirmatively to the officer's question about declassification without requesting specifics.

As we were leaving the building after the presentation, two men in civilian clothing, who recognized Ashcroft, asked him if he'd ever talked to a man named John G. Tiffany who had worked at WPAFB.

I recalled that, according to Kevin Randle and Donald Schmitt's research, Tiffany's father was the man dispatched from Wright Field to retrieve the Roswell materials and possibly the space alien bodies at Fort Worth. Tiffany claimed his father picked up metallic debris and a large cylinder that reminded his father of a huge thermos bottle.

Ashcroft said he had not talked to Tiffany's son and he later explained to us that the son was undoubtedly tired of answering questions about his father's story and would refuse to be interviewed.

After we left the building, I asked Ashcroft if he'd ever contacted Brigadier General Arthur Exon, the Base Commander of WPAFB in the 1960s, for information about UFO investigations on-base. Ashcroft responded that as commander of the base, Exon was responsible only for maintenance of base infrastructure and would not have been privy to activities of various agencies on-base.

* * *

The above information gave us the even stronger impression that Project Blue Book was a public relations endeavor rather than an investigative project. For example, as Quintanilla noted, some authorities at that time thought UFOs were Soviet in origin. However, one would expect that if UFOs were thought to be Soviet, the military would have investigated at a much higher level. It was difficult

The Roswell Incident book by Charles Berlitz and William L. Moore. The first book about the UFO crash at Roswell in 1947

to think that even Quintanilla thought Blue Book had sufficient security and resources to investigate Soviet technology. One would expect UFO evidence to be sent to an agency that could investigate it scientifically, such as WPAFB's Air Force Materiel Command its chief research and development branch, rather than to Project Blue Book. Likewise, radar visuals would probably have gone to agencies specializing in radar signatures. In 1947 when UFO investigation began, WPAFB had at its disposal some of the world's best American and German scientists. If materials or valid observations had been collected, these would probably have been sent to WPAFB. But there would be no reason for the Air Force to give its best evidence to Project Blue Book, which lacked the technical specialists, the equipment and the secured area to conduct appropriate investigations.

Moreover, Ashcroft's unwillingness to interview Tiffany showed a lack of interest in this information because the Tiffany account is integral to the Roswell reports. Likewise, we viewed Ashcroft's response to the question about Exon as ridiculous; the fact that Exon was responsible for maintenance of base infrastructure in no way precluded knowledge of Roswell.

Others with direct knowledge about Blue Book have also been skeptical about it as an investigative project. Hynek reported in his 1998 book, *The UFO Experience: A Scientific Inquiry,* that during a visit to Blue Book headquarters he happened upon some cases by accident when he saw material lying on a desk outside the files. These cases were not included in information shown to him by Blue Book personnel. He had access to Project Blue Book files only when he requested data about a specific case. According to Jennie Zeidman, Hynek often commented that he knew the best cases were withheld. In fact, she described the desperate emphasis or hush-hush of Blue Book as being in an environment of ludicrously slipshod security.

* * *

Jones and I have interviewed family members of former Project Blue Book employees. One said that her parent, who worked for Project Blue Book, though some of the cases involved real UFOs and others did not.[16] This parent had overheard conversations while working for Project Blue Book and based on these, the parent thought an alien crash at Roswell really did happen. The parent said some material was still sensitive and that talking about it was not permitted. This account is compatible with the *NAIC Alumni Days Operation Blue Book V-7512* video, in which one speaker said some Blue Book material remains classified. Thus, the actual level of some of today's Blue Book information remains unclear.

Such information reinforces the idea that Project Blue Book was simply a public relations maneuver rather than a scientific investigation. Many skeptics disagree, however, believing it was an important government-backed study group and that it disproved the notion that UFOs were extraterrestrial.

Jones and I have also conducted interviews with Ashcroft about his involvement in the search for Roswell-related materials at WPAFB.

In 1993, US Representative Steven Schiff of New Mexico began looking into the possible government cover-up of information about the Roswell incident—which, of course, took place in his state. In 1994, he prompted a General Accounting Office investigation to obtain files from the Department of Defense (DOD), an organization that UFO investigators think has custody of some important Roswell documents. Bruce Ashcroft was one of several DOD employees who were asked to locate Roswell documents.

Ashcroft's task was to determine whether the NAIC maintained files and materials about the Roswell event. In addition, Ashcroft had developed a personal interest in the topic and had spent his own time and money collecting and analyzing Roswell information from outside sources, keeping these personal investigations separate from work done for his employer. He had interviewed numerous experts, including leading Roswell investigator Stanton Friedman, Roswell researcher Robert Todd and writers Philip Klass (a noted skeptic) and Karl Pflock. As a result of his research, Ashcroft admitted that an extraterrestrial explanation might account for particulars of the Roswell story if corroborating information and evidence could be located. But while he expected a mundane explanation, Ashcroft acknowledged that reports of alien bodies presented a problem, so he was keeping an open mind.

If the truth did involve alien technology, then material taken from the Roswell debris field was extraterrestrial in source and probably represented technology beyond what was then state-of-the-art. Government-sponsored materials research would thus have been affected by investigations of this material, as the government would surely have tried to replicate it. Ashcroft studied reports from materials research projects undertaken by the Air Force between 1947 and 1951, but he said he found no evidence of new research directions that might have resulted from Roswell material as it is described in UFO literature.

Ashcroft notes that one explanation for the dearth of Roswell information in government files might be that the event was deemed unimportant by those involved with it; thus, critical documents might have been discarded. Ashcroft found no reports on the Roswell event and no references to it in any files he searched and these files included those of his own organization, those at the Air Force library and archives at Maxwell Air Force Base in Alabama and those at the military records center in St. Louis. He also looked at secondary records (such as reports on expenditures, related-project reports and facility reports) but found nothing directly or indirectly connected to Roswell.

One wonders, however, if Ashcroft has been play-acting a role assigned to him as part of a government cover-up. It's impossible to know, but Ashcroft treated Jones and I and the subject of UFOs, with politeness and respect and on more than one occasion he criticized the Air Force's handling of the UFO issue.

* * *

The possible Roswell debris would likely have been sent to WPAFB because of the base's central position in both aviation and space exploration. WPAFB's reputation lends high credibility to its research. It is named after the Wright brothers of Dayton, Ohio, which is known throughout the world as the "Birthplace of Aviation" because this is where the brothers changed the course of human history when they invented the airplane. Indeed, those from this Midwestern region have played a crucial role in aviation and space exploration–including John Glenn, the first American to orbit the earth and Neil Armstrong, the first person to walk on the moon. It is the government's chief aeronautical research agency and the largest and most organizationally complex base in the Air Force. Developments of the base's Aeronautical Systems Center include such legendary airplanes as the P-51 Mustang, the B-17 Flying Fortress and the B-52 Stratofortress and more recently, the B-2 stealth bomber and the F-22 Advanced Tactical Fighter. WPAFB was a Strategic Air Command (SAC) base, meaning that nuclear missiles were stored there during the Cold War.

WPAFB is composed of Wright Field, south of Ohio's State Route 444 and of Patterson Field, north of Route 444 and divided into three areas: A, B and C. Area A contains what was once called the Air Technical Intelligence Center (ATIC), which housed the first official studies done on UFOs, such as Project Blue Book. It employed J. Allen Hynek, Ph.D., noted astronomer and chair of the astronomy department at Northwestern University, past Project Blue Book consultant and a prominent writer, who is often called the "Father of UFOlogy."[17]

Project Blue Book is WPAFB's best-known government agency for UFO investigation, but it has had several predecessors. Historically, these agencies date back to the first sighting reports. In January 1948, the Air Force established its first group, Project Sign, to study the UFO reports that flooded in from around the country in the aftermath of the sightings by Arnold and others. At that time the government considered UFOs to be possibly extraterrestrial; for example, Project Sign's "Technical Report No. F-TR-2274-IA Unidentified Aerial Objects Project 'Sign,'" discussed the possibility that UFOs were from another planet.

Moreover, their following "Estimate of the Situation," concluded that "based on the evidence, that they [UFOs] were alien spacecraft, or to put it in the terms of the time, interplanetary craft."[18]

By February 1949, however, Project Sign was dissolved and its staff generally replaced. A new project was formed, Project Grudge, so called because high-ranking Air Force officers disagreed with Project Sign's conclusions that extraterrestrials could be behind the UFO sightings. The staff at Project Grudge was substantially more skeptical than the Project Sign crew and Project Grudge was more representative of the government's new UFO-debunking policy.

In his *Report on Unidentified Flying Objects* (1956), Captain Edward Ruppelt, former head of Project Blue Book, said Project Grudge had a two-fold program of UFO debunking: (1) explaining away every UFO report and (2) saying the Air Force had solved all UFO sightings. Project Grudge personnel expected this dual policy to end UFO reports. But because eyewitness testimony often could not easily be explained away and because Air Force personnel could not answer all questions, the military contracted Battelle Memorial Institute. In 1952, the Air Force's UFO study project underwent another reorganization and the name was changed to Project Blue Book. This new project typically included supervisors such as Ruppelt, four other officers, two aviators and two civilians, as well as three scientists who'd worked full-time on the earlier Project Bear and others who'd worked part-time.

Ruppelt thought that the most interesting, best documented and most informative sightings stubbornly resisted conformist explanations. Indeed, many of the sightings Blue Book investigated were not explainable even after rigorous scrutiny. Ruppelt left Blue Book convinced that the extraterrestrial hypothesis deserved serious consideration. Many others, such as Temple University's David Jacobs, Ph.D. in his 2000 *UFOs and Abductions: Challenging the Borders of Knowledge,* have described the controversy around the idea that UFO phenomena deserved serious study. Nevertheless, Blue Book was downgraded and its investigations became increasingly incompetent.

* * *

Another iconic aspect of WPAFB, which may be partly related to its UFO activities, is its extreme security. This security is legendary and prevents any direct investigation of WPAFB by most UFOlogists. Legends circulate concerning highly placed persons, even presidential candidates, who have been barred. One such story is about Arizona senator and presidential candidate Barry Goldwater, who once asked General Curtis LeMay, Chief of Staff of the Air Force, if he could see the "Blue Room," said to be the holding room for UFO evidence at WPAFB. Goldwater said he was rebuffed in the strongest terms. Similar stories are told about Laurence Rockefeller and FBI Director J. Edgar Hoover.

Several authors, such as Michael Hesemann and Philip Mantle, have told how on November 1, 1995, after futile attempts to end the civil war in Bosnia-Herzegovina, leaders of the opposing factions arrived in the US for a peace conference. The conference was not held in Washington, D.C. or at Camp David, but at WPAFB in part because of its security. By November 21, the participants had crafted the Dayton Agreement, a treaty that was signed three weeks later. Insiders claim the pressure that brought about the agreement was the "alien card": leaders were shown something that made their own civil war look petty by comparison. Indeed, informants from Dayton whom I've interviewed claim that on the night before the leaders agreed to the treaty, residents of Dayton saw substantial UFO activity in the skies above WPAFB.[19]

Indeed, WPAFB is one of the world's most secure areas. Many of its complexes are surrounded by tall chain-link fences with barbed wire at the top and attached signs that read, "It is unlawful to enter this area without permission of the Installation Commander. . . . While on this installation all personnel and the property under their control are subject to search. This area is patrolled by military working dog teams and entered at guard posts."

The National Air and Space Intelligence Center (NASIC) (formerly the National Air Intelligence Center, or NAIC) to which Ashcroft invited us for the NAIC conference is particularly interesting. Its headquarters, Building 856, appeared to me to be the most secured on WPAFB. It is so secure that, although located inside WPAFB's secured areas, it has its own high-security zone, with rooftop cameras pointing in all directions and machines that resemble traffic lights surrounding a wide area of the periphery. This building complex is highly important to the UFO field because, under the acronym ATIC, it once housed Project Blue Book and the other UFO studies taking place there. Because it has been said that government UFO work is the most secure in the government, perhaps it still houses the fabled "Blue Room," and similar projects.

The Air Technical Intelligence Center (ATIC), which housed Project Blue Book, was later called the Foreign Technology Division, FTD, where photo analysis and

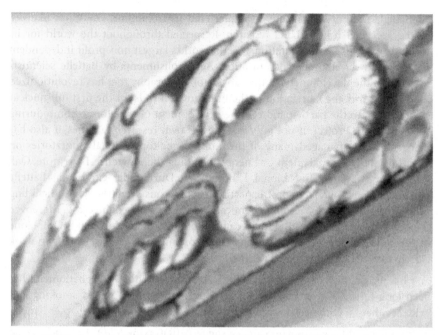

The real "Little Green Men," of WPAFB. During World War II, part of WPAFB served as a prisoner of war camp for between 200 to 400 German soldiers. These POW artists painted huge murals depicting gargoyle-like figures out of Germanic folklore, such as this giant figure that appears to be watching who enters the large doorway. Could these figures be the source of the stories about the Little Green Men at WPAFB?

study of foreign aerodynamic, ballistic missile and space vehicle systems took place. It became the National Air Intelligence Center (NAIC) and in 2003 the name was changed to the National Air and Space Intelligence Center (NASIC). I asked Ashcroft about the reason for its high security and he said that it is where the information from satellites is processed. Because of my experience working on satellite photography in the DIA, I was aware of the high security associated with this work and I also thought that this type of center might be the one that processes UFO information (which would come under the category of foreign flight information). Thus, one of the area's functions along with identifying aircraft might be the identification of unknown objects, such as UFOs and it might still house a modern agency whose work is similar to its former UFO investigation function. This security is also likely why photographic information may be stored in the vault structures under WPAFB.

* * *

Battelle Memorial Institute, headquartered in Columbus, Ohio, has likewise played a crucial role in UFO research. Respected throughout the world for its scientific expertise and reputation, it is the world's largest non-profit independent research and development organization. Accomplishments by Battelle scientists range from the development of the process of xerography that has revolutionized the entire world, the fabrication of the uranium fuel rods for the first full-nuclear scale reactor, to the participation in the development of the atomic bomb during the Manhattan Project. It not only operates its own research facilities, it also has managed or co-managed many of the atomic age's top national laboratories on behalf of the US Department of Energy, including the Lawrence Livermore, Oak Ridge and Brookhaven National Laboratories. During the Cold War, Battelle personnel were a who's who of expertise in numerous scientific fields, including metallurgy, nuclear physics and chemical and mechanical engineering. Moreover, the institute is adjacent to the main campus of Ohio State University (OSU), one of the nation's largest universities and this proximity allows its scientists to work closely with their counterparts at Ohio State.

Because of such expertise, Battelle's association with UFO phenomena has been long-term. This enabled Jones and I to be the first to report smoking gun evidence that UFO material was analyzed here, to be discussed in Chapter Nine.

Moreover although much evidence suggests that many UFO study projects at WPAFB were simply public-relations endeavors, some research conducted under Project Blue Book is highly significant and this was the work done at Battelle Memorial Institute.

For example, under Project Blue Book, Battelle conducted an extensive study of UFO phenomena. The results of this massive statistical analysis were presented in a report, *Project Blue Book Special Report No. 14 (Analysis of Reports of Unidentified Flying Objects)*, also known as *SR-14*. Even today, *SR-14* represents the largest such study ever undertaken and reigns as perhaps the most significant collection of evidence that UFO phenomena represent something real.

It investigated two of the most prominent theories that have been used to disprove UFO phenomena: (1) UFO reports result from a lack of reliable information and witnesses and (2) UFOs are known but misidentified objects. Blue Book scientists at Battelle tested these two theories by analyzing sighting reports and data using rigorous scientific statistical methods, as described by Bruce Maccabee, Ph.D., in his 1979 work, *Historical Introduction to Project Blue Book Special Report #14*.[20]

The first theory, that unexplained UFO sightings are caused by a lack of information or by inaccurate perceptions, suggests that when reliable observers and a large amount of information are available, the number of unexplained sightings will decrease. The results of the Blue Book study by Battelle scientists were the opposite of those expected. Based on 3,201 of the most reliable sightings (selected from approximately 7,200), the most reliable report category ("excellent") had a higher percentage (33.3 percent) of unknowns than the least reliable report category (16.6 percent). In addition, 38 percent of the "excellent" sightings were by military personnel, compared to approximately one-quarter of the sightings in the "poor" category. This large study therefore refuted the idea that UFO sightings result from a lack of reliable information and observers.

The second theory is that UFOs are really known but misidentified objects. If this were true, one would expect characteristics of UFOs generally to match those of conventional objects. For example, a certain percentage of conventional flying objects are aircraft with predictable lighting arrangements and a certain percentage are meteors; therefore, the frequencies of such characteristics among UFOs should correspond to these percentages. In the Battelle study, the frequencies of certain characteristics of UFOs and Identified Flying Objects (IFOs) were evaluated according to a standard statistical procedure (the widely used "chi-square"). In five of six categories, the hypothesis that UFOs are misidentifications of conventional objects was disproved. Battelle scientists determined that by every available criterion, the characteristics of the UFOs differed from those of the IFOs, that better qualified observers reported sightings of longer durations and that when more information was available, it was more likely that a report would defy explanation.

In other words, by the standard statistical methodology used in scientific studies, some UFO phenomena very likely represent something real, despite the government's representation that *SR-14* found nothing. Additional discussion of Battelle's activities will follow in Chapter 9.

* * *

Although one of the most common ideas about UFOs is that Blue Book was a government agency that investigated UFOs and found nothing to them, after conducting research and talking to WPAFB personnel, Jones and I think that Blue Book and similar projects were public relations ventures designed to thwart popular interest in UFOs. Projects Sign, Grudge and Blue Book were all likely housed at WPAFB because it had the expertise to analyze UFO data and had participated in this from the beginning. The best data did not, however, go directly to Project Blue Book. It more likely went to specialists and scientists in secured areas and who worked in fields related to the specific nature of the information. What this means is that some agency was actually collecting the good accounts, as Hynek reported. Kenneth Arnold's experience, discussed in the previous chapter, suggested that such upper echelon agencies were generally housed in Washington DC.

One study—that done by the Battelle Memorial Institute, *SR-14*—is probably the most important scientific UFO study ever made and its findings indicate that some UFO phenomena are real, but the government massaged these findings.

CHAPTER THREE

UFO Crash Accounts

EXACTLY seventy years ago perhaps the world's most famous UFO mystery began when it appeared that an object shooting through an electrical storm, was struck by the approximately five billion joules of energy of a lightning bolt and then crashed in the desert on the outskirts of Roswell, New Mexico.

In spite of countless investigators pouring over the evidence from this crash that might have even included aliens, the mystery has never been solved.

Although we don't know for certain if extraterrestrials crash—or even if they exist—we do know that UFOs crash. Many crashed UFOs are probably military devices, but until the government allows us to view all of its files, we won't have definite evidence.

This event continues, even today, to be investigated and we have uncovered a remarkable new account of this crash as will be described below.

Perhaps the best -known UFO crash is the Roswell one. Many books have been written about Roswell, WPAFB and Hangar 18 by authors, such as Stanton Friedman, William Moore, Kevin Randle, Donald Schmitt, Karl Pflock, Charles Berlitz, Robert Wooten and Karl Korff. Many of these people have impressive credentials; for example, Berlitz, who is listed in the

Charles Berlitz – courtesy Rick Hilberg

People's Almanac as one of the 15 most eminent linguists in the world, won the Dag Hammarskjöld International Prize for non-fiction in 1976 for his book on the Bermuda Triangle (which sold over 20 million copies) and he has written additional best sellers about anomalous phenomena.

Japanese fugo balloon

Many ideas have been postulated about what Roswell was. Some think the object that crashed at Roswell was a balloon, possibly a Japanese Fugo fire balloon. During World War II, between November 1944 and April 1945, Japan deployed these balloons with the intention of setting fire to North American farms and forests. The WPAFB museum includes a Japanese Fugo balloon display with information, photographs, balloon parts and a sample of the rice paper from which the balloons were made. Based on this display, one can see that a crashed Fugo would be easily identified and fit into one 12 feet by 5 feet by 4 feet crate, with room to spare.

UFO writer James McAndrew, in his 1997, *The Roswell Report: Case Closed*, points out that the American government has repeatedly claimed the Roswell debris was from an American "Mogul" balloon. Project Mogul was a top-secret US military operation from 1947 through 1949; it involved using high-altitude balloons to

'Project Mogul' was a series of rubber weather balloons and tinfoil radar "kites" strung together in a row for carrying listening devices aloft

detect atomic bomb tests by the Soviets. Based on the dates of a timetable of Mogul balloon releases shown to Bill Jones and me by Bruce Ashcroft and based on known Mogul landing sites, there's no reason to attribute the Roswell event to Project Mogul. In addition, a look at the balloon-like appearance of the Mogul balloon on display at the UFO Museum and Research Center in Roswell, New Mexico, leaves little doubt that anyone could confuse it with a UFO.

Perhaps the most interesting part of the Roswell story focuses on the space-alien bodies reportedly found at the crash site. McAndrew's report claimed the supposed bodies were human-shaped dummies used to test high-altitude parachutes. However, dummies used in projects such as the Air Force's Operation High Dive were man-sized, while eyewitness accounts of the Roswell incident described the alien bodies as being small and child-sized. In addition, the dummies were made of wood and furthermore, Operation High Dive did not begin until the 1950s–some of these dummies are displayed at the UFO Museum and Research Center in Roswell. In spite of the US government's repeated attempts at debunking and covering up reports about the Roswell incident, members of the American public continue, after all these years, not to accept the official explanations.

A recently uncovered Roswell account differs from others, but contains material that might be more in line with the actual evidence than the early ideas. Both the government presentation that the Roswell crash was that of a balloon and other ideas that it was an extraterrestrial vehicle are based upon circumstantial evidence. However hard evidence exists that something was sent to WPAFB–because radio announcer Joe Wilson said on-air that he had just spoken to the officials at Wright Field and they were expecting a delivery. This would suggest that something real had been found, because a Mogul balloon or other government device would have been easily identified and there would be little reason to send it to WPAFB. Some accounts also tell that quite a bit of debris was sent. One account that might be compatible with some of this evidence, but differs from other accounts, could be one uncovered by Philip Mantle. This is the report of Big Springs Deputy Sheriff Charles H. Forgus of Howard County, Texas, who was interviewed in 1999 by Los Angeles private investigator Deanna Bever (DB) and another interviewer (LR).

Unlike other eyewitness accounts where few people actually reported seeing bodies, this witness reported seeing the craft and the bodies in a crash that appeared significant enough to report.

Forgus was traveling with the sheriff in July 1947, from Texas to Roswell to pick up a prisoner. They heard on the police radio about a crash near Roswell and went to see it. The crashed object was about 100 feet in diameter, perfectly round and in a canyon where it appeared that it had crashed onto the wall. He thought there are about four beings, around five feet tall with large eyes and feet like ours. Their skin was brownish and he didn't see any blood. Their bodies were being picked up by a lift attached to a crane and swung into a truck

He said there were about three or four hundred military people there; he didn't know from which branch but said they were not Air Force. He and the sheriff watched for a while and the military people saw them. Later they were told to leave. He said that a government person came around to talk to him later, but he told him to shut up and go away.

Portions of a rough transcript of the video tape of Deanna's June 21, 1999, interview show what Mr. Forgus' observed of the crash in his own words:

> When we got there, the land was covered with soldiers. They were hauling a big, a creature. Hauling him away.

> What I seen of him looked just like the one we see on television, with big eyes. There was a big round thing in the canyon. It was about 100 feet across. They put that on a truck and hauled it away. They wouldn't let us get very close to it either. So we headed up to get the prisoner in Roswell and back to...

> LR: So you were on your way from to Roswell to pick up a prisoner and you happened to be at that place......

> CF: It already had crashed. They were taking them out. There were

soldiers there....about 3 or 4 hundred of them. They wouldn't let you get very close. They were keeping all the people away. People were coming out there.

LR: What did the saucer (we'll call it) look like?

CF: It was a big round thing. Across the middle it was about 100 feet.

LR: Did you see any lights around it?

CF: No, they went out when it banged into the wall in the creek. It was like a mountain on the side of the creek.

LR: Did you see any creatures: How many did you see?

CF: Yeh, I saw them. I think I seen about four (of them).

LR: Were they covered up?

CF: Mostly. I saw the legs and feet on some of them.

LR: What did the feet look like? Do you remember?

CF: They looked like our feet....

LR: Did you tell anyone about it?

CF: The Army was there and military soldiers were there.

LR: Did they tell you not to say anything?

CF: No, they didn't tell me nothing. They wouldn't let you get close to 'em.

LR: Did they actually see you observing what was going on?

CF: Sure, they saw me lookin' at them.

LR: And they didn't tell you to not say anything.....

I was riding with the Sheriff when we went to get the prisoner.

He didn't order nobody except me to go with him. The UFO was already down when we got there. We went and got the prison afterwards. We heard about it on the radio.

LR: What did you hear on the radio?

CF: That the thing had crashed.

LR: But they didn't know what 'the thing' was?

CF: No. But you would think that when people hear something like this, it scares the heck out of them. This came out of the POLICE

RADIO. We were on the way through there (to pick up the prisoner) when we heard it on the police radio. It was a big distance from to Roswell...you can look on a map and see it.

LR: So let me ask you this. When you guys were driving down the road and you were listening to the police radio......

CF: Yeh.....

LR: Do you remember what was said on the radio about whatever it was... Do you recall?...

LR: How long do you think you were at the site? (Note the cookoo clock goes off at noon)

CF: Probably about 20 minutes. We see them haul them (the bodies) out there, out of the canyon up to the trucks....putting them on the tow trucks so they could haul them.

DB: Did anyone try to get you to leave the scene.

CF: No....they told the Sheriff that we had to go. That was good enough for us....He's the boss.

LR: When they were taking the beings (we'll call them), were the beings laying on the ground around the saucer?

CF: Yeh, they were lifting them up with a crane that they had and picking them up and swinging them to put them on the truck. The bodies must have been 5 feet tall.

LR: Did you see the heads?

CF: Yeh....they were covered. They eyes looked like the ones we see on television and the pictures of them.

LR: What color was the skin?

CF: As much as I could tell....the skin was a brownish color.... Like they were in the sun too long.

LR: From the time it crashed until the time you got there, do you know how much time went by? From the time you heard it on the police radio until you got there?

CF: About two hours.

LR: Did you see any writing or engraving on the saucer?

CF: I wasn't that close to it?

LR: If you were say 12 feet away from the beings, how far were the beings away from the saucer. Were they thrown pretty far?

CF; We couldn't see that well because of the trees. It was in a riverbank. It slammed into a river bank. I say them lifting one up with the crane.

LR: Did anyone else talk to you about what was going on?

CF: There were some solders, but I don't think they were from the Air Force.

LR: Where do you think they were from then?

CF: I don't know. They were wearing uniforms. I didn't pay no attention cause I just wanted to go with the Sheriff to get the heck out of there before something happened.

LR: When you guys were in the car to go pick the guy up, did you discuss or talk about what you had seen with the Sheriff?

CF: No. I didn't know what they were and he didn't either or where they came from or nothing.

DB: Did you see any blood on the bodies?

CF: I don't know.... I guess they were dead....

LR: Has anyone ever talked to you or asked you to talk about what happened...like to the Government, cause there's a lot of research going on now because of the cover-up.

CF: There was one that came around and I told him to shut up and not come around. I don't know who they were. That was when I was Deputy Sheriff.

LR: When you saw the saucer, can you remember in your mind what it looked like. Can you draw it?

CF: No....you draw it?

(Note: Charlie had LR draw because he broke his arm and can't use it). He directed LP to draw a circle (not an oval). Then he directed LR to draw another circle with the circle. This was a drawing of the top of the saucer. Charlie was standing on top of the opposite side of the bank of the dry creek bed where the saucer had crashed.

LR: Were you standing above it?

CF: I was standing on the back side. The saucer hit the bank on this side of the creek and I was standing on the other side of the bank, at the top of the hill. I was looking down at the site. . . .

LR: So you had a 'bird's eye view', that's why you were able to see the top of it?

CF: I didn't have a 'bird's eye, I've got my own eyes (he laughs)

LR: LR shows Charlie the drawing. LR says, if this is the top (of the saucer), how much higher were you.

CF: Probably about 20 feet above it.

LR: So, that's why you saw the top (of the saucer). And you say, that from here to here (across the top of the saucer - diameter) is about 100 feet.

CF: It was evenly round.

LR: So it was absolutely round.... Not oval shaped and you were 20 feet above it, that's why you saw the top.

LR: did you see the fingers and hands?

CF: No, they were covered up. But I saw the head.

LR: But you said you saw the feet.

CF: Yeh, later on, when they were passing by I saw the feet. I could see them lifting it up with the crane. They wouldn't let you close enough when they were putting' them into the truck. When they were lifting them on the crane you could see them laying' on that thing.

LR: You said the body was covered. Were the arms laying on the stomach under the cover?

CF: When the wind blew, the cover went back so you could see the face. The same way with the feet.

Forgus made a special effort to note to Deanna "not to believe what others will say - he and the Sheriff did witness the Roswell crash scene."

If there were several hundred military people and large trucks with cranes, this must have been a sizeable operation. He said they had tow trucks and used a crane for lifting things.

The fact that Forgus couldn't identify the branch of the military people, but knew it wasn't the Air Force might also help to identify the time period. This is because The United States Air Force didn't become a separate military service until September 18, 1947, with the implementation of the National Security Act of 1947. Thus, he may have seen the crash before that date.

Major Hector Quintanilla

Charles H. Forgus and wife Marlene circa 1985

It appeared that they told few people about the event. Forgus said that he and the sheriff did not discuss the event after they left the site, because they didn't know anything about it. He also did not discuss it after he returned to Big Springs, because he said that no one was interested (they probably would be if they had heard of Roswell).

It was unclear what had crashed and whether it was called a saucer. Most of the time in the interview, Forgus referred to the object as "the thing." He said they drove there because, "they heard on the radio that a thing had crashed." The interviewer at one time said, "We will call it a saucer."

So far, I have not found evidence that any 100-foot diameter round craft or test craft was flying in 1947. It is unknown why they would use a lift and a crane to move the bodies.

It was also unclear in the video who the sheriff was. Forgus referred to "the sheriff" several times without giving the sheriff's name. In the video, the interviewer filled in the sheriff's name as Jess

Army of the United States
Honorable Discharge

This is to Certify, That C. H. FORGUS, 6 956 420 Technical Sergeant

Headquarters Company, 1052nd Engineers

ARMY OF THE UNITED STATES
is hereby Honorably Discharged from the military service of the United States of America.
This certificate is awarded as a testimonial of Honest and Faithful Service to this country.

Given at Separation Center
Fort Bliss, Texas

Date 27 September 1945

ARTHUR L. HILL

Major, CWS

ENLISTED RECORD AND REPORT OF SEPARATION
HONORABLE DISCHARGE

1. LAST NAME - FIRST NAME - MIDDLE INITIAL	2. ARMY SERIAL NO.	3. GRADE	4. ARM OR SERVICE	5. COMPONENT
Forgus, C. H.	6 956 420	T/SGT	CE	RA
6. ORGANIZATION Hq Co 1052nd Engineers	7. DATE OF SEPARATION 27 Sept 45	8. PLACE OF SEPARATION Sepn Cntr Ft Bliss Tex		
7. PERMANENT ADDRESS FOR MAILING PURPOSES P.O. Box 961 Big Spring, Tex	9. DATE OF BIRTH 28 Jan 1918	10. PLACE OF BIRTH Aspermont, Texas		
11. ADDRESS FROM WHICH EMPLOYMENT WILL BE SOUGHT See 9	12. COLOR EYES Brn	13. COLOR HAIR Brn	14. HEIGHT 5-11	15. WEIGHT 170 LBS	13. No. DEPEND. one

16. RACE	17. MARITAL STATUS	18. U.S. Citizen	21. CIVILIAN OCCUPATION AND NO.
Single Married Other	X	YES / NO X	Laborer Highway 9-32.31

MILITARY HISTORY

22. DATE OF INDUCTION	23. DATE OF ENLISTMENT	24. Date of Entry Into Active Service	25. PLACE OF ENTRY INTO SERVICE
	5 Jun 40	5 Jun 40	Ft Bliss Texas

SELECTIVE SERVICE DATA 26. Registered Yes / No 27. Local S. S. Board No. 28. COUNTY AND STATE Not Shown

29. HOME ADDRESS AT TIME OF ENTRY INTO SERVICE See 9

30. MILITARY OCCUPATIONAL SPECIALTY AND NO.	31. MILITARY QUALIFICATION AND DATE
Salvage Driver 454	Marksman (Rifle) 15 Jan 43

32. BATTLES AND CAMPAIGNS

New Guinea Bismarck Archipelago

33. DECORATIONS AND CITATIONS Good Conduct Medal SO 31 Hq 1052 Eng 45 Asiatic-Pacific Service Medal American Defense Service Medal Philippine Liberation Ribbon

34. WOUNDS RECEIVED IN ACTION None

35. LATEST IMMUNIZATION DATES				SERVICE OUTSIDE CONTINENTAL U. S. AND RETURN		
SMALL POX	TYPHOID	TETANUS	OTHER (typhus)	DATE OF DEPARTURE	DESTINATION	DATE OF ARRIVAL
9Jun43	5Jul40	9Jun43	8 Aug 44 typhus	3 Jul 43	SW Pa	24 Jul 43
				26 Oct 44	United States	21 Sep 45

37. TOTAL LENGTH OF SERVICE					38. HIGHEST GRADE HELD
CONTINENTAL SERVICE			FOREIGN SERVICE		
YEARS	MONTHS	DAYS	YEARS	MONTHS	DAYS
3	1	4	2	2	19	T/Sgt

39. PRIOR SERVICE None

40. REASON AND AUTHORITY FOR SEPARATION Convenience of the Government RR 1-1 (Demobilization) AR 615-365 15 Dec 44

41. EDUCATION (Years) Grammar / High School / College

42. SERVICE SCHOOLS ATTENDED Navy Div Sch

PAY DATA

43. Longevity for Pay Purposes			44. Mustering Out Pay		45. Soldier Deposits	46. Travel Pay	47. TOTAL AMOUNT, NAME OF DISBURSING OFFICER
YEARS	MONTHS	DAYS	TOTAL	THIS PAYMENT			
5	5	23	300	100	None	17.65	$242.74 L. N. Fields MajBD

INSURANCE NOTICE

IMPORTANT IF PREMIUM IS NOT PAID WHEN DUE OR WITHIN THIRTY-ONE DAYS THEREAFTER, INSURANCE WILL LAPSE. MAKE CHECKS OR MONEY ORDERS PAYABLE TO THE TREASURER OF THE U. S. AND FORWARD TO COLLECTIONS SUBDIVISION, VETERANS ADMINISTRATION, WASHINGTON 25, D. C.

48. Kind of Insurance			49. How Paid		50. Effective Date of Allotment	51. Date of Next Premium Due (One month after 50)	52. Premium Due Each Month	53. INTENTION OF VETERAN TO
Nat. Serv.	U. S. Govt.	None	Allotment	V. A.				Continue / Discontinue
X			X		30 Sept 45	31 Oct 45	6.70	X

54. REMARKS (This space for completion of above items or entry of other items specified in W. D. Directives)

Lapel button issued
ASR Score (2 Sept 45) 98

Print

55. SIGNATURE OF PERSON BEING SEPARATED	57. PERSONNEL OFFICER (Type name, grade and organization - signature)
C. H. Forgus	Helen J. O'Neil 1st Lt WAC

WD AGO FORM 53-55
1 November 1944
This form supersedes all previous editions of WD AGO Forms 53 and 55 for enlisted personnel entitled to an Honorable Discharge, which will not be used after receipt of this revision.

Filed for record

Charles H. Forgus military discharge papers

58

Slaughter. However, Slaughter was not sheriff in 1947. The list of Howard County Sheriffs showed that Slaughter had been sheriff from 1928 until 1941. He was re-elected in 1952 and served until 1957. R. L. Wolf had been sheriff in 1947. Because Forgus usually said "the sheriff" rather than giving a name, he might have not remembered for sure to which sheriff he was referring. Also, because Slaughter was sheriff in the years before and after 1947, he might have continued to be addressed as sheriff. Forgus was a deputy sheriff under Slaughter in 1957 according to the *Big Spring Weekly Herald*, but the length of his service is unknown. I contacted the Big Springs sheriff department, but their records didn't go back that far. However, he likely could have ridden with the sheriff regardless of whether he was a deputy.

The police work of Forgus, Slaughter and Wolf have been written about in the *Big Spring Weekly Herald* in articles that identified their police positions at various times.

Forgus' discharge certificate showed that he had been a Technical Sergeant. In the 1052nd Engineers. The Big Spring Weekly Herald in several articles described the 1052nd Engineers. He entered service in 1940 and left the service in 1945 with an honorable discharge from Ft. Bliss, Texas. Afterwards he became a deputy sheriff at Big Spring, the county seat of Howard County, Texas. He was 81 when interviewed, but in the video, his mind was clear and he appeared in good health.

Could this be the real Roswell crash that perhaps has been covered up by stories, such as those about debris in several areas including the Foster ranch, or is it simply a recollection of a long ago plane crash?

Roswell has had a strong cultural impact because it occurred simultaneously with the events that inaugurated the Cold War (to be discussed later).

Randle and Schmitt's 1991 *UFO Crash at Roswell* inspired a 1994 television film, *Roswell*, which starred Martin Sheen and received a Golden Globe Award nomination for Best Mini-Series. Additional notable films referring to the Roswell incident include the following: *Hangar 18, Independence Day* and *Indiana Jones and the Kingdom of the Crystal Skull*.

Thomas J. Carey and Donald R. Schmitt's 2009 *Witness to Roswell: Unmasking the Government's Biggest Cover-Up* and Timothy Green Beckley's 2003 book, *MJ-12 and the Riddle of Hangar 18: The New Evidence*, among many others, were best sellers. Several novels have been written about the Roswell incident, by such authors as Whitley Strieber, Sonny Whitelaw and Colonel P. J. Corso. In addition, a 2011 book by Annie Jacobsen, *Area 51: An Uncensored History of America's Top Secret Military Base*, theorizes that the Roswell object was a Russian spacecraft with child-size aviators. These aviators, according to Jacobsen, were developed in human experiments by the notorious Nazi doctor Josef Mengele. Jacobsen also asserts that Joseph Stalin recruited Mengele and that Stalin sent the craft into US airspace in 1947 to spark public hysteria.

Television series about Roswell have included one called *Roswell* that aired from 1999 to 2002 and the series *Seven Days*. Episodes of the *Futurama* TV series, an episode called "Little Green Men" on *Star Trek: Deep Space Nine* and several other series episodes have dealt with Roswell.

Several popular songs have also mentioned Roswell and the American rock band the Foo Fighters named its record label Roswell Records.

In addition, Roswell has been featured in comics, games and toys. Moreover, a Roswell UFO Festival takes place each year and the Roswell UFO Museum and Research Center attracts many visitors.

* * *

On December 9, 1965, a flaming, hissing object careened across Canada and the northeastern US raining debris that started fires in Ohio and caused shockwaves, sonic booms and a possible crash in Kecksburg, Pennsylvania.

The Kecksburg UFO Incident is named after Kecksburg, Pennsylvania, which is about 30 miles southeast of Pittsburg. It is one of the best documented of all crashes because, unlike many crashes where the only evidence consists of debris, there were many witnesses to the actual crash.

The incident began when a streak of light flashed through the sky on December 9, 1965. Thousands of people in at least nine states and Ontario, Canada, saw the flash, including airplane pilots, weather observers, Lake Erie Coast Guardsmen and residents of Idaho, Indiana, Ohio, Pennsylvania, West Virginia and New York. These witnesses saw an orange ball move across the sky, according to a report the following day in the *Columbus Dispatch*. Times listed for the sightings were 4:40 p.m. in Indiana, 4:44 p.m. in Oberlin, Ohio and 4:50 p.m. in Erie, Pennsylvania.

Kecksburg UFO discussed in the newspapers

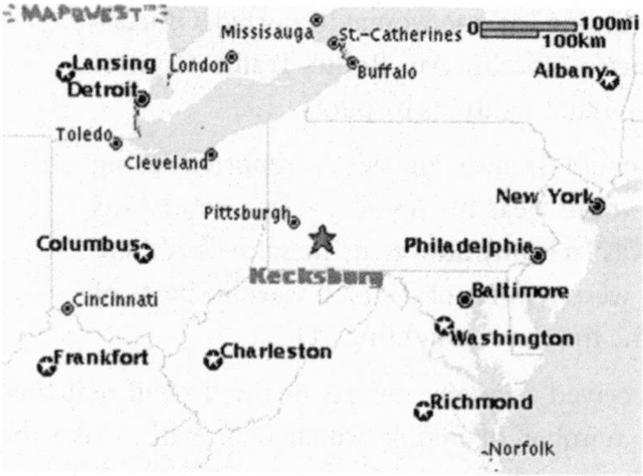

Map showing the area of the alleged UFO crash at Kecksburg

Several Columbus, Ohio, residents reported seeing it, including a weather observer who said he saw an object that looked like a meteor—but the object moved too slowly to have been a meteor.

Meteors, even exploding meteorites, do not normally cause fires, especially in this area in December when the weather is damp and cold. However, the meteor-like fireballs seen on the day of the Kecksburg incident started at least 10 grass fires near Elyria, Ohio and were thought to be the cause of a fire in Kecksburg, according to story that appeared on December 10 in the Cleveland newspaper, *The Plain Dealer*. Lieutenant Jack E. Trumbles of the Elyria Fire Department said two engine companies rushed to an area near the west branch of the Black River on West River Road soon after 5:00 p.m. to extinguish 10 small fires in a 1,000 square-foot area. The Associated Press reported that state police in Pennsylvania were called to a wooded area near Kecksburg to investigate a fire.

Eyewitness, Raymond Rawlings, of Painesville, Ohio, was flying his small plane over Perry, Ohio, when he saw an object in the sky to the west. He said it seemed to disintegrate at about the same height at which he was flying, 2100 feet and particles fell from the object. Parts of the object reportedly crashed into Lake Erie, north of the Detroit River. Other pieces fell on a Lorain, Ohio, schoolyard and into a swampy wooded area of Columbia Station in Lorain County, Ohio. The object must have been quite large to have had so many parts come down and still be large enough to land and start fires after burning in the earth's atmosphere.

In an article titled "'Fireball' Slams into Country from Lake Erie to Eaton," Elyria's *Chronicle Telegram* reported the next day:

> A crackling, hissing fireball . . . slammed into Lorain County last evening at dusk. Although no fragments had been recovered, thousands of observers saw chunks slam into the earth. . . . Wire dispatches report the fireball was seen in nine states. . . In Pennsylvania a team of Air Force, state police and scientific personnel were combing an area 30 miles southeast of Pittsburgh for an object

which came to earth "smoldering," as one woman reported. Officials at Federal Aviation Agency's Oberlin Air Route Traffic Control Center reported seven individual sightings by pilots. . . .

In Eaton Township, 11-year-old Brenton Hartley . . . reported seeing a flaming ball crash into woods near his home. . . .The woods was "full of smoke" and there was " a funny odor to it," he said—but there were no flames. . . . There were reports of a shock wave in parts of Western Pennsylvania at the time of the sightings. (1, 3)

Sheriff's deputies said they received so many reports of the fireball that they didn't bother to log them all. A number of people watched fireballs strike the ground. Some reported seeing flaming chunks drop into Lake Erie and into a schoolyard.

Michigan State University astronomers Von Del Chamberlain and David Krause investigated the fireball after the fact and published their conclusions two years after the incident. They noted that early reports gave debris landing sites that ranged from western Michigan to Pennsylvania. They mentioned that the object reportedly moved in a northeasterly direction and disappeared over land 15 miles southeast of Windsor and that the fireball was very bright, with an apparent

Model of the Kecksburg UFO near the site of the incident

magnitude rating of at least -15. Assuming the falling object was meteoric in origin, Chamberlain and Krause used photographic triangulation to calculate its trajectory and orbit. They concluded that the object descended at a steep angle, moved from southwest to northeast and probably crashed on Lake Erie's northwestern shore at 4:43 p.m. Loud sonic booms were heard at intervals in the Detroit and Windsor area. A dust train that followed the object persisted 30 minutes or longer. The Geophysics Laboratory of the University of Michigan at Willow Run Airport recorded a shock phenomenon on a seismograph shortly after the fireball was seen. This shock pulse was presumably generated at the burst point near the end of the trajectory. Chamberlain and Krause noted that no meteorites associated with the fireballs have ever been found.

Today investigators still don't know if an object actually landed. Substantial anecdotal evidence, however, suggests that something did land in Kecksburg and some people think Project Moon Dust, a UFO retrieval team possibly stationed at WPAFB, retrieved whatever crashed in the small woods near that town.

Jenny Randles, in her 1995 book, *UFO Retrievals: The Recovery of Alien Spacecraft*, reports that hundreds of witnesses in southern Canada, Michigan, Ohio and Pennsylvania observed the object and that its passage took at least six minutes, making it much slower than a meteor. Indeed, its calculated speed was only 1,000 miles per hour and even this might be an overestimate. Unlike a bolide or fireball, which would typically explode high in the air, this object caused shock waves: several pilots spoke of being buffeted as the thing passed. Sonic booms were reported at Port Clinton, Ohio and ground vibrations similar to those of an earthquake were felt at Acme, Pennsylvania. The dust trail remained visible for as many as 20 minutes and was filmed by a witness in Pontiac, Michigan. During the final few miles of the sighting, the object's trajectory appeared to turn east. If true, this would further disprove the theory that the object was a bright meteor, because a meteor does not change course.

Randles also points out that researcher Ray Boeche found, in Freedom of Information Act (FOIA) documents, a memo about the Kecksburg Incident that was sent by a Project Blue Book investigator to his superior at WPAFB. The memo notes that a three-man team was dispatched to Kecksburg to investigate and retrieve an object that started a fire. The memo also confirms that even before authorities arrived in Kecksburg, they knew something retrievable had crashed there. Pennsylvania UFOlogist Stan Gordon, in a further investigation, found additional witnesses and he has told us (the MidOhio Research Associates, MORA) that despite criticism he is continuing his investigations.

The investigators found that a fire department team from Kecksburg had come within 200 feet of the object before the military turned them away. Witnesses reported that they'd seen, on the ground, a strange object that had fallen from the sky. Some said it was bell-, conical-, or acorn-shaped. One witness said that the object looked like a large bullet embedded in the ground and that blue sparks flew from its surface.

That night a retrieval team from the Aerospace Defense Command set up a direct link with the North American Aerospace Defense Command (NORAD) from the fire station. This interest by aerospace authorities caused speculation that the object was a military satellite and many thought it might have been the Soviet Cosmos 96 satellite. However, the Cosmos 96 had crashed in Canada earlier that day at 3:18 a.m.—13 hours too early.

Randles also mentions a 1967 account from an Air Force guard stationed at Lockbourne Air Force Base (now Rickenbacker International Airport), located near Columbus, Ohio, which is between Kecksburg and WPAFB. He was on patrol at the base when, in the early hours of December 10, 1965, when a flatbed truck arrived via a little-used back gate. On the flatbed was a conical object covered by a large tarp. The guard was told to shoot anyone who tried to get close to it. After the truck left, he was told its destination was WPAFB.

Another witness, a building contractor in the Dayton area, spoke to our Ohio UFO investigators. This witness reported that on December 12, 1965, he was asked to take a load of 6,500 bricks to a hangar inside WPAFB. The hangar was well guarded, but he managed to sneak a look inside where he saw a bell-shaped device about 14 feet high. The men inside the hangar were wearing white protective "radiation-style" suits and gas masks.

Richard Seifried, an author who was the director of MUFON of Ohio for many years, told me that a patrol officer said an acorn-shaped object, covered by a tarp and on a truck, entered the rear gate at Rickenbacker Air Force Base, outside Columbus, Ohio.

Seifried also added that not far north of WPAFB is a factory that produced bricks of all types. This company was contacted by the Air Force and asked if they could manufacture bricks that absorbed radiation. They said they could. When the bricks were delivered, one man looked behind a tarp and saw an acorn-shaped object (what is now thought to have been the Kecksburg object). He was told by authorities not to do this again. This man said he spoke to the civilian guard who allowed the object to enter WPAFB Field through the large Fairborn gate.

The US government took a debunking position on the Kecksburg incident. Project Blue Book documents indicate a three-man team investigated the crash but found nothing. In 2005, with the fortieth anniversary of the crash imminent, NASA released an official statement claiming the Kecksburg object was a Russian satellite. This incident has been featured in numerous television documentary programs, including the following: an episode called "Kecksburg UFO" on the History Channel's *UFO Hunters*; a two-part episode of *Unsolved Mysteries* called "Kecksburg UFO"; a *Sightings* episode called "UFO crash in Kecksburg, Pennsylvania, in 1965"; and a Sci-Fi Channel documentary titled *The New Roswell: Kecksburg Exposed.*

Whatever the object was, to have been seen over such a wide distance it must have started burning at a very high altitude. Eyewitness and newspaper reports indicate the object fell quite slowly—several minutes occurred between the first reports and the last—and the object seems to have hit supersonic speed only near the end of its fall in Ohio and Pennsylvania, where residents heard sonic booms. Thus, this appears to have been a controlled landing. These sonic booms indicate it was a solid object. It seems to have left more debris than would result from an ordinary meteorite or from the disintegrating heat shield of a space capsule. The object seen in Kecksburg was acorn-shaped and solid like the space capsules of that era, but if it was a space capsule, no country has ever claimed it.

Today one current theory is that it was a General Electric Mark 2 Re-entry Vehicle launched by the Air Force as a spy satellite that fell out of orbit, but the government has not confirmed this. Regardless of what is was, it shows the government's impressive ability to lie and cover-up and the UFOlogists' impressive ability to investigate.

* * *

One pre-Roswell event is so interesting that novelist Dan Brown in his 2009 best seller, *The Lost Symbol,* may have used some of its elements. It concerned not only UFOs, but perhaps some of the most important actors and events in the twentieth century. Although UFOlogy is typically said to have begun around 1947, UFO reports have been made from as far back as ancient times. This 1939 experience was by a highly reliable witness, Cordell Hull. Bill Jones and Eloise G. Watson discuss this case at length in their *International UFO Reporter* article, "Pre-World War II 'Creature' Retrieval?" and Bill Jones and I have investigated it extensively.

Cordell Hull – US Secretary of State

Cordell Hull of Tennessee was one of the greatest statesmen of the twentieth century. He was elected to the US Senate in 1930, chaired the Democratic National Committee and became Secretary of State under President Franklin Roosevelt in 1933. Hull was our longest-serving Secretary of State, occupying the position for 11 years. In 1944, just before ratification of the United Nations (UN) Charter, Roosevelt was so impressed with Hull's ideas that he offered him the seat of Vice President. Hull has been called the "Father of the United Nations"; indeed, he received the Nobel Peace Prize in 1945 for helping to found the UN. He died in Washington, D.C., in 1955 and today the state office building in Nashville bears his name. Hull would have no motive for fabricating a UFO story—especially at a time when accounts of flying saucers and their space-alien passengers were not yet part of our culture.

In early December 1999, CUFOS received a letter from Lucile Andrew of Ashland, Ohio, the daughter of Cordell Hull's cousin, Reverend Turner Hamilton Holt. The letter read as follows:

> Today I want to share some knowledge that has been, by request, kept secret in our family since sometime in World War II. This concerns something my father was shown by his cousin Cordell Hull, the Secretary of State under Franklin Roosevelt. Snip, my father, who was young, brilliant and sound of mind, told us this story because he didn't want the information to be lost.
>
> One day when my father was in D.C., Cordell swore him to secrecy, took him to a sub-basement in the US Capitol Building and showed him an amazing sight:
>
> (1) Four large glass jars holding four creatures unknown to my father or Cordell.
>
> (2) A wrecked round craft of some kind nearby.
>
> My father wanted my sister and I to make this information known long after he and Cordell were dead, because he felt it was a very important bit of information. . . . We hope that you will research this information. The jars with creatures in formaldehyde and the wrecked craft are somewhere! Cordell said they were afraid they would start a panic if the public found out about it.

As a follow-up for CUFOS, Bill Jones and I interviewed Lucile and her sister Allene about the crash story. Lucile told us Holt and Hull were born in Pickett County, Tennessee and were cousins and friends. Holt had a doctorate in theology from Ashland Theological Seminary in Ohio and was a minister at the Shenandoah Christian Church in Greenwich, Ohio. He was a community leader and in 1956 he wrote a book entitled *Life's Convictions*. He married Vina May Clark and they had three daughters, two of whom claim their father told them the story about space-alien creatures.

Lucile informed us that her letter to CUFOS retold the story she'd heard from her father when she was a teenager. She acknowledged that at that time she was too young to pay much attention to it, but her sister Allene was told the same story. Holt was not the sort of person to invent a wild story and the two sisters felt they'd followed their father's wishes in divulging the story. Each assured us she remembered the story independently. Holt described the entities in the glass jars as "creatures," a term common for his day. He never referred to them as "aliens" or "extraterrestrials," and he never said where they had come from.

Lucile thought Holt was shown the jars by Hull in the late 1930s, probably in 1939. Holt said Hull described the "wrecked round craft" as being of a material that was "silver metallic," and that it was a vehicle that was in pieces and that appeared to have been taken apart. Lucile said Hull told Holt that the material was not of a color he'd seen before and that for lack of a better word Hull called it "silver."

Barbara A. Wolamin, curator of the US Capitol Building (where Hull said the jars and the spacecraft were stored in a sub-basement) chuckled after Jones told her the story. She had never heard about "creatures" in jars being stored at the Capitol, she said, but she did confirm that a sub-basement was indeed divided into storage rooms in the 1930s.

Perhaps this story is the genesis of a passage in Dan Brown's *The Lost Symbol*, which describes a Capitol Building sub-basement as follows: "There's no place in Washington more secure.... It's the symbolic heart of our nation" (242).[21]

After Cordell Hull left government service he wrote his memoirs in two volumes, but no reference to the incident appears in these pages or in his papers in the Library of Congress. Jones contacted numerous experts and libraries, but there's been no confirmation of Lucile's story. If our government did indeed possess the bodies of space-alien "creatures" and an extraterrestrial spacecraft in 1939, such prior knowledge of aliens and their aircraft would have helped prepare authorities for the Roswell event and could have resulted in the beginning of a much earlier cover-up (possibly why the higher authorities in the Arnold event appeared unconcerned). Clearly, this is a story that deserves further investigation.

Interesting material about the story continues to surface. In September 2009, Lucile's niece Margaret Gramly sent Ohio researcher Linda Wallace a copy of a

1935 letter from President Roosevelt to Reverend Holt. In it Roosevelt asks for Holt's spiritual counsel. A number of passages in Roosevelt's letter demonstrate his humanistic concerns. For example, he writes, "I am particularly anxious that the new Social Security Legislation just enacted ... providing for old age pensions, aid for crippled children ... shall be carried out in keeping with the high purposes with which this law was enacted."[22] Some of his interest in social legislation may have sprung from his own health problems, which were largely unknown by the general public at that time.

Gramly also sent Wallace an undated (but presumably from circa 1935) church bulletin draft about an upcoming "Workshop on World Order." The bulletin mentions "United Nations" delegates being at this workshop. Wallace remarked in an email to me:

> Perhaps the term "United Nations" was in the Washington lingo prior to the official inception or perhaps the possibility exists that the original Roosevelt letter was an organizational introduction to the concept of a "Workshop on World Order" and the resulting workshop actually materialized after Roosevelt's January 1, 1942, Joint Declaration of the United Nations.... Isn't it funny how far back the term "World Order" goes. The stories of crashed unidentified objects being contemporaneous with the formation of the UN are again synchronistic.[23]

The two anachronistic expressions in the material Gramly sent to Wallace are "United Nations" and "World Order." The January 1, 1942, "Declaration by United Nations" contained the first official use of the term "United Nations," which Roosevelt had suggested. As for the term "World Order," after looking at Wallace's material, Bill Jones said he recalled coming across information about that "Workshop on World Order." He thought Richard Nixon (as a young adult) and Edward Condon (long before he directed a US Air Force study of UFOs, generally known as the *Condon Report* (see Chapter Nine) attended. Jones had no recollection of where he'd seen this information, however.

Roosevelt's impact as a leader was tremendous and worldwide; for example, his initiatives resulted in the Social Security program and he helped to pull the nation's economy out of the great depression. Roosevelt and Hull were powerful forces whose actions led to the formation of the UN on October 25, 1945. If the Cordell Hull story is true, one wonders if the American government's awareness of aliens and their spacecraft provided a stimulus to create the UN and for attempts to unite the world into a World Order.

* * *

Several UFO crash stories have been associated with the Defense Supply Center, Columbus (DSCC) in Columbus, Ohio. During World War II, the facility was the largest military supply installation in the world and it played a substantial role in that war effort. Today it remains the largest supplier of weapon-systems parts to the US Armed Forces and to our allies around the world.

In one version of this account, UFO writer Kevin Randle mentions an event that occurred north of Columbus late in the summer of 1952. Vivian Walton, a worker for the Signal Corps, decoded a classified message about a crash near Columbus. Walton was later shown photographs of a crashed "flying saucer" by a co-worker. Walton described the saucer in the photo as 30 feet in diameter with almost no damage. She said the retrieval team had trouble entering the spacecraft, which was unoccupied and that it was taken to WPAFB.

Another UFO writer, James Moseley, also describes this crash. Moseley notes that late in the summer of 1952 a DSCC employee reported she had information about a UFO that had crashed north of Columbus. She said that a few days after the crash an alert was sounded at the DSCC installation. She and others were told during an official briefing that the alert was prompted by the fear of a UFO attack following recovery of a strange and unidentified aircraft. She said UFO artifacts

James Moseley & Allan Manak

had passed through DSCC on their way to WPAFB and that rumors circulated throughout the center about the recovery of five-foot space aliens that resembled humans.

Roundtown UFO Society (RUFOS) founder Pete Hartinger and I investigated a possibly related event. Hartinger received the information from a close relative that I later interviewed separately. His informant, a DSCC supervisor, was a decorated war hero who served in the Pacific during World War II; as such, he is considered a reliable witness. His sighting occurred at DSCC in the early 1950s during daytime. He was standing on a warehouse dock when he observed in the sky a strange circular object with two fins on its rear. It was grey and its diameter roughly equaled the length and wingspan of a commercial airplane. He could see only the underneath part of the object and not the top. He was pointing it out to two men when it swooped down over the DSCC's warehouses. It came in so low, at an altitude of 500 to 700 feet, that he thought it had come from a hangar at the nearby Curtiss-Wright aircraft manufacturing plant.

He told the other men that this object must be "ours" because it was flying so close to the ground.

The object flew slowly down the main street of DSCC; he stood directly in front of it as it came down the street. It turned east before reaching Building 42 and Building 41 and it flew away behind some storage sheds. His sighting lasted about three minutes and several other people also saw the object, but later he could not recall their names. There was a vapor trail behind it and he did not hear it make a noise. He told his wife about this sighting later that day and she subsequently confirmed this.

Soon after the incident—he thought it was the next day—one of the buildings that had been unsecured suddenly became highly secured. Its windows were covered up and no one was allowed inside. The area outside the building was roped off. He thought his sighting might have occurred around the time of the incident described by James Moseley.

For many years, Hartinger's informant thought the flying object he saw was some kind of American aircraft; however, after studying various UFO sighting reports, he now has his doubts. He says he has never seen another aircraft resembling the one he saw that day. He thinks the object may have buzzed DSCC because UFO artifacts were stored there.

Timothy Good and I discussed this sighting and, in his 2007 *Need to Know: UFOs the Military and Intelligence*, he compared it with several similar UFO intrusions over military installations during the early 1950s. He notes that in one case, when Mustang fighters were scrambled from WPAFB to intercept a UFO that was visible and tracked by the base, the object was thought to have been checking on a craft that had been stored at the base.

Another person interviewed by Pete Hartinger and me reported seeing a large saucer-shaped object carried on a flatbed truck as part of a military convoy down East Broad Street near DSCC in Columbus. The object was covered with canvas and was accompanied by motorcycle police. The informant said the event probably occurred in 1954; he suspected the convoy might have been transporting a UFO from DSCC to WPAFB.

Yet another informant who had worked at DSCC reported that generals and other high-ranking officers at that facility showed films about UFOs to her and to others. These films chiefly depicted UFOs in flight through mountainous areas. She recalled the officers also presented information about space-alien babies.

This informant thought the American government uses psychological warfare on those it wants to discredit and that these people may end up in asylums (see the discussion of Bennewitz Affair in Chapter Nine). The informant reported hearing about a 1941 UFO crash and her information agrees with Pete Hartinger's data about a 1941 UFO crash. She further noted that astronaut Neil Armstrong—an Ohio native, commander of the Apollo 11 mission and the first man to walk on the moon—is interested in UFOs and this is corroborated by information from several other sources (as discussed in Chapter Eight).

In a follow-up investigation, I visited DCSC in 1992; although it was secured, to enter the facility at that time one needed only to state, at the gate, the name of a contact person. I walked unescorted to meet my contact. On the way back, I was able to wander around to view the general layout of facility and did not feel I was being observed. Moreover, I accidentally parked my car in a secured area before anyone noticed. The area generally matched the descriptions given by Hartinger's witness, although I was unable to find the buildings to which he referred.

* * *

Although the following account doesn't involve a UFO crash, it tells of the study of alien debris and of an airplane crash, while possibly in pursuit of a UFO. On October 22, 1954, a dazzlingly bright cigar-shaped object hung motionless above Jerome Elementary School in Marysville, Ohio, for approximately 45 minutes. It left behind small white tufts covering a three-mile radius. Some of these white tufts were subsequently brought to the principal, Mr. Warrick and to a teacher, Mrs. Dittmar. Dittmar sent some of the material to WPAFB, according to Ohio UFOlogist Lillian Crowner Desguin in her book *UFOs: Fact or Fiction* (1992). Desguin notes that a

Battelle laboratory worker later found a jar marked "Marysville, Ohio." Desguin identifies this worker as "J. P." in her book; his real name is Jack Pickering. Pickering said that the jar was in the possession of a colleague at Battelle. The colleague said no one had been able to identify the substance; the colleague also did not divulge who was paying for the analysis. Pickering was allowed to examine it under a microscope: each thread consisted of four or five smaller threads. Bill Jones investigated this incident and was told the material (which might be the substance, sometimes called "angel hair," occasionally found after UFO sightings) had covered a large area where it hung from power lines and trees. Jones interviewed Pickering, but he never learned the name of Pickering's Battelle colleague.

Jones adds that Pickering was involved in the 1948 Mantell UFO Incident, during which Thomas Mantell, a Kentucky Air National Guard pilot, crashed and died while pursuing what was thought to have been a UFO. In 1977, Pickering reported that he'd heard transmissions between Mantell and the tower at Godman Field at Fort Knox, Kentucky, on January 7, 1948, as the event unfolded. Pickering was stationed at Lockbourne Air Force Base south of Columbus at the time and for some reason the transmissions were sent from Godman to Lockbourne. Later that night he and others at Lockbourne saw a UFO descend and circle that base.

* * *

One might think it would be difficult to locate people who claim knowledge of UFO artifacts, but the reality is that in Ohio—especially around WPAFB—such people seem to be everywhere. For example, while returning from a trip to the University of Cincinnati where Kevin Randle was promoting his book, Bill Jones and I stopped at a restaurant. A waiter saw our copy of *The Truth about the UFO Crash at Roswell* and he told us about a relative of his who held a high position at WPAFB. The relative claimed alien artifacts and alien bodies were stored there. The waiter said that at one time the relative even knew exactly where they had been kept.

Although it might seem odd that so many stories about crash debris and aliens come from Ohio, in the 1940s–1960s, Ohio was one of the nation's leading industrial states. Some of its industries were not only among the world's best, but they were close to WPAFB. Thus, it's only natural that if alien debris existed, it found its way to Ohio. However, during that era most people, including members of the media, were not yet aware of Roswell and other crash stories; thus, they would have had no reason to associate strange substances with UFOs.

* * *

Arnold's account and those included here have had a tremendous impact on

72

our culture. And as French UFOlogist Jean Sider and I theorized in a series of articles we published, rather than material events, such crashes might have been staged to influence our culture.

Indeed Sider thinks that the Roswell crash might have been the most important event in all of UFO history and maybe even in the history of human society since the coming of Christ. This importance is due to the Roswell incident's influence on our culture and because the incident occurred at precisely the same time as the events that inaugurated the Cold War.

Sider has theorized that the UFO at Roswell was in fact a highly sophisticated decoy disguised as an alien spacecraft event. The event was staged, says Sider, to convince American and Soviet authorities of the reality of the threat of world destruction by the powers themselves and of the possible threat from extraterrestrial invaders at that crucial time. The intention behind the Roswell incident, in Sider's view, was to impress upon world leaders the need for unity and a peaceful resolution to their political differences. The cultural impact of some of these ideas can be shown in that both James Oberg, one of the world's leading popularizers and interpreters of space exploration and Philip Klass, a noted UFO debunker, immediately commented on these articles.

Similarly, in the Cordell Hull story, the account of the preserved alien creatures and their spacecraft was synchronous with monumental changes in the human worldview, such as the development of the UN.

CHAPTER FOUR

The Forties and Fifties: Sputnik – Atomic Installations and UFOs Over The White House

THE 1940s and 1950s saw many dramatic and complex UFO encounters. However, people today think of those decades as times when people simply saw flying discs. This is because either the era's reports of landings, human-appearing entities and sightings over the White House were so threatening that people didn't think they were true, or the official agencies concerned with UFOs allowed the public and most scientists to hear only the sanitized accounts.

These years also included periods when sightings suddenly increased unexplainably. UFOlogists use the words "flap" and "wave" to designate sudden unexplained increases in UFO reports. Flaps occurred in the US (and sometimes worldwide) in this period in 1947, 1952 and 1957 and later in 1965 through 1967 and in 1973.

First atomic bomb in 1947

Some of the sightings of this era occurred over the country's most sensitive areas, including a 1952 Washington, DC. "invasion" UFO wave when UFOs flew over our nation's capital. A series of sightings in 1957 may have been the most widespread and unusual of all. And these incidents punctuated an important milestone in the earth's history: on November 3, 1957, earthlings became extraterrestrial when the Soviet Sputnik II satellite carried the first earthly passenger into orbit—a dog named Laika. At this time, sightings occurred almost simultaneously near our country's most sensitive areas, where the first atomic bombs were designed and manufactured. Additional sightings took place in diverse locations worldwide ranging from Levelland, Texas, to Australia's atomic testing area (no similar flap occurred with Sputnik I).

* * *

The Washington, DC, UFO incident involved UFOs that flew over our nation's capital. According to Captain Edward Ruppelt, head of the Air Force's Project Blue Book from 1951 to September 1953, no UFO report in history gained more attention than these Washington sightings, as we discovered during our investigation that included interviewing the family of one of the scrambled jets pilots.

In July 1952, several visual and radar-based sightings occurred in the Washington area, including at Washington National Airport and at Andrews Air Force Base. These events led to security concerns because the UFOs ignored restricted zones and flew right over the White House. Indeed, the White House fly-over resulted directly in the creation of the Robertson Panel, a committee formed by the CIA to investigate UFOs (to be discussed in Chapter Nine).

On July 19, 1952, at 11:40 p.m. a Washington National Airport air traffic controller noticed seven strange blips on the radar of the sky southwest of the city. The objects were obviously not standard airplanes because they alternately dawdled at 100 miles per hour and accelerated to 7,000 miles per hour. As the night progressed, other controllers saw these and other objects on radar and in the sky and several airline crews saw lights in the locations where UFOs were indicated on radar. Officials at the Washington Air Route Traffic Control Center (ARTC)— the group responsible for overflights, arrivals and departures for Washington-Baltimore, New York City and Philadelphia—phoned Washington National saying they had blips on their short-range radar, as did Andrews Air Force Base nearby.

Ruppelt later reported that although airline pilots are typically reluctant to report UFOs, several did that night. One pilot noted that a light was following him. It tagged along after his airplane to within four miles of touchdown. This was confirmed on radar. Another UFO showed on radar at three different facilities before it disappeared. Controllers at ARTC told radar operators at Andrews that they had spotted an object directly over the Andrews radio beacon. Andrews's radar operators and other aviators saw at least one huge fiery-orange sphere in the sky.

Within hours the objects moved into every sector of the radar screens in the Washington area. Alarmingly, some flew through prohibited areas over the White House and the Capitol Building. ARTC called for Air Force interceptors to investigate.

Finally at around daybreak, two fighter jets arrived from Newcastle Air Force Base in Delaware, but by then the UFOs were gone. This delay in the jet's arrival suggests a cover-up.

The Washington event made front-page headlines across the country. Seven days later, just as the excitement began to cool, on July 26 at 8:15 p.m. some new blips appeared on radar screens at Washington National and Andrews. Pilots and ground personnel confirmed the sightings of the new objects, which were traveling at 100 miles per hour. Soon UFOs were again appearing in every sector of the local radar screens.

As before, a call went out for jet interceptors and as before, there was a delay. At 11:30 p.m. two F-94s finally flew over Washington, but as the jets arrived the objects disappeared.

Meanwhile Langley Air Force Base in Virginia received calls about bright rotating lights of changing colors. Langley's control tower operators saw the same lights and called for an interceptor. An F-94 arrived; its pilot saw one of the lights and tried to chase it, but the light suddenly went dark. The jet had locked on to the object several times via radar, but each time, the radar lock-on was broken and the object sped away. A few minutes after they had left the Langley area, the UFOs reappeared in the sky over Washington. Another F-94 steered toward the objects, but as the jet approached, the objects sped away.

According to Ruppelt, the radar room staff at Washington National thought the UFOs were solid metallic objects. He said the radar operators were well qualified— these individuals dealt in human lives and brought thousands of people safely into the airport every day—and they could definitely distinguish between a real aircraft and a weather balloon, which they had often seen. Ruppelt added that UFO activity throughout the country was extremely high that summer, yet the national media concentrated on the Washington sightings.

Ruppelt never explained why, in both cases, the fighter jets took so long to arrive. Such delays certainly provide evidence of a cover-up, or government knowledge of these events. There is likely a classified reason for the delay, because these events would be of high importance.

The Air Force had an official explanation for the UFOs, however: the events were a mirage caused by a meteorological phenomenon known as a "double temperature inversion." Atmospheric scientists including University of Arizona meteorologist James McDonald, Ph.D., subsequently rejected this theory; the temperature inversions did not correlate with the UFO sightings.

Ohio UFOlogists gained first-hand information about the Washington UFOs from an informant called "Cathy Johnson" (not her real name) during an interview about another sighting. Johnson said that Lieutenant Colonel Charles Harris Cooke was her first husband's father. He told people that he was one of the pilots who chased the Washington UFOs and she thought that he'd worked for Project Blue Book. She thought that he was second behind the lead pilot. She recalled that he talked to his family about the case from time to time and that he was upset because the government hadn't briefed him and his fellow pilots about UFOs. The pilots thought they were going after Soviet planes invading US air space. He said that when the pilots arrived over Washington, the silvery thing they saw in the sky was not what they expected.

Cooke died in Cooperstown, New York, in 1973, seven years after retiring from the Air Force. Johnson recalled that on the day of his funeral, people who identified themselves as CIA agents taped off his house for four hours and wouldn't let anyone enter. They removed many of his files from a locked cabinet, she said and much of the material is thought to have concerned UFOs.

Lieutenant Cooke was interested in UFOs and he unofficially studied the reports that were later passed to Project Blue Book. On August 7, 1966, he published an article in the *Washington Evening Star* strongly voicing his opinion that some UFOS were extraterrestrial machines.

This series of sightings is considered by some as one of the largest and most significant of all time in terms of its credible reports and the data obtained.

* * *

In the 1940s and 1950s, some highly publicized strange sightings took place in the region near the Ohio River. One of these was the Flatwoods, West Virginia sighting.

On September 12, 1952, strange lights and objects in the sky were witnessed in Ohio and eastward into Virginia. Thousands of people in West Virginia saw the display. These lights marked the beginning of the Flatwoods Monster Incident.

Flatwoods monster Press coverage

SEPTEMBER 23, 1952

Half an hour past sunset in Flatwoods (in Braxton County, West Virginia), some people saw a bright object pass overhead. It blazed across the sky, emitting a trail of sparks that resembled red balls of fire. Then it came to rest on a hill.

The witnesses climbed the hill and among the trees they observed a red pulsating object 25 feet in diameter. A nauseating smell permeated the scene. One shined a flashlight and caught something in its beam. His dog growled and its hair stood on end as the group saw two greenish-orange eyes glowing in the dark on the blood-red face of a "monster." It was 10 feet tall and it wore a monk-like robe with a hood draped over its head. The monster hissed at them before floating toward the landed object. Terrified, the group raced down the hill. Some became hysterical and others were later treated for shock. One suffered severe vomiting and convulsions.

Later the local sheriff led a posse armed with shotguns to the scene. They saw no sign of the bright object or the crimson-faced monster, but a sickening odor lingered in the air. The posse found parallel skid marks and a large circular area of flattened grass where the object had rested.

The following day, also in Braxton County, a similar incident occurred near Frametown, West Virginia. George and Edith Snitowski were driving through a wooded area with their baby when their vehicle inexplicably stalled. The Snitowskis had no advance warning of automotive problems, but their battery was suddenly dead and the engine would not turn over. As George tried to start the car, an unpleasant odor, like a combination of ether and sulfur, spread through the air, making the baby cry and cough.

George saw a bright light in the woods and got out to investigate. As he walked toward the light, he felt prickling sensations all over his body. He stopped and headed back to the car and on the way he repeatedly lost his balance. As he reached the car, his terrified wife pointed to a 10-foot humanoid figure standing around 30 feet away. The family locked themselves in their vehicle and the figure disappeared into the woods moving by gliding rather than by walking. The light in the woods rose, swinging back and forth like a pendulum gathering momentum. Then it shot out of sight, leaving a glowing trail behind it.

George again turned his key in the car's ignition and the vehicle easily started.

* * *

A similar incident took place three years later near the towns of Kelly and Hopkinsville, Kentucky. The Kelly-Hopkinsville Encounter—also called the Kelly Green Men Case—is one of the best-known and best-documented of all 'Close Encounters of the Third Kind' incidents (in which humans encounter alien beings and not just UFOs).

Artist's impression of the Hopkinsville goblin

This incident was investigated not only by local police, but also by military officers from Fort Campbell. It remains one of the best-known and best-documented cases in the history of UFO incidents.

* * *

Many UFO sightings in the period between 1940 and 1960 involved military or government personnel, including WPAFB.

Sightings by government officials have a high credibility. However, after the passage of Air Force Regulation 2002 in 1954, which made it a security violation for members of the armed forces to discuss a UFO sighting with the media or the public, the number of publicized sighting reports from the Air Force radically declined. In his 1995 *Alien Identities: Ancient Insights into Modern UFO Phenomena*, Richard Thompson includes a list of sightings by US Air Force employees; this list was taken from Richard Hall's 1964 book, *The UFO Evidence*. It showed evidence of numerous UFO interactions. In 20 of the 91 cases mentioned by Thompson and Hall, a UFO seemed deliberately to follow an Air Force plane or to fly at low altitude over a US military base. In 24 of the 91 cases, an Air Force plane chased a UFO, was chased, or was repeatedly "buzzed" by one. These statistics are difficult to reconcile with the official Air Force conclusion that UFOs have never posed a military threat.

Budd Hopkins; Mark Rodeghier, scientific director and president of the J. Allen Hynek Center for UFO Studies; Richard Hall, called "the Dean of Ufology," author of The UFO Evidence, NICAP's assistant director; Jennie Zeidman; and others. (Credit: Jennie Zeidman)

In the 1950s numerous sightings occurred in the Midwest and often near WPAFB. For example, on March 8, 1950, two F-51 pilots and several airline pilots near Dayton observed a round UFO. It was also seen from the ground and was tracked on radar before it ascended and disappeared into the clouds. On June 1, 1951, a unit chief at WPAFB observed a flying disc making right-angle turns in the sky. A year later on July 23, 1952, Air Force Captain Harold W. Kloth, Jr., saw two bluish-white objects change course in the sky over South Bend, Indiana. Two years after that, on July 11, 1954, Air Force jet bomber crews over Hunterdon, Pennsylvania, watched a flying disc keep pace with their four bombers.

On May 24, 1954, a UFO briefly accompanied an Air Force plane near Dayton when the crew of an RB-29 Super fortress bomber watched a brilliant, circular UFO fly below their plane at an estimated speed of 600 miles per hour. The crew photographed the object, but this photo was never released to the public.

UFO literature about Dayton and its vicinity in the 1950s abounds with cases of Air Force planes chasing, being chased by, or being buzzed by UFOs. Over Dayton on August 1, 1952, Air Force pilots (a major and a first lieutenant) chased a UFO detected by radar; they saw and photographed a circular flying object. Also over Dayton, on an unspecified date in 1954, an Air Force lieutenant colonel and a senior pilot chased two UFOs that hovered then flew away. On July 23, 1954, the Ground Observer Corps in Franklin, Indiana, reported a UFO and two jet pilots from the 97th Interceptor Squadron saw four large glowing objects in the sky. As the jets closed in on one of them, it veered away and left the scene (this incident has been officially denied). On June 16, 1955, UFOs were sighted over a wide area of the eastern US Dozens of interceptor pilots were scrambled from many points and gave chase without result. Two months later on August 23 over Cincinnati, Ohio, three flying discs were detected by radar and chased by Air Force jets that failed to catch them.

* * *

In spite of its repeated denials, the US military has spent substantial resources investigating UFO events. While seeking witnesses to a UFO sighting near Delaware, Ohio, Bill Jones and I found evidence of this when we stopped at random to interview a highly respected neighbor that I knew well.

When we asked about UFOs, he related his experiences as a UFO investigator for the Navy in the late 1940s and early 1950s. Luke Laprad (not his real name) is a respected community leader and owner of a large, well-known business in Columbus, Ohio. He served in the Navy for a decade, spending his last few years at NATO's Incirlik Air Base outside Adana in southern Turkey. When we asked Laprad for the number of the unit he was assigned to, he replied, "It didn't exist."

We pressed him for the name of his unit, even if unacknowledged at the time and he responded, "I can talk about this stuff in general, but I am sure the details are still secret." The secrecy is the result of Laprad's role as an aircraft navigator in secret overflight missions. These missions took his unit into the Soviet Union's air space to make aerial photographs of Soviet military installations and other important locations. Higher-flying U-2 reconnaissance aircraft in the mid-1950s eventually replaced the unit.

As we questioned him about UFOs, he said, "If you twist my arm, I can tell you that I used to investigate those things." He went on to describe the secondary purpose of his unit and that purpose was every bit as secret as the primary one.

"Back in those days," he said, "UFOs were considered to be a very important matter. When the areas of the Soviet Union, which were assigned to us, were clouded over inhibiting aerial photography, we were frequently assigned to fly to various locations around the world to help indigenous personnel conduct UFO investigations. Many of these missions were to South America. There was a lot going on there, apparently."

Laprad said these assignments involved specific investigations. The men would fly to a country, pick up a team of investigators and fly into a designated region to take reports from the residents. He said his team acted as "truck drivers" for groups of indigenous military personnel who lacked their own aircraft. Because he spoke neither Spanish nor Portuguese, Laprad was unable to learn much about the reports, copies of which were flown with them back to Turkey and were subsequently sent to the Pentagon (but apparently not to Project Blue Book) by way of the NATO base in Oslo, Norway. When asked why the reports were sent via such an indirect route, he replied, "For diplomatic purposes." He said that the reports were classified as "secret" before being forwarded, that his group did no analysis of the reports and that no information about the purpose of the reports ever came back to his group.

We eagerly pressed Laprad for information about the specific sightings he investigated, but he declined to answer, saying the data might still be classified.

The information from Laprad that reports were sent to the Pentagon, but apparently not to Project Blue Book, is compatible with information from Arnold, Lawrence Coyne (discussed in Chapter Six) and Hynek suggesting that the government: took the UFO situation seriously; had separate high-level, secure agencies that investigated the reports; and used Project Blue Book simply to dupe the public.

Jones and I first investigated this case in 1996. Later I discussed it with Timothy Good, who also described it in his chapter on Naval intelligence in *Need to Know: UFOs the Military and Intelligence*.

This military encounter took place in 1957 at Ellsworth Air Force Base in Rapid City, South Dakota. Between 6:30 and 7:00 p.m. on a late spring day in 1957, Airman Second Class Wallace Fowler saw an object hovering over his head. It was saucer-shaped and silver in color. On top of the saucer was a dome with portholes behind which he could see moving shadows. The larger lower part of the saucer was metallic in appearance and it was constantly changing colors. The object, which he estimated to be about the size of a house, hovered motionlessly.

Fowler later recalled that he thought that it couldn't be an airplane, because he had never seen an airplane stand still like this. After this standoff for about 2 to 3 minutes, he remembered saying to himself that You can come down here if you want, mother fxxxer. Then it will be just me and you. Now strange as it may sound the thing took off as if it was reading his mind, going straight up with unbelievable speed. He did not hear any noise, nor did he see any exhaust.

After the object was out of sight, Fowler ran for the hangars and the base control tower. As he neared the hangars he saw a number of pilots running toward their planes—others had obviously seen the object. When he entered the hangar he heard all the telephones ringing and there was a lot of activity as people ran to prepare the aircraft for take-off. Fowler went up into the control tower, where more telephones were ringing.

After the airplanes took off, Fowler heard a controller speak to one of the pilots. Fowler reported that he heard the pilot say that the thing acted as if it is playing games. It just sits and waits on us and when we get close it takes off.

The pilot replied that it was ahead of them and seemed to be waiting for them again. The controller advised them to watch their altitude. The pilot noted that the object appeared to be metallic.

Fowler then said that all of a sudden they heard a crash and the tower could no longer contact the pilot. Soon Fowler and some others were asked to leave the tower. Before he and everyone left, an officer told them to not talk about what they had seen and heard. Later that evening when his friends returned from town, he learned that people there had seen an object as well.

Fowler, a parachute rigger, reported that little was said about the incident, but he remembered a pilot saying a plane that pursued the object had turned up missing and its wreckage was never found. Fowler added that he wished someone would find out which family lost a loved one in 1957 at Ellsworth.

Timothy Good and I discussed this report and in *Need to Know* he compared it with a UFO seen in 1956 over Ellsworth Air Force Base. Members of the 718th Squadron, 28th Strategic Reconnaissance Wing, at Ellsworth while on a photoreconnaissance training flight, made this sighting. Twenty-two men were on board a Convair RB-36H Peacemaker bomber, when a saucer-shaped object appeared in the sky. It was about 100 feet in diameter, with a dome on top and portholes around this dome. On its sides were many separate light sources, each of a different color. It flew just a few hundred yards off their wingtip for five to eight minutes and its existence was confirmed by radar. The men photographed it. When they landed, they were required to submit their logs and equipment to an intelligence unit called Reconnaissance Technology. The men were told not to discuss the incident.

* * *

Another category of UFO is small objects. Since Kenneth Arnold's initial sighting, numerous small UFOs have been reported, especially between 1940 and 1960.

Small UFOs are reported far less frequently than larger objects. This may be because small UFOs are seen less frequently, or because observers mistake them for phenomena such as ball lightning, "spook lights" (or "ghost lights"), swamp gas and even ghosts. Because many people consider UFOs to be aircraft piloted by aliens, they may not recognize smaller objects as being UFOs.

Reports of small UFOs reveal them to be even more inconsistent with known phenomena than larger UFOs, because the power sources for the smaller objects are harder to explain. For example, according to the government study, "Technical Report No. F-TR-2274-IA Unidentified Aerial Objects Project 'Sign' AMC Wright-Patterson Air Force Base (B1UFO 1947)": "No reasonable hypothesis of the true nature of balls of light . . . has been developed that explains the behavior reported" (9).

Jennie Zeidman is a Columbus, Ohio, pilot and UFOlogist told me about a small UFO incident that took place in Ohio shortly after midnight in June 1979. During this incident a 31-year-old physician saw a randomly pulsating light outside her house. The light passed through a sealed window to a spot where the witness was preparing to go to sleep on a family room sofa. No storm or electrical activity was taking place at the time to explain the light. In addition, although yellowish-white like a firefly, the object lacked a firefly's characteristic soaring flight while illuminated. Either it was on, the witness said, "as bright as a 60-watt bulb" and illuminating the entire room, or it was off and invisible in the diffuse light from an adjacent hallway. The light emanated from the entire object, not from a specific part of the object (as in a firefly's light). As it passed three feet in front of the witness, she equated the shape and size to a large paper clip held at arm's length. The total observation time was probably less than a minute. As soon as she could maneuver around the light and out into the hall, the witness fled in terror, accompanied by her agitated dog.

Artist's impression of the sightings of green fireballs

Zeidman wrote about a larger object in the same article. A woman who was using the telephone saw a slender, luminous, submarine-like object, of intense blue color, fly rapidly through an open window. It headed for a wall, reversed itself, flew into another room, halted in front of the witness, changed aspect, changed course, moved down a corridor and finally exited through another open window. Two additional witnesses viewed it and the sighting lasted about five seconds.

"Green fireballs" are a type of small UFOs that came to public attention in the 1940s when meteor expert Lincoln LaPaz, Ph.D., headed an investigation on behalf of the American military. Because of extensive US government reports about the phenomena, green fireballs are among the best-documented examples of unidentified flying objects.

Early green fireball sightings occurred chiefly in the southwestern United States (US), especially in New Mexico. The sightings alarmed the US government, because the fireballs were often clustered around sensitive research and military installations, including Los Alamos National Laboratory, Sandia National Laboratory and White Sands Proving Ground.

Lincoln LaPaz PhD - investigator of the green fireballs reports

The first atomic bombs were designed and manufactured as part of the Manhattan Project during World War II at Los Alamos and they were tested in the desert at the White Sands Proving Ground near Alamogordo. The WSMR is the country's largest military installation. At a time when the US was developing its atomic capabilities, the green fireball phenomena appeared to be attracted to atomic installations. LaPaz concluded that the objects displayed too many anomalous characteristics to be meteors and that they were artificial—possibly secret Soviet spy devices. Many people of high repute, including LaPaz and the scientists at Los Alamos, saw them and so they were generally considered to be real phenomena and not figments of someone's imagination or part of a hoax. Secret conferences to study green fireballs were convened at Los Alamos and in Washington, D.C., by the Air Force Scientific Advisory Board.

Although researchers in the 1940s theorized that green fireballs were Soviet in origin, the Soviet Union was not immune to green fireball sightings. Several decades later, on September 7, 1984, the pilot of a Soviet Aeroflot airliner flying over Minsk (in what today is Belarus) observed a bright light in the sky. A blob-like object shot out of it. The object, which the pilots guessed was at 100,000 feet, emitted wide green beams that lit up the ground miles below like huge searchlights and that cast a greenish tint over the landscape. One of the beams swung around and projected light straight into the cabin of the Soviet airplane—causing weird effects inside, including multiple lights of different colors and fiery zigzags. The beams outside changed shape to mimic the plane. Another nearby plane also saw the object. In addition, it was picked up on radar and seemed to cause radar interference.

The US government's concern about green fireballs led in December 1949 to the establishment of Project Twinkle. This system of observation stations was discontinued two years later, however, when the government decided green fireballs were natural in origin. LaPaz and others disputed this hypothesis.

Zeidman, during an interview, recorded an interesting comment from LaPaz, that UFOs are the Fifth Horseman of the Apocalypse. His meaning is unknown.

Green fireballs have also been reported in other areas. Ohio researchers Frank Reams, a pilot for Lane Aviation at Columbus International Airport and Barb Spellerburg investigated a December 1991 sighting near Troy, Ohio (outside Dayton), by a man who saw a green fireball appear to crash. A month later in the same area on a perfectly clear day, he and his daughter saw another UFO. This one was four times the length of an airliner, it made no noise and it had no wings or tail. The daughter saw a green flash and the object disappeared. The next morning, five green military helicopters came over the area where the object had disappeared. The witnesses reported that they'd never seen such a formation of helicopters in that area.

Foo fighter photo during WWII

A year later on October 9, 1992, a large, low, green fireball traveled along route I-70 over central Ohio. It was in sight for some time and a number of people photographed it.

OSU professor William Allen told me about seeing a green fireball and described it in an article he published in *Readers Digest*. The fireball reached its zenith, fell through the sky and disappeared behind a tree line. Allen didn't hear it hit ground, but he saw a faint puff of smoke drift in the sky just above the trees.

As in the Soviet Aeroflot incident mentioned above, green fireballs are sometimes associated with beams of light and some UFOlogists think that both are aspects of the same phenomenon. For example, green beams of light that appear simultaneously with UFO phenomena may act as "tractor beams"—devices that attract one object to another from a distance—as in the Schirmer case described in Chapter Five and the Coyne case described in Chapter Six.

Allied pilots, who referred to them as "foo fighters," saw other small UFOs during World War II. These were observed (at around the same time that green fireballs were attracting attention in the US) over both Europe and the Pacific. Foo fighters appeared to Axis pilots, as well and each side thought the objects were the other's secret weapons. But when hostilities ended, no one claimed them.

Foo fighters in the mid-1940s were typically small luminous spheres that appeared near planes at night and that sometimes escorted Allied military aircraft through the sky. Some pilots reported small balls of light that kept pace with their planes. Others described discs and globes of up to five feet in diameter. Foo fighters appeared in colors ranging from white to orange to red and sometimes they changed colors during flight. Foo fighters were typically seen outside of aircraft, but on some occasions they reportedly entered and moved slowly around inside a plane's fuselage.

"Spook lights," "ghost lights," "will-o'-the-wisp," "ignis fatuus"—all of these are names for small UFOs in the form of ghostly lights appearing at night or at twilight. (Perhaps they're seen only at night or twilight because they're not visible during daytime.) Missouri physicist Harley Rutledge, Ph.D., investigated such small UFOs in his 1973 study (discussed at length in Chapter Six).

* * *

Mysterious lights have sometimes been seen in the same form and place repeatedly over many years. The phenomenon has been associated with specific places in various parts of the country including Marfa, Texas; Putney Hill, New Hampshire; and the Missouri-Kansas-Oklahoma border.

Probably the best-known example is the Texas, "Marfa Lights." These are unexplained lights, or "ghost lights," seen near US Route 67 east of Marfa, Texas, on Mitchell Flat. Now a tourist attraction, they've also been observed above the nearby Chinati Mountains and as far north as El Paso and as far south as Mexico.

The Marfa Lights are typically described as brightly glowing basketball-size spheres that float either just above the ground or high in the air. Their colors include white, yellow, orange, red, green and blue. They sometimes hover a few feet above the ground, they sometimes move laterally at low speeds and they sometimes shoot around rapidly in different directions. They frequently appear in pairs or groups, can divide or merge and can disappear and reappear. Sometimes they move in regular patterns. The people I interviewed told me that sightings may occur around 10 to 20 times a year and the lights are nocturnal only. Some writers say the Marfa Lights display typical characteristics of UFOs, including intelligent behavior.

I've looked for the Marfa Lights phenomenon from the Marfa Official Viewing Area, from Marfa itself and from the Davis Mountains to the north. I've been to the Marfa airport a number of times, met some of its employees and even taken a glider ride from it once. I've watched the sights from the viewing area and interviewed people who claim to have seen objects. I think that tourists watching from the Viewing Area often confuse car headlights coming over west Texas mountain roads with the Marfa Lights. I've stayed in the Davis Mountains a number of times in a place that had an excellent view of Marfa out of picture windows and spent some time watching and filming it in different conditions, such as lightning storms at night.

Marfa lights, Texas, USA

The only time I have seen an unusual light display over Marfa was from the Davis Mountains. This light was very bright, looked extremely large and flew low over the town for around 30 minutes very late at night. It was brighter than any of the town's lights and during its flight pattern would sometimes disappear and then reappear. I also made a videotape of it and it showed up clearly. I called the Marfa airport, but they reported seeing nothing that night. They were probably closed when it was there, but hadn't heard anything about it. Because it showed up large and clear in my video, someone must have seen it. I think this was on September 4, 2012, at around 11:30.

The lights were seen by one of my co-workers, a trained and skeptical scientist who was a former university professor and geology department head. At the time of his encounter, he'd never heard of the Marfa Lights. He, his family and a group of scientists were traveling at night along a dark, deserted road in Texas. He and his family were in one car and the other geologists were following in another car. He saw a light approach his vehicle and appear to follow it. This light seemed large and close and it frightened him. When his car later stopped, the occupants learned the passengers in the other car had also seen the light and thought it was following them.

The Marfa Lights are also known worldwide because the area is an "art Mecca" to which people come from around the globe to see world-class art and architecture, as well as the classic town square. The region was the filming site for several iconic films, including *Giant, No Country for Old Men, There Will Be Blood* and it was the setting for the play *Come Back to the Five and Dime, Jimmy Dean, Jimmy Dean* and its film adaptation.

The Marfa Lights themselves have been featured in various media. These include the following television shows: *Unsolved Mysteries*; an episode of *King of the Hill* called "Of Mice and Little Green Men"; and an episode of *So Weird*, a Disney Channel original series. The lights inspired David Morrell's 2009 book *The Shimmer* and they're referred to in the 2009 song "Obfuscation" by the musical group Between the Buried and Me. Because they are so widely known and cultural phenomena, Presidio County has built a large viewing station on US 67 near the site of an old air base and, each year, people gather for the annual "Marfa Lights Festival."

A phenomenon similar to the Texas Marfa Lights is the New Hampshire "Putney Hill Globes." These were seen as early as the mid-1700s and accounts of them have been around for so long they have become folklore. Between 1750 and 1800, numerous witnesses reported seeing lighted balls or luminous globes floating through the air in a forested area north of Putney Hill near Hopkinton, New Hampshire. The slowly drifting globes displayed a seemingly intelligent behavior. In one report, the globes followed a traveler, halted when he stopped to look at them and resumed following him when he continued on his way. The globes were said to stay at least 50 feet from whomever they followed.

The "Hornet Spook Light" is named after a community that once existed near the Missouri-Kansas-Oklahoma border. This light varies in size from that of a baseball to that of a bushel basket. Like other spook lights, its movement is erratic: it may travel rapidly down the road and climb to the level of the treetops, or it may swing slowly up and down and from side to side. It varies in color and may explode and scatter sparks. It has chased vehicles and when pursued it vanishes just before the pursuing car makes contact with it. It's bright enough easily to light up the surface of a road and its intensity is often compared to that of a car's headlight. Locals have seen it in their backyards, outside their bedrooms and beside their porches.

Lights in the sky are sometimes associated with seismic activity. Indeed, "earthquake light" is the term for a glow that can appear in the sky during an earthquake. Researchers including Michael Persinger have theorized that all UFOs result from "earthquake light" and similar phenomena, although this theory is not generally accepted.

* * *

"Waves," or "Flaps," (increased UFO reports) were another characteristic of the period between 1940 and 1960. Some of these were enormous ones that took place nationally and others were more localized. For example, there was an abrupt, huge increase in the number of UFO sightings around November 3, 1957. This was interesting because it occurred when Sputnik II carried Laika the dog into orbit-the momentous first time earth-life had gone into space. Because this was done by Russia, Americans knew about it until they read or heard about a day or so later. However, reports from all over the world began to flood in immediately on that date, so the media had not influenced the wave.

Thus, like other UFO sightings, these near-simultaneous sightings support the idea that UFO reports are associated with real phenomena and are not caused by media attention. With the launch of the Sputnik I on October 4, 1957, Americans suddenly became space- and sky-conscious and citizens strained to catch a glimpse of the satellite—but there was no increase in UFO reports on that day and the next and there were only five substantial UFO cases in the US during October. With the launch of the dog-carrying Sputnik II the following month, however, authorities were suddenly inundated with UFO reports. And these sightings began even before word of the Soviet launching was flashed to the US—thus, it is difficult to link them to reactions to Sputnik II or to press coverage of the event.

These UFO reports were chronicled by independent sources such as Richard Hall in *The UFO Evidence* and Leonard Stringfield in *Situation Red*. In addition, an unusually high number of radiation cases (which adversely affected the health of witness) and of electromagnetic cases (in which cars were temporarily immobilized) were reported during that period. Some UFOlogists feel the UFO activity might have been an alien demonstration to highlight the launch of Sputnik–when earth life entered space.

Many of the November 1957 UFO reports described red or reddish-orange egg-shaped objects that were sometimes associated with electrical failures. Publicly, the Air Force was unconcerned and it collected information on reports that were obviously of the moon, stars, planets, aircraft, balloons and the northern lights. Rather than separate the November reports into unidentified and identified flying objects, the Air Force did not distinguish between the two types of reports, explaining away all the UFO sightings as being mistaken IFO observations.

Perhaps the most famous November 1957 incident is the one that took place in Levelland, Texas. On November 3, 1957, authorities received numerous independent reports of one or several large UFOs in Levelland. Between 10:40 p.m. and 1:30 a.m., people in the area saw reddish or bluish-green objects stopping on roadways and suddenly departing. The objects seemed to cause "electromagnetic effects" in nearby vehicles: the cars would not function properly and sometimes the engine and headlights turned off and could not immediately be restarted. (Although this seemed like science fiction then, such remote-control devices are available today)

Witnesses included Sheriff Weir Clem, who saw a brilliant red object move across the sky at 1:30 a.m. In addition, as Levelland Fire Chief Ray Jones watched an object at 1:45 a.m., his car's lights went off and his engine sputtered.

Other people around Levelland experienced similar incidents that night. Many called police. By morning, authorities had received a large number of independent reports of a glowing object or objects that came near vehicles. After the local media reported the matter, the sheriff's office received over 100 calls from other residents who'd seen objects during the three-hour period of its activity.

Project Blue Book later explained the Levelland, Texas, incidents as having been caused by lightning strikes and lightning balls. But these explanations are stranger than the phenomena itself, for several reasons. First, there was no electrical storm that night. Second, as Jenny Randles points out in her 1987 book, *The UFO Conspiracy: The First Forty Years*, ball lightning is extremely rare. Moreover, it does not form repeatedly, it is thought to never be as wide as a road, it does not remain stable for minutes at a time and it has no effect on car engines and lights. Additionally, on November 4 there was a repeat of the Levelland events. This repeat occurrence makes extremely unlikely the Project Blue Book theory of freakish natural phenomena.

* * *

An extended world-wide military survey seemed to accompany the November 3, 1957, "wave." New Mexico was the state where the Roswell UFO drama unfolded a decade earlier. The area was highly critical and historic, for it gave birth to the atomic age. The first atomic bombs were designed and manufactured during World War II at New Mexico's Los Alamos National Laboratory and were exploded in 1945 at the White Sands Proving Ground.

The area near Alamogordo and White Sands, New Mexico is strategically important. Rockets and missiles were also secretly developed and tested in this area and this was a region where green fireballs had baffled top US scientists in the 1940s. Nearby was Las Cruces where Clyde W. Tombaugh, the only twentieth-century scientist to discover a new planet Pluto (now considered a dwarf planet), experienced his own UFO sighting.

At White Sands, New Mexico, at about the time of the Levelland, Texas, events – around 3:30 a.m. November 3, 1957 – military policemen Corporal Glenn Toy and Private First Class James Wilbanks were patrolling the White Sands Missile

Range in New Mexico in a Jeep. They noticed a very bright egg-shaped object, 75 to 100 yards in diameter, high in the sky. The object descended to 50 yards above a bunker used during the first atomic bomb explosion. Then it blinked out. A few minutes later its light flared up again, becoming as bright as the sun. Then the object dropped toward the ground on a slant about three miles away.

A search party was unable to find any trace of the UFO.

The report by Toy and Wilbanks and another report by First Lieutenant Miles Penney, commanding officer of the Stallion Site Camp north of the White Sands headquarters, of a similar sighting were issued to the press on November 4. In addition, Toy reported, in an open session with public information officer William Haggard and several reporters, that the landing looked completely controlled.

At 8:00 p.m. on November 4, Specialist Third Class Forest R. Oakes and another specialist third class named Barlow were on another Jeep patrol two or three miles west of the atomic bomb bunker when they sighted another UFO again hovering above the bunker. Oakes described it as 200 to 300 feet long and very bright. As the two watched, the UFO climbed at a 45-degree angle with its light pulsating on and off—just like the UFO at Levelland. Moving slowly and sometimes stopping, it traveled away and gradually diminished to a star-like dot in the sky.

Seventeen hours after the second White Sands/Alamogordo sighting, high-altitude research engineer James Stokes saw an elliptical-shaped UFO maneuver in the sky. He was driving toward El Paso, Texas, on Highway 54 near Orogrande, New Mexico (15 miles from the Missile Test Center at the southeast corner of the Proving Ground) when his engine failed. As he coasted to a halt, he noticed other cars ahead of him stopped on the roadside (no information exists about whether they also had engine failure). People were looking up and pointing to the sky.

Stokes saw a large, whitish, egg-shaped object moving in and out of the clouds to the northeast. It made a shallow dive, turned and crossed the highway a few miles ahead and flew into the clouds, causing them to disperse. As the object passed at its closest, Stokes felt a heat wave that made his skin tingle. When he reentered his vehicle and checked the engine, it worked—but the battery was steaming.

I also did some investigating at the White Sands Missile Range and discovered that odd happenings occur to this day. I videotaped an interview with a government employee there about some of these reported happenings. He said that something, maybe some sort of flying objects, could affect people's compasses there (an effect noted at the time of Arnold's sighting). He said that people did not know why, but that rangers would be out in the dunes and suddenly get false readings. He added that they did not know all the types of testing that is taking place, but that it was not just missile testing, but testing of high intensity lasers and other equipment. It was interesting that he seemed to link lasers with effects on compasses. I interviewed him in 2013, but did not ask how long such effects had been going on.[24] He also mentioned that because Holloman AFB, Fort Bliss and Alamogordo surround the area, that all kinds of testing has gone on and added that it still does.

In addition, there are interesting bases in this desert area. I found an old trail, followed it and videotaped it to a base. It was just south of Orogrande and near the site of Stokes sighting. Unlike other such bases, this one did not even seem to have a name, or any identifying information posted. It was in the mountains and some distance from the road. A somewhat illegible old sign on the way there appeared to say no trespassing or photography was allowed. It is off Rt. 54 and not in a populated area. I could drive only on a trail to the south of it, because it was well-fenced. I saw no people, but a number of buildings. Several large active radar units and buildings on the mountains surround it and there are several buildings where its trail connects to Rt. 54. A large tube enters it from the road. This is very close to the location where Stokes saw his 1957 UFO. Although the area appears isolated, there appear to be a number of military installations in the mountains, or off the road.

Holloman Air Force Base also has had great influence. It was featured as not only a UFO landing site, but a location of contact with UFOs in several highly influential films–a 1974 documentary, "UFO's: Past, Present and Future," narrated by Rod Serling and a 1976 televised documentary report "UFOS: It Has Begun" written by Robert Emenegger and presented by Rod Serling, Burgess Meredith and José Ferrer. Experts such as Col. Hector Quintanilla, Dr. J. Allen Hynek and Dr. Jacques Vallée and other government spokesmen, presented information. Some have even said that President Eisenhower met aliens here.

Amazingly, similar events occurred also at other atomic installations and military bases across the country and world at this time. During the November 1957 wave–from November 1 to 7–objects appeared to survey military and nuclear sites.[25] Often these military sites were designated as nuclear. In many instances, electro-magnetic effects were prevalent, objects had a glow or haze about them, the predominant shapes of objects were ovoid, egg or torpedo-shaped and many of the objects landed on roads.

Often sightings were very reliable because in many instances multiple witnesses were involved and many of the witnesses were military personnel, reporters, state troopers and scientists.

A clear pattern seemed to emerge in the military sightings including those of nuclear installations. First, in the case of Pantex (the subject of the article), a manufacturing entity was targeted; second, in the case of White Sands, a testing facility was targeted; and third, in the case of Kirtland and Amarillo Air Base, an end user of nuclear weaponry was targeted. These sightings included all the links in a chain from the manufacture, to the testing, to the delivery and were surveyed in one week. The suggested a highly concentrated effort to study U.S. weapons capability.

* * *

However, these events actually appeared to extend around the globe. In far-away Australia nuclear weapons tests were underway in the Maralinga desert in September and October 1957. And at about the same time as the Alamogordo sighting—the exact date is unknown, but some UFOlogists think the events were simultaneous—a close encounter with a UFO occurred in Australia.

Royal Air Force Corporal Derek Murray, a photographer for the Australian Home Office and a highly reliable witness, gave a firsthand account of what happened. He was in a Maralinga canteen with some colleagues at 4:00 p.m. when a man rushed in claiming a UFO was hovering over the test site. Murray and his colleagues laughed, but the man was so sincere that they went outside with him. They could not believe what they saw.

It was a metallic, silver-blue craft with a flat base, a top dome, plates on its sides and square windows. The on-duty air traffic controller also saw the object; he called other airfields but nothing unusual had been reported. For security reasons, all cameras at the test site were locked up, so Murray and the others were unable to photograph the object. After 15 minutes, the UFO shot upward at a fast speed. It departed at sunset.

Jenny Randles reports on this Australian incident in *The UFO Conspiracy*. She adds that there appeared to be a pattern among three events: Murray's sighting, the sightings near White Sands and Alamogordo.and the launch of Sputnik II. She added that for the UFOs almost simultaneously to arrive as earthlings made their first forays into space and to hover over both the world's first nuclear test site and the site of Australia's tests underway at the time, suggests that an intelligence was at work.

Meanwhile, at still another military base, Fort Itaipu in Brazil at 2:03 a.m. also on November 4, 1957, another close encounter also took place involving a UFO. At 11:00 p.m. two sentries saw what they thought was a new star as it burst forth in a cloudless sky; soon they realized it was a flying object and it was coming straight toward their facility. Within seconds, it was over the fort. The object stopped abruptly, slowly drifted down and hovered 120 to 180 feet above the highest turret.

The size of a large Douglas aircraft, it was disk-shaped, encircled by an eerie glow and emitting a humming sound. After a minute an intolerable heat wave struck both soldiers, as had happened with Stokes and the air filled with the humming sound.

Soldiers rushed to reach their battle stations, but the lights all over the fort suddenly went out, as did the rest of the electrical system. The emergency circuits also failed. Then electric clocks set to ring at 5:00 a.m. began to clamor at 2:03. Both sentries had severe burns.

Also in Brazil, what is often considered the first abduction report took place. The Antonio Villas Boas case occurred on October 15, 1957. Boas reported that a luminous egg-shaped object landed near the tractor with which he was plowing his family's farm. He tried to escape via this tractor, but its lights and engine went dead. He attempted to

Brazilian abductee Antonio Villas Boas

run but was dragged aboard a craft and into interior rooms lighted by fluorescent white lights. He was stripped, covered with a strange gel and put into a room into which some kind of gas was being pumped and this gas made him violently ill. A strange woman – who had almost white hair, large slanting eyes, a triangular-shaped face and blood-red underarm and pubic hair – soon joined him. They had intercourse and the woman subsequently pointed to her stomach, then to Boas and then toward the sky. Next he was taken on a tour of the spacecraft. Afterward, he suffered nausea,

US abductees Betty & Barney Hill

headaches and skin lesions and those who later examined him thought he might have been exposed to radiation. At that time, UFO abduction phenomena were generally unknown. Such phenomena did not receive widespread publicity until the Betty and Barney Hill abduction case was reported in 1966. Because the case was well documented and because of its early date, the Boas case is now considered one of the world's most important abduction cases. In addition, Boas, who was a law student, is quite credible. He later became an attorney, married, had four children and stuck to the story for his entire life.

* * *

Also in a section of the Midwest, for example in Ohio, Indiana, Illinois, an independently reported spike of similar and near-simultaneous sightings also occurred in 1957, with many UFOs being reported at around the same time and often with radiation effects.

In his 1994 *Regional Encounters*, Indiana UFOlogist Francis Ridge discussed a similar flap that began on November 2, 1957, in the Indiana-Illinois area. On November 6, Rene Gilham and other witnesses heard a disc over Terre Haute make a sizzling sound as brilliant beams of blue light shot downward from it. Gilham was underneath the object at the time and he later experienced symptoms consistent with radiation exposure. After he was treated in a Sullivan, Indiana, hospital, Air Force officers interrogated him and advised him not to discuss the sighting. This event was preceded on October 15, 1957, by an incident in which Robert Moudy of Foster, Indiana, saw a large, flat oval-shaped UFO shoot overhead as the engine of his combine died.

Another example that fit a pattern seen among several UFO events was the sighting of a bright, unidentified flying object, followed by physical symptoms in the witnesses that suggested radiation exposure. On the snowy, windy night of November 10, 1957, Mrs. Leita Kuhn of Madison, Ohio, had been going back and forth between her house and dog kennels to check on an overheating stove. Suddenly she saw a huge glowing object about 60 feet above the ground. It was about 40 feet wide and 10 feet thick with a dome on top. A phosphorescent light seemed to flow from the dome and this light was so bright it hurt her eyes. Puffs of apparent exhaust appeared around the bottom and these became increasingly more visible. She fled into the house. When she next looked out the window at 1:55 a.m., the object had disappeared.

One of her dogs was very frightened and Mrs. Kuhn stayed up all night with it (it subsequently died of cancer). Several days later a rash developed over Mrs. Kuhn's body. She sought medical treatment for the skin rash and for eye irritation from the object's blinding light; because of suspected radiation effects, she was advised to report the UFO to Civil Defense. She did so, becoming the third American to report an injury or burn from watching a UFO. Her doctor thought the rash might have been related to what she had seen.

She developed a variety of strange physical conditions, such as an abnormal craving for sweets and water, over the next two years. Some of these were physically painful and some emotionally disturbing. Such conditions may have been the result of exposure to radiation, because exposure can produce effects in various parts of the body, such as rapidly growing cells in the skin and the digestive tract.

In November 1957 in Ohio, according to UFOlogist Leonard Stringfield, two witnesses he called "Mr. and Mrs. J." were watching television. Suddenly there was interference as the picture went into waves and then blacked out. Seconds later a strong, eerie light came through their window. They saw a large, squat object about 20 feet in diameter hovering over their back yard. As Mrs. J. watched through the window, her husband went outside to investigate. The object moved directly over him as he stood frozen in disbelief. He fled inside and immediately became ill and feverish. Within 48 hours he was dead. Medical examination showed intense radiation damage and his internal organs were reportedly "fried."

Such accounts and even physical symptoms suggesting radiation exposure have occurred in association with other UFO reports. An excellent example of radiation exposure associated with UFO activity is the Cash-Landrum Encounter, an event extensively investigated by John F. Schuessler in his 1998, *The Cash-Landrum UFO Incident*. Although this encounter took place in Texas more than two decades after the Levelland incident, it and the simultaneously occurring Rendlesham Forest Incident together have supported the notion that UFOs can and do produce radiation.

Several types of radiation have been associated with UFOs. Some types seem similar to microwave radiation, which causes intense heat. This kind of radiation may result in burned areas of vegetation, such as those described in a burn area by Budd Hopkins in his 1987 *Intruders: The Incredible Visitations at Copley Woods*. In other cases, ionizing radiation, resembling gamma rays, seems to be present, because subjects experience symptoms similar to those caused by atomic bombs, such as nausea and hair loss. Radiation such as gamma rays is emitted from a source. For the radiation to exist and to affect its surroundings, the source must be present; so if the source is a UFO, the rays should affect matter only when the UFO is there. Therefore, for an area to remain radioactive after a UFO has left, the object must have left radioactive material behind.

* * *

Press coverage of the Cash – Landrum case

As shown in this and other chapters, some UFO events have coincided with certain momentous occasions. November 3, 1957, is one of the most significant dates in the history of the earth because it is when earthlings became extraterrestrial. The date may not be as deeply etched into America's national consciousness as, say, the Kennedy assassination; indeed, Americans didn't even know it had happened until they read the next morning's paper. However, the date also marks substantial UFO activity in the US and elsewhere in the world. If UFOs are connected with intelligent beings, these beings may have been aware of the Sputnik II launch. They may have been trying to call attention to themselves to deliver a crucial warning. During the Levelland and White Sands incidents, for example, the UFOs seemed to be showing off as they manipulated car lights and engines. Some UFOlogists feel that as we entered space, unearthly beings sought to heighten our awareness of the power of atomic energy—and to send a message discouraging the use of that energy for destructive means.

REPORT OF SEPARATION FROM THE
ARMED FORCES OF THE UNITED STATES

AIR FORCE

2. SERVICE NUMBER AF 14 405 158

A/1C(P) 1 Mar 55 Reg AF

Expiration Term of Service AFR 39-10

16 July 55 Release from Active Military Service

Houston, Mississippi

Nellis Air Force Base, Las Vegas, Nevada

unknown   Male   Caucasian   Brown   Brown   5'11"   163

Bd#10 Houston (Chickasaw), Mississippi

Not Applicable

FE 4yrs

17 Jul 51 Grenada, Miss.

Hq ConAC (NARS) Denver 6, Colorado

3381 Pearl St, Houston, (Chickasaw) Mississippi

National Defense Service Medal - Good Conduct Medal

4935th Air Base Squadron (ARDC)

Med Dept. Meat & Dairy Inspection   Sep 51   Nov 51   Not Applicable   None

None Indemnity

$644.74 $124.56   Not Applicable   Not Applicable

UP Section 6(a) Appendix

C. H. KOOLAGE, CAPT USAF   8225-481

GEORGE W SCOTT
CWO., USAF Pers Officer

Not Applicable

Single   04   00   None

Academic

3 Pearl St., Houston, Mississippi

214   INDIVIDUAL'S COPY (TO BE DELIVERED TO THE INDIVIDUAL BEING SEPARATED)

John Scott's Air Force discharge paperwork that shows that he worked in Area 51. He was released from Active Military Service with a place of separation, Nellis Air Force Base, Las Vegas, Nevada and his most significant duty assignment was the 4935th Air Base Squadron. The 4935th Air Base Squadron's mission was to support United States Atomic Energy Commission (AEC) nuclear testing at the Nevada Proving Grounds, and the Nevada Proving Grounds at that time contained Area 51. (Area 51 is also known as Groom Lake.)

DEPARTMENT OF THE AIR FORCE
HEADQUARTERS 81ST COMBAT SUPPORT GROUP (USAFE)
APO NEW YORK 09755

REPLY TO
ATTN OF: CD

13 Jan 81

SUBJECT: Unexplained Lights

TO: RAF/CC

1. Early in the morning of 27 Dec 80 (approximately 0300L), two USAF security police patrolmen saw unusual lights outside the back gate at RAF Woodbridge. Thinking an aircraft might have crashed or been forced down, they called for permission to go outside the gate to investigate. The on-duty flight chief responded and allowed three patrolmen to proceed on foot. The individuals reported seeing a strange glowing object in the forest. The object was described as being metalic in appearance and triangular in shape, approximately two to three meters across the base and approximately two meters high. It illuminated the entire forest with a white light. The object itself had a pulsing red light on top and a bank(s) of blue lights underneath. The object was hovering or on legs. As the patrolmen approached the object, it maneuvered through the trees and disappeared. At this time the animals on a nearby farm went into a frenzy. The object was briefly sighted approximately an hour later near the back gate.

2. The next day, three depressions 1 1/2" deep and 7" in diameter were found where the object had been sighted on the ground. The following night (29 Dec 80) the area was checked for radiation. Beta/gamma readings of 0.1 milliroentgens were recorded with peak readings in the three depressions and near the center of the triangle formed by the depressions. A nearby tree had moderate (.05-.07) readings on the side of the tree toward the depressions.

3. Later in the night a red sun-like light was seen through the trees. It moved about and pulsed. At one point it appeared to throw off glowing particles and then broke into five separate white objects and then disappeared. Immediately thereafter, three star-like objects were noticed in the sky, two objects to the north and one to the south, all of which were about 10° off the horizon. The objects moved rapidly in sharp angular movements and displayed red, green and blue lights. The objects to the north appeared to be elliptical through an 8-12 power lens. They then turned to full circles. The objects to the north remained in the sky for an hour or more. The object to the south was visible for two or three hours and beamed down a stream of light from time to time. Numerous individuals, including the undersigned, witnessed the activities in paragraphs 2 and 3.

CHARLES I. HALT, Lt Col, USAF
Deputy Base Commander

Halt memo

CHAPTER FIVE

The Sixties – Police Chases, Mothman and Close Encounters of the Third and Fourth Kind

THE 1960s were a time of astonishing and well-documented UFO cases. It was the Cold War era and many UFO events included a peculiar involvement by the US military or other government officials. Some occurrences involved not only UFOs, but strange phenomena such as "monsters," humanoid" sightings and police chases. Several incidents were so impressive that they inspired popular books and major Hollywood movies: Steven Spielberg's *Close Encounters of the Third Kind* and *The Mothman Prophecies* starring Richard Gere come immediately to mind.

This was also the time when abduction phenomena received widespread publicity, especially the Betty and Barney Hill case of 1961, which was first widely publicized through John Fuller's best-selling 1966 book *Interrupted Journey: Two Lost Hours Aboard a Flying Saucer* and was later the subject of the 1975 made-for-television movie, *The UFO Incident*, starring James Earl Jones and Estelle Parsons.

Also, during this decade, the government made a study of the UFO reports previously collected from the public by the US Air Force in several projects the best known of which was Project Blue Book. This 1969 report was Edward U. Condon's, *Scientific Study of Unidentified Flying Objects* generally known as the Condon Report. It concluded that nothing should be done with further reports because they would not contribute to science. After this the government ceased officially collecting reports from the public, but Air Force regulations for reporting UFOs that could affect national security continued to the present day.

* * *

An icon of the 1960s is the monster known as "Mothman," and the UFO-related phenomena associated with Mothman events.

In the mid-1960s, the area around Point Pleasant, West Virginia, was abuzz with reports of a huge primeval beast. It had blazing red eyes, large bat-like wings and the ability to fly or levitate. Frighteningly, it sometimes followed people down the highway to Point Pleasant. These events also occurred in an area of great importance to the historical development of America.

Author John Keel arrived at Point Pleasant in December 1966 and began collecting reports about the bird- or bat-like entity that people called Moth-man. These reports included apparitions, monsters, mysterious lights, unearthly noises, UFO

Drawing of the Mothman

US author and researcher John Keel

phenomena, "Men In Black" (MIB), ghost-like beings and other hellish entities that haunted the pastoral Ohio River valley. Keel had spent a year traversing the valley as he collected stories about the monster and he and others thought its appearance presaged a disaster. No one was sure what the disaster would be, but people expected it soon.

Almost as if accountable to these predictions, on December 15, 1967, the Silver Bridge—a 700-foot bridge across the Ohio River at Point Pleasant, West Virginia,—suddenly collapsed; 37 vehicles were crossing the bridge at the time and 46 people died. The collapse is still considered the nation's worst highway-bridge disaster. In 1975, Keel published *The Mothman Prophecies and* it became the best-known account of events associated with the Silver Bridge collapse.

This towering suspension bridge was historic and important. It was built in 1928 as a two-lane eyebar suspension type bridge, 2,235 feet in length and called the Silver Bridge because it was the nation's first aluminum painted bridge. After the collapse, many questioned why the bridge would suddenly drop into the river. Three reasons commonly heard were: a sonic boom caused the event, the "Curse of Chief Cornstalk" was fulfilled by the collapse, or the bridge fell due to structural failure.

Many people reported a sonic boom either just before the bridge fell, or simultaneously with its fall.

Alternatively, some residents associated the collapse with the Curse of Cornstalk. Chief Cornstalk was the Native American commander during the 1774 Battle of Point Pleasant, an important turning point in American history that some consider the first battle of the American Revolution. It is linked with the opening of what was then the Northwest Territory (and the American Midwest) for white settlement. Chief Cornstalk later signed the Treaty of Camp Charlotte and according to legend, with his dying words he placed a curse of death and destruction on the Point Pleasant area because whites were taking Native American land and killing and abusing the Indians. (Another noted Native American, Tecumseh, lost his father during the Battle of Point Pleasant. Tecumseh—who later founded a great Indian confederacy, which was the Native American equivalent of Washington, D.C., but in a territory greater than that of the US of the 1810s—also put forth several prophecies about the nation.)

The third theory of structural failure involved the bridge's eyebar construction. The bridge used eyebars—straight metal bars, each with a hole or "eye" at each end. A single steel eyebar was found to have been cracked. The crack had widened, causing the collapse of the entire bridge.

Some of these events involved UFOlogy's original foundations and establishers. For example, Gray Barker, who wrote *The Silver Bridge* in 1970, linked the bridge collapse

Gray Barker – courtesy Rick Hilberg

107

with the appearance of Mothman. He was the first to do this, as his book preceded John Keel's by five years. Barker, from West Virginia, was also a pioneering UFOlogist: in his 1956 book *They Knew Too Much About Flying Saucers* he was among the first to describe these mysterious MIB figures who according to UFO conspiracy theorists intimidate witnesses into keeping silent about UFOs. Barker is also the author of *MIB: The Secret Terror Among Us*.

Another key UFO trailblazer was also involved in these events, Albert Bender. In 1952, he founded the first worldwide civilian UFO investigatory group, the International Flying Saucer Bureau (IFSB) and its magazine, *Space Review*. This group led to important spinoff organizations, such as the Aerial Phenomena Research Organization (APRO), Civilian Saucer Investigation (CSI), National Investigations Committee on Aerial Phenomena (NICAP) and MUFON, which include the world's top UFO groups. He had served in the Air Force and was a company supervisor.

In 1962, he collaborated with Barker on the book, *Flying Saucers and the Three Men*. This resulted from his 1953 discoveries that caused him to think that he had finally found the truth the UFO phenomena and its cover-up. He planned to reveal this information in the October issue of the *Space Review*, but he was visited by three MIB. They terrified Bender to the point where he not only did not publish the report, but quit UFO investigation altogether. He left a warning to those engaged in saucer work, to be very cautious. This is similar to the Arnold's events (mentioned in Chapter 1) at the beginning of UFO study, which also involved MIB.

Albert K. Bender

This warning was so strong that Bender withdrew from UFO investigation. This withdrawal was so complete, that the UFO field did not even notice that this original founder was still alive; he died very recently at age 95 on March 29, 2016.

Even before these events, the story of a flying monster was legendary among ancient Native Americans in the area of the Mississippi and its tributaries (such as the Ohio River, on which Point Pleasant is located) long before the arrival of Europeans. For example, near the city of Alton,

Pisa petroglyph

Illinois, there was once a rock engraving, or petroglyph, of a flying entity called the "Piasa Bird." This work, discovered in 1673, was of a horned monster with red eyes, a face like a person's, a long tail and wings. The monster was also called "a bird that devours men," "Storm Bird," or "Thunder Bird," by Native Americans, who considered it dangerous.

Our local Ohio UFO research group, MORA, investigated whether Point Pleasant was still the center for strange events but was told that nothing unusual had happened in recent years.

The idea of "Men in Black" gained cultural prominence; for example, a 1997 movie *Men in Black*, starring Tommy Lee Jones and Will Smith, was based on Lowell Cunningham's comic book about a secret organization that suppresses and monitors paranormal activity on earth. A *Men in Black* TV series and a 2002 sequel followed the film.

* * *

EDITORIAL VIEW
Paperwork jingle still steer-
's the government offices around
by to James Kilpatrick.

THE WEATHER
Cloudy and colder tonight.
Low in mid 20s. Saturday partly
cloudy and colder. High in the
upper 40s.

The Athens Messenger

Monster No Joke For Those Who Saw It

By ROGER BENNETT
Assistant News Editor

They think it's a big joke.
They think we can go out there
and it come out for us.

"I" in the red-eyed, winged-
back, six - foot manlike t h i n g
which has turned a remote section of Mason County, W. Va.,
into a dusty, car - packed thrill
show.

"They" are the hundreds of
curious sightseers, who h a v e
jammed a 10,000 - acre tract of
Point Pleasant each night since
the creature was sighted by two
married couples last
week.

The sightseers knew there
took such a thing, but they
hadn't dared to miss a chance
looking it.

The people who've seen it so
far, especially Mr. and Mrs.
Roger Scatberry and Mr. and
Mrs. Steve Mallett, are afraid
they'll see it again. But they
keep looking.

"I hope others do see it. I
hope it scares them as much as
it did us. Maybe then they'll believe the thing exists and we're
not dreaming," Mrs. Mallette
said.

The two couples first spotted
the creature Tuesday in the
sprawling - marshy area which
contains the McClintic Wildlife
Sanctuary and a huge abandoned TNT plant. Most of the property is government owned.

Tuesday night the area was
alive from the lights of cars
and flashlights as the curious

traveled up and down the main
of dirt roads. Police officials estimate more than 1,600 persons
were searching the area prior
to midnight.

Every intersection was jammed with parked cars and
small clumps of laughing, jos-
ting young adults. Huge abandoned powder plant build-
ings rang with the shrieks of
youngsters seating themselves
more in the pitch - black plants
than the people standing in the
narrow roadways.

Volunteer police officers and
firemen — creeping through the
crowds — have no major fear.
They estimated that each car
in the area had at least one
gun. One officer heard an auto-
matic rifle bark several times

Thursday night behind one of
the many buildings.

Early sightings — besides
that of the two couples — have
seen several things in common. The
description includes two red
eyes about six inches apart,
wings with 10-foot span and always manlike; with stocky legs.
These sightings came f r o m
Cheshire, Rutland, several persons at an isolated home near
the TNT plant and one in God-
dridge County, W. Va., east of
Parkersburg.

The Scatberrys and the Mal-
lettes said they believe the
thing "didn't mean to harm
us," even though Mrs. Scatberry had to be treated for
shock, only to chase them away.
At one time the creature came
within 100 feet of their car.

In all they spotted it five
times the first night. They've
seen it twice since. The first
night it chased their car at
speeds up to 100, gliding above
and behind the vehicle. It coul-
and a stand closing in a "tree-
ard played at a high speed or
legends of a mouse."

What is it? They don't know
but they're sure—
"One thing that
leels is the pigeons.
Since he appeared from
disappeared from
ed police plant but
where the creature
roosts," one said.
"Pigeons can be
either hidden
throughout the
the huge double
power plant.

Press coverage of the mothman sightings

Another event of the 1960s, the Portage County UFO chase, one of the world's most dramatic and best-verified UFO encounters, was perhaps one of the world's most important UFO events. It involving a police chase and multi-state sighting and is thought to have inspired the UFO pursuit sequence in Stephen Spielberg's *Close Encounters of the Third Kind*. In addition, it helped spur the creation of the Condon Committee, a group that undertook a government-supported investigation of UFOs (see Chapter Nine).[26] Our investigation showed that even today information about it is evolving. I have remained in contact with one of its original investigators, Rick Hilberg.

And because the facts indicate that authorities knew about the UFO before it reached Ohio and there appeared to also be a cover-up at is termination (possibly around Sharon Massachusetts), a cover-up may have been in place at the beginning and throughout the events, as will be described.

On April 17, 1966, police chased a rapidly moving UFO across multiple state jurisdictions. The event was very credible because

US researcher Rick Hilberg

it involved police officers. Law enforcement personnel are highly accurate and believable witnesses because they're trained to observe incidents in detail, to avoid responding emotionally to situations and to focus on "just the facts" when describing an occurrence. In addition, because police departments keep careful records, UFO cases involving law enforcement are well documented. Moreover, local police tend to resent or disdain their federal counterparts and so they are less likely to engage in the kinds of cover-ups associated with the US military, the FBI and the CIA.

The UFO may have first been seen in Michigan. The police chase ended south of Pittsburg, Pennsylvania, but the object may have been sighted later in the Massachusetts area. However, the event has come to be named after the Ohio County where its pursuers spotted the object. It is also known as the Spaur/Neff case after the two officers who led the chase.

In the early morning of April 17 when three Benton Harbor trash collectors in southwest Michigan were startled by a flying object of such dazzling brightness that they couldn't look straight at it. Ohio police were notified to be on the lookout for this object, according to an article published in the *New Castle News* in Pennsylvania on April 18. Thus, the authorities already knew something about the object.

The chase itself began just before 5:00 a.m. Deputy Sheriff Dale Spaur and Mounted Deputy Wilbur "Barney" Neff, both of the Portage County Sheriff's Department, were chatting with a utility pole repairman when, to their amusement, they overheard a police radio report about an Akron woman who'd seen in the sky a bright object as big as a house. As the dispatcher and police personnel on the radio laughed at the report, Spaur, Neff and the repairman joined in.

Minutes later the deputies responded to a call to investigate an abandoned automobile by the side of the road between the towns of Randolph and Atwater, on Route 224 south of Ravenna, Ohio. When they arrived, the officers noticed the car was filled with radio equipment. Painted on its side was the emblem of a triangle and a bolt of lightning. Above this were the words "Seven Steps to Hell."

The deputies left their scout car to investigate. That's when they first saw the bright object in the sky. As it rose from the horizon, it approached them, hovered 75 feet overhead and bathed them in light.

Spaur later gave this account during an interview with Air Force Major Hector Quintanilla, head of Project Blue Book:

> I always look behind me so no one can come up behind me. And when I looked in this wooded area behind us, I saw this thing. At this time it was coming up ... went up to about treetop level, I'd say about

one hundred feet. It started moving toward us. . . . It was so low that you couldn't see it until it was right on top of you. As it came over the trees, I looked at Barney and he was still watching the car . . . and he didn't say nothing and the thing kept getting brighter and the area started to get light. . . . I told him to look over his shoulder and he did.

He just stood there with his mouth open for a minute, as bright as it was and he looked down. And I started looking down and I looked at my hands and my clothes weren't burning or anything, when it stopped, right over on top of us. The only thing, the only sound in the whole area was a hum . . . like a transformer being loaded or an overloaded transformer when it changes. . . .

I was petrified and, uh, so I moved my right foot and everything seemed to work all right. And evidently he made the same decision I did, to get something between me and it, or us. . . . So we both went for the car, we got in the car and we sat there.

The UFO moved east and paused again. By now the object was about 250 feet away and still shining brilliantly. Spaur later described it as an oval, about 40 feet in diameter and about 21 feet thick, with a rounded bottom from which a conical spotlight shined onto the ground below. It returned and Spaur and Neff, now in their cruiser, punched the microphone button and told Sergeant Henry Shoenfelt at the Ravenna police station that the object was there. "He comes back with . . . 'Shoot it!'"

Spaur said:

After we got to thinking it over, it wasn't such a good idea to shoot it. . . . It was low and it was big and great God Almighty . . . it just moved right up and stopped; . . . it wasn't two hundred fifty feet in front of the car. And everything was lit up . . . it was big as a house! . . . like looking down the middle of hell. . . . It was very bright; it'd make your eyes water.

Sergeant Shoenfelt asked if they had a camera and he asked if they could follow it or stay with it until the police could get a camera there.

The two followed the light along Route 183 and then on Route 224, where they paced beside it at 86 miles an hour. By now it was 300 to 500 feet in the air and it lit the ground under it. They again were able to clock its speed and reported that it was traveling 103 miles per hour.

After that they crossed the Berlin reservoir and traveled into Mahoning county; Spaur said it came back toward them:

112

And when it did, it angled, you could see it silhouetted against the sky and the beam of it was . . . going straight behind it. . . . And you could see the whole back third of a metallic object . . . you could see it just as plain as . . . and I thought then we could identify it. . . . I could see only one projection. And all this I kept radioing back. Everything that I seen, I gave it to the other cars and Bob at the radio; I gave it to the other counties as I was going. . . . It changed direction probably two or three times. . . . I never seen anything like it. It was a monster.

At one point the object stopped and waited for them to catch up:

It lost probably half its altitude, so help me God, it went down over [Route] 51, waited as we came up to it, it went right up to the left, it went right straight up about five, six, seven hundred feet and took off again, right at the same pace.

The chase was witnessed by both civilian and government personnel. On April 18 several local newspapers, including the *Albany Times Union* and the *New Castle News,* reported that hundreds of area people watched the object and that jets had been scrambled. Many accounts said six or seven police departments reported the object. In an article titled "No Reports UFO Seen in County," the *Albany Times Union* stated that reports also came from Air Force Reserve pilots, based at Youngstown, who said they attempted to follow the object but that its speed was too slow for their jet trainers That same day the *New Castle News* in Pennsylvania noted that as soon as the reports started coming in, jet pilots at Youngstown Airport were up in the skies, but the jets were too fast for the UFO.

Law enforcement personnel throughout the area were aware of the UFO because calls from civilians flooded the switchboards of sheriffs' offices and police stations along the route. Gerald Buchert, a police chief in Mantua, Ohio, reported that he photographed the object.

One person who monitored the police broadcasts was Patrolman H. Wayne Huston of East Palestine, Ohio and he radioed to the deputies that he would join the chase. Soon he saw the bright light streak through the sky with Spaur and Neff in pursuit. Huston joined the chase and the three officers crossed the Pennsylvania state line near Rochester. The UFO was now headed southeast, but Spaur and Neff, who'd been chasing it at a high speed for nearly 80 miles, were out of their jurisdiction and low on gas. Their superiors radioed to them to abandon the chase at 5:30 a.m.

Meanwhile in Salem, Ohio, eight miles south of the UFO's path along Route 224, policemen Lonny Johnson and Ray Esterly were listening to police radio reports and watching for the object. At about 5:30 a.m., they spotted it. They reported that it was two miles away and hovering at an altitude of 10,000 feet—the same altitude as a commercial jet that was passing at the time. As they watched, two smaller jets approached it. When the jets and the object disappeared, these two officers drove back to headquarters.

At about 5:20 a.m. in Conway, Pennsylvania, 30 miles south of New Castle, another police officer, Patrolman Frank Panzanella of the Conway Pennsylvania Police Department, was on patrol when he saw a stationary object shining brightly in the sky. Unsure of what he was seeing, Panzanella stopped his car and got out to watch it as Spaur and Neff pulled up.

Spaur, Neff, Huston and Panzanella stood and watched the UFO, which was hovering at 3,500 feet. They could see the moon in the sky above it and a bright star near the moon (later determined to be Venus). Panzanella saw an airplane pass below it and radioed his police dispatcher, John Beighey of Rochester, to ask him to contact the Greater Pittsburg Airport. The air traffic controller there confirmed that the object was being monitored on airport radar. Within minutes, the officers heard police radio chatter about jets being scrambled to intercept the object. In a statement to the Air Force, Panzanella later wrote:

> I saw 2 other patrol cars pull up and the officers [Neff, Spaur and Huston] got out . . . and asked me if I saw it. I replied SAW WHAT! Then pointed at the object and I told them that I had been watching it for the last 10 minutes. The object then moved out towards Harmony Township approximately 1,000 feet high, then it stopped then went straight up real fast to about 3,500 feet. I then called the base station told the radio operator to notify the Pittsburgh Airport. . . . The operator got the airport on the line and told them what happened, . . . we kept watching the object and at that time a passenger plane passed to the left.

Panzanella gave the following account to investigator William Weitzel of the National Investigations Committee on Aerial Phenomena (NICAP):

> John Beighey, the Rochester Base Radio Operator, or a voice going into his microphone, said, "They're sending two [jets] up." Also heard a voice saying the object was on radar. . . . The radar report was heard before we saw the plane fly under the object. I also saw two streaks of smoke or something in the sky, like jet contrails, apparently coming in such a way that, if continued, the streaks would have circled the object. The front of the growing streaks was to the object's left, above the object.

Spaur mentioned the same incident in his report to Project Blue Book's Hector Quintanilla:

> We could see these planes coming in. . . . When they started talking [on the radio] about fighter planes, it was just as if that thing heard every word that was said; it went PSSSSHHEW, straight up and I mean, when it went up, friend, it didn't play no games, it went straight up.

As Spaur, Neff and Huston prepared to drive back to Ohio, Panzanella said he intended to wait around to see if the object would return. However, the dispatcher from Rochester radioed to Panzanella with a request that the Ohioans come to the Rochester station for a police interview. Panzanella sped off to catch them. Just before he did, Panzanella spoke via police radio with Patrolman Henry Kwaianowski of Economy Borough (just east of Conway); Kwaianowski reported seeing a metallic, football-shaped object flying at the same altitude as two jets.

Spaur, Neff, Huston and Panzanella went to the Rochester station, where Spaur spoke briefly by phone to an unidentified man he later identified as "some colonel." This colonel tried unsuccessfully to persuade Spaur that he had simply misidentified some normal phenomenon. The colonel eventually agreed to report the event to WPAFB, headquarters of Project Blue Book.

The Portage County incident received considerable media attention. Scientists contacted Spaur the same day as the chase. And of course, the US government became involved. As an article published six months later in *The Plain Dealer* put it after this chase, Spaur's daily routine was washed away immediately through public ridicule.

Spaur, Neff and others had described many interesting, unique and specific aspects of the object. For example, Spaur and Neff observed that if their police cruiser had to slow for traffic or road conditions, the UFO would slow, too, as if it were waiting for them to catch up with it. They had related this observation to others via radio. However they were not the only ones to observe this interactive behavior. As reported in the *New Castle News*, two local married couples surnamed Matteo and Roth, who were driving when they first sighted the same UFO, thought at first that it was a reflection. But when they stopped and rolled down the window, they still could see it. When they stopped, the object stopped. When they moved the car, the object began moving. They repeated this and observed the same results. As they followed it for several miles, they watched it move from one side of the car to the other. Mrs. Roth described it as very frightening.

In his interview with Quintanilla, Spaur gave many specific answers further describing technical details about the object. About changes in object's light intensity, he said:

> It would maneuver, this part [the part shining the light] would be a real bright, blue light, or a white-blue light, like a mercury vapor or something; a white light. The only thing that would change is, it would get brighter when it would go up and then it would seem like it would lose part of its intenseness, of the light as it would come back down to us.

He also described the appearance of the object's upper portion: "You could see it very plain and it was like an aluminum top that's been used for a while; it was definitely a silver, or light color, but it wasn't like chrome." This account is similar to Kenneth Arnold's 1947 description of the objects he saw. Spaur also said that when the object maneuvered, "The nose part of this thing . . . when it was going forward . . . would be down. . . . If it wanted to go straight up, it would level out. . . . It was all, beautiful maneuvers; they were clean." It also appeared to gain altitude as it passed over cities: "When we got to Canfield, it went up, to about, I'd say pretty close to two thousand feet. . . . After it cleared the area of Canfield . . . it came back down."

* * *

The government investigation begun by "some colonel" continued the next day, April 18. Major Hector Quintanilla interviewed Spaur and his fellow witnesses several times before announcing, on April 22, that the officers had experienced an optical illusion, had become confused and had chased an Echo communications satellite and the planet Venus. The Air Force denied that jets were scrambled to pursue a UFO that morning.

Spaur and Neff's superior, Sheriff Ross Dustman of Portage County, defended his deputies, saying the object was not a satellite and not Venus; Venus would not be 50 feet above a road and moving from side to side. Portage County Judge Robert Cook (an acquaintance of Spaur's and Neff's) also supported the deputies' judgment; he contacted the US Congressional Representative from Ohio, William Stanton and characterized the Air Force investigation as grossly unfair to the two deputies. Stanton wrote a letter of complaint about the Blue Book investigation to Defense Secretary Robert S. McNamara and demanded that the Air Force Commanding General reopen the investigation. When the Air Force refused, Stanton went to the Pentagon and spoke to Air Force Lieutenant Colonel John Spaulding, who agreed to send an investigator to the scene.

To everyone's dismay, that investigator was Quintanilla. The official conclusion, called the "Echo/Venus Explanation," remained unchanged. This explanation was highly questionable, however, because several witnesses saw both Venus and the object at the same time. Numerous officials disagreed with the "Echo/Venus Explanation," including OSU astronomy professor J. Alan Hynek, Ph.D., University of Arizona atmospheric physicist James E. McDonald, Ph.D., Portage County Sheriff Ross Dustman and NICAP investigator William Weitzel.

Meanwhile, although Spaur, Neff, Huston and Panzanella asserted they'd heard radio confirmation that the UFO was tracked by radar at the Greater Pittsburgh Airport, officials at the airport denied that such tracking had occurred and that such a statement had been made via radio.

After the Project Blue Book investigation of the Portage County case, the officers found their lives had changed forever.

Immediately after the UFO event, deputies Spaur and Neff had been tired and shaken. Neff's wife Jackelyne said that she hoped she would never see her husband like he was after the chase. He was real white, almost in a state of shock. He had been through the wringer. Spaur's wife Daneise reported that she'd never seen her husband more frightened. He acted strange and listless, she said. He just sat around and was very pale. Later, he got real nervous. He would disappear for days and days, when she wouldn't see him.

Patrolman Wayne Huston, who'd been with the East Palestine police department for seven years, quit his job within six months of the chase, changed his name and moved to Seattle where he became a bus driver. He admitted he quit because of the incident. People, including the local authorities, had laughed at him. City officials don't like police officers chasing flying saucers.

During the months after the event, the wife of Portage County Deputy Wilbur Neff said that people ridiculed him. He doesn't talk about it now. Once he said that if the thing landed in his back yard, he wouldn't tell a soul.

Deputy Sheriff Dale Spaur, the primary figure in the incident and the only one named in the Blue Book report, suffered the most. In addition to experiencing persistent nightmares, he was ridiculed mercilessly for months and hounded by the media. One night two months after the encounter, he was driving alone at night in his cruiser when he thought he saw the UFO again. A month later, during a flash of tension and confusion, he shook his wife violently, leaving bruises. She filed assault charges; he was jailed and lost his job.

In October 1966, six months after the UFO chase, *The Plain Dealer* reported that Spaur's wife had filed for divorce. Spaur had taken a job as a house painter. Strapped by child-support payments, he was living alone in a dingy motel room, eating cereal and a single daily sandwich. He had lost 40 pounds. He was broke.

In utter desperation Spaur turned to God for help. On the first Sunday that Spaur attended services at a local church, the minister, eager to help him feel welcome, introduced him to the congregation as that man who chased flying saucers. Spaur felt he had become a freak.

Huston, Neff and Spaur clearly felt mentally strained from the incident and its aftermath. Like many disaster survivors and combat soldiers, they seem to have suffered what today would be called post-traumatic stress disorder (PTSD). They may even have experienced a mental anguish similar to that reported by alien abduction victims. But instead of receiving the help they needed, they were ridiculed.

* * *

Over the two days following the Spaur sighting, numerous UFO sightings occurred in Massachusetts, including the Sharon Saucer case, named after the town of Sharon, Massachusetts. UFOlogist, Diana DeSimone of Newton, Massachusetts, has suggested to me that this case might have been included the same object that Spaur and Neff chased.[27] The Sharon Saucer, reported in Raymond Fowler's 2001, *UFOs: Interplanetary Visitors*, was seen in the city of Sharon, just south of Boston.

The Sharon Saucer case involved multiple reports over a two-day period in New England; these reports began 13 hours after the Portage County chase ended. Moreover, the location of the sightings is consistent with the movement of the Portage County UFO, for Sharon and its surrounding area lie almost exactly due east of the greater Akron area and the Portage County object moved eastward fairly consistently.

An object that may have been associated with the Sharon Saucer was spotted in Danvers, Massachusetts—formerly known as Salem Village and the site of the notorious seventeenth-century witch trials. The Danvers sighting occurred on April 17, 1966. Starting at around 7:15 p.m. witnesses observed an oval-shaped UFO; later an oval object was spotted in the sky over nearby Peabody. Witnesses said it hovered above a school. On April 18, near Peabody, witnesses reported an oval object that reacted to searchlights by zigzagging, accelerating straight up and disappearing.

On April 19 at 12:15 a.m. near Sharon, police received reports of a silent object that appeared over the tree line. As in the Spaur case, the witnesses included the police: four officers and several other witnesses reported the sighting. An object appeared above the tree line at about 200 to 300 yards away from the observers. It was a very bright large mass of white light with a round appearance and it made no noise. It stopped and hovered above the tree line for two or three minutes while a plane passed overhead; then it moved off. It had a red light in the front and one in the rear; a wide section of white light extended between the red ones. It flew so low that it seemed to pass right over witnesses' heads. Additional witnesses in the area also reported a similar object. At around the same time, an object with a piercing hum and a dazzling violet light appeared in Stoughton, Massachusetts. Witnesses there described an oval object, with red lights at both ends that descended into dense woods. Other nearby witnesses said a helicopter and five airplanes circled a landed UFO near Bellingham.

As in the Spaur case, officials denied the object existed.

Fowler reported that during April 1966 the sky had seemed to burst from the weight of UFO reports. However, the average person had no inkling about these reports because radio and television newscasts were silent on this topic. A friend of Fowler's, who was employed at a Boston radio station, told him that during that hectic period, his supervisor would not allow him to include UFO reports arriving by Teletype on the newscasts.

Fowler added that several days after the Sharon sighting, Air Force personnel from Hanscom Field in Bedford, Massachusetts, made an official inquiry into this event. He also found that the Air Force had instructed the Sharon police not to comment on the incident; thus, the sighting received little publicity.

Police were told to maintain a separate, nonpublic log for further UFO reports in the area. An investigator named Ernie Reid discovered the fact that a separate police log was being maintained for UFO reports at the time of the Sharon sighting. Reid headed a detective agency and was studying for his doctorate in criminology. He told the police that their blotter was within the public domain and he threatened to complain to the district attorney's office. The police chief decided he'd rather face the Air Force than the district attorney and Reid was given the data.

During his investigation, Reid and others discovered that several additional sightings had been reported on the same date. Six reports had been made in the area of the Sharon encounter on the same night.

The use of a separate police log is, by itself, evidence of a cover-up; in conjunction with reported government actions during the Spaur case, the Sharon account suggests that a cover-up plot had been in place from the beginning of the Spaur sighting.[28]

* * *

Early in 1997, Bill Jones and I began a re-investigation of the Portage County UFO Case. We learned that Portage County deputies Dale Spaur and Wilbur Neff had both died. One of the two other police officers, who joined in the chase—either

119

Patrolman Wayne Huston, or Patrolman Frank Panzanella—had also died, but we did not learn which one.

Mantua, Ohio, Police Chief Gerald Buchert, who had photographed an object, had also passed away. Jones telephoned Buchert's son and asked if anyone in his family would be willing to discuss the events of that night in 1966. The son was pleasant, but he insisted no one wanted to talk. He did, however, point out that once when his children were playing the game *Trivial Pursuit*, they saw their grandfather's name as an answer to one of the game's questions. The children asked to know more and the parents told them the story, but it had not been discussed in the family since. When asked why the family refused to talk about this part of its history, the son replied it was too upsetting and painful. Yes, the family still had the photographs, but he insisted that the photos would stay with the family.

We tried to reach witnesses, as well as the spouses of the deceased officers, to learn what has occurred in their lives since the event, but we were unable to make contact with any of them. Jones and I had ended the article we wrote with the statement that, beyond yielding a question for the board game of *Trivial Pursuit*, perhaps this painful and life-changing affair should just pass into history.

However, this case has had such important ramifications that it did not pass into history and it may remain active. For example, on April 5, 2008, I received an email from a Washington state investigator about another re-investigation of the Spaur case. He made the following remark about why the event was important:

> I have never failed to make the Dale Spaur case a premiere case because it so aptly illustrates the Actual Reality as faced by pilots, military personnel, average citizens and cops. Then there is the Official Reality that is created in the media, this time via a villain called Major Quintanilla of Blue Book.

* * *

On December 3, 1967, 20 months after the Portage County UFO chase, another police officer, Herbert Schirmer in Ashland, Nebraska, experienced a close encounter. Although the government study called the *Condon Report* (see Chapter Nine) devotes just two pages to this event in a hard-to-find section titled "Case 42—North Central Fall 1967," UFO researcher Jenny Randles, with many others, felt that it had merit and included it in her *The UFO Conspiracy*. It is now considered an important abduction case.

Schirmer was on patrol when he saw an object that emitted a screeching sound. It hovered a few feet above the road, swayed from side to side, then climbed upward and disappeared. This was all that he initially could remember about the event.

During the Condon committee study of his case, which was conducted after the investigators learned of his sighting, Schirmer became aware of a discrepancy in his report. He could not account for 20 minutes of time. His notation in the police logbook for the time when he returned to the police station was inconsistent with the time when he should have returned to the station right after his

Police officer Herbert Schirmer

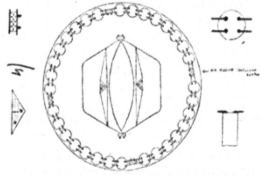

The most mysterious sketch was of the propulsion unit. Schirmer was told that this worked on a principle of 'reversible electromagnetism'. Shown is a series of wire-connected cannisters, surrounding a glowing cone in the centre.. The triangular objects appeared to be computers.

The spaceman appeared to be 4½-5 feet tall. He wore a close-fitting, hooded, silver-grey uniform, black boots, belt and gloves. On the left chest was a red emblem of a winged serpent. The man's proportions were normal. Looking down, the eye would normally 'see' a picture of a person with a large head and small feet but the conscious mind compensates for this perspective problem.

Details of the UFO and the entity witnessed by police officer Herbert Schirmer

sighting. To help Schirmer remember what happened during the missing 20 minutes, Leo Sprinkle, Ph.D., of the University of Wyoming, hypnotized him.

Under hypnosis, Schirmer recalled that the engine and lights of his car had become inoperable. The UFO was at the top of an incline and a strange force from the UFO had "towed" his car up to it. Two beings emerged from the object. One carried a "box," and from this box a green glow was projected all over Schirmer's car. Feeling as if in a trance, Schirmer found himself getting out of his vehicle.

One of the beings stood next to him and communicated in a deep tone that was slow and ponderous. The message Schirmer received seemed to come without being spoken, as if it were transmitted telepathically. The being asked, "Are you the watchman of this town" and Schirmer replied that he was.

After he was led up and onto the catwalk that ringed the UFO, Schirmer was taken inside. Here he saw what he described as a baby saucer, a remotely controlled device for observing what was happening on earth. It was about the size of a hubcap. The being said the device transmitted sound and sight to a screen on the larger ship. (UFOlogy is full of descriptions of small UFOs, which perhaps are similar devices. Schirmer may be the first to report having seen such a device inside a UFO and having learned about it from a space alien.) Schirmer was told that the aliens had a breeding analysis program and had used some humans. (Alien breeding programs similar to the one Schirmer mentioned have been reported many times since then.)

Schirmer was shown what he called a "vision." (This vision may have been a hologram, the concept of which was unknown to him in 1967). This "vision" resembled a projected image of a sun and six planets. The being said that it and its colleagues had come from another galaxy and were watching earth closely. It communicated that someday Schirmer himself will see the universe as the being has seen it. However, it added that he would only remember viewing the UFO from the outside.

Schirmer was a highly respected police officer that had served as a US Marine and he did not experience the harassment undergone by Spaur and Neff after their Air Force investigation. Indeed, after Schirmer's UFO experience, he became the youngest man ever to rise to head of the town's police department. Because of this accomplishment, one can assume his superiors did not question his judgment or his account of the incident.

Sprinkle was so profoundly impressed he spent the next 20 years investigating alien abduction cases. He is one of the world's leading experts on close encounters of the fourth kind (abductions) and for many years, he was considered the only academic figure devoting any time to studying or researching abduction accounts. He once described one of his speculations about the meaning of the UFO phenomena to me:

My speculation is that UFOLKS are providing Humankind with instructional events (UFO sightings), in a gradual manner, so that we can discover the relationships between physical, biological, psychosocial and psychic levels of reality. Then we can build flying saucers & become UFO occupants for another planet, etc., etc.[29]

* * *

What is perhaps the best-known of all abductions, the Betty and Barney Hill case, also occurred in the 1960s and was widely publicized through John Fuller's *Interrupted Journey*. One of the first abduction investigators was an Ohio schoolteacher and amateur astronomer, Marjorie Fish. During the hypnotic

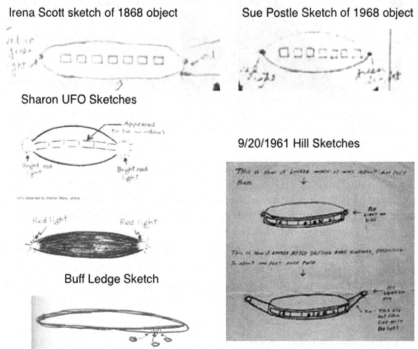

Irena Scott sketch of 1868 object

Sue Postle Sketch of 1968 object

Sharon UFO Sketches

9/20/1961 Hill Sketches

Buff Ledge Sketch

A photo of Betty and Barney Hill's original sketch of a row of windows on the object they saw, showing the smaller lights on both ends (done on September 20, 1961 right after the sighting, and published in "Betty and Barney Hill: Where the Debunkers Went Wrong"). The Hill's original sketches of their sighting are similar to other objects reported at about the same time and location; such as of the Sharon Saucer (http://www.ufoevidence.org/cases/case548.htm), the events reported by Walter Webb in his 1994 book "Encounter at Buff Ledge", and of a sighting in Massachusetts 1968 by Sue Postle and Irena Scott (IUR 9-10/1990)

sessions of Betty and Barney Hill, Betty recalled seeing a "three-dimensional" star map that was shown to her by the aliens. She later drew a version of the map from memory. In 1969, Fish used this drawing as a basis to make her own three-dimensional star map in an attempt to locate the home planet of the aliens. She made a model of the stars with distances between stars corresponding to Betty Hill's map and she sought to determine the location of the home planet by inspecting this model. She identified the map as being of the double star system of Zeta Reticuli. Later, when computers could be used in this type of work, computer analysis roughly replicated her work.

What is perhaps the best-known of all abductions, the Betty and Barney Hill case. Betty Hill is here seated on the left - courtesy Phyllis Budinger

More recently, chemist Phyllis Budinger analyzed Betty's dress. She told me that the pink stains in the areas that Betty said were touched by her non-human captors were coated with a biological material of mostly protein and a small amount of natural oil. The protein seemed to break down the fiber structure. She thought that her analysis supported Betty's account.

Another interesting aspect to this sighting is the report of a row of windows and of lights on both ends on the row of windows. The drawings of this are similar to other reports, such as of the Sharon Saucer, the events reported by Walter Webb in his 1994 book *Encounter at Buff Ledge* and of a sighting in Massachusetts.[30][31]

* * *

In late autumn 1966—about a half year after the Portage County UFO chase and a little more than a year before the Schirmer incident—the Ohio Penitentiary was the site of several independent sightings of a UFO.

The Ohio Penitentiary was a fortress-like 23-acre site with a series of buildings enclosed by 30-foot rock walls. It stood near downtown Columbus, Ohio, just east of Neil Avenue (now the prosperous Arena District). Opening in 1834, it is legendary for numerous reasons. In 1930, hundreds of prisoners were burned alive in the worst fire in US prison history. By the 1960s, it had hosted several luminaries. One was American author William Sydney Porter, who wrote under the pen name O. Henry. While serving time for embezzling, he produced numerous stories including "The Gift of the Magi." Another inmate was Confederate General John Hunt Morgan, known for leading Morgan's Raid into Kentucky, Indiana and Ohio—the deepest penetration into the North of any uniformed Confederates. Yet another convict was Chicago gangster Bugs Moran, whose gang members were gunned down by Al Capone's associates in the Saint Valentine's Day massacre and who popularized the "drive-by shooting." Other notable inmates included Dr. Sam Sheppard, an Ohio physician whose trial for murdering his pregnant wife generated headlines comparable to those of the O. J. Simpson trial and whose case inspired *The Fugitive* TV series and film and several members of John Dillinger's gang. The prison was closed in 1983 and before it was demolished in 1998 it served as the setting for the 1985 made-for-television movie *Love on the Run*, starring Stephanie Zimbalist and Alec Baldwin.

H. White (not his real name) worked at the Ohio Penitentiary as a guard from 1965 through 1967. A former GI (he later returned to the military and retired from the Marine Corps as a captain), he was 31 years old at the time of the incident described below. For years he never spoke externally of the event because of the penitentiary's policy not to divulge what happened inside the prison to outsiders. Later, however, he opened up to our group's UFOlogists Frank Reams and Barbara Spellerberg during their investigation of the Ohio Penitentiary sighting; Reams found him to be down-to-earth and not prone to exaggeration.

On a clear autumn night in 1966 at 2:00 a.m., White was in the tower at the northeast corner of the prison's perimeter walls when he saw a bright, large, circular object rise from the south across the nearby Scioto River. It reached an estimated altitude of 100 feet. White said the object had a domed central section, but he couldn't make out any windows or other features because of its bright light. The UFO moved rapidly toward the grounds inside the perimeter walls, where it paused and hovered at a low altitude, barely higher than the walls, lighting up the yard as if on a sunny day. The object was no more than 50 feet from White. Most of the 75 employees on duty that night saw the object; indeed, many of them screamed in terror.[32]

White recalled that the prison captain on duty that night called Lockbourne Air Force Base (now Rickenbacker Air National Guard Base) and the municipal airport, Port Columbus, to ask if their personnel were aware of aircraft near the prison and if anything unusual had appeared on radar. The answer was no. White said that to his knowledge no one officially reported the event and that at the time no one investigated what had happened.

White later recalled the name of the guard in the northwest tower that night; Reams contacted this guard. He did vaguely remember the event, however—particularly the bright light.

Reams also contacted the Ohio Department of Corrections during his investigation; he was told that if records from the 1960s existed, they'd be in storage and not easily found. Reams uncovered additional information about this sighting in May 1994, after MORA produced, on the Columbus public access cable channel, a television program featuring this Ohio Penitentiary case.

After the program, Ralph White (no relation to H. White, the pseudonym of the primary witness), who was working in the state correctional system and who thought he could put MORA in touch with others who knew about the event, contacted an individual from MORA. Ralph White helped Reams contact Frank Miller, a former Ohio Penitentiary employee who'd also seen the TV program. (Miller eventually uncovered the names of others who had witnessed the UFO and were willing to talk; these names included Dave Stokes, Russell Brisnston and someone called "Joseppi.")

Miller began work at the penitentiary in 1968 and he said that seeing the show brought on chills because he remembered that that year he'd overheard several guards discussing the 1966 event. According to Miller (the supervisor who was on duty the night of the sighting), a man named Captain Smith, mysteriously committed suicide soon after the event.

While investigating another UFO sighting, Bill Jones and I encountered the daughters of Roy Beck, a prison guard supervisor who described a similar UFO incident at the Ohio Penitentiary, which may have involved the same object. They said Beck told his family that he'd seen a flying saucer over the prison and that the event convinced him UFOs were real. The daughters weren't sure when this happened, because they were children at the time, but they thought it was in 1949 or 1950.

As the saucer had moved over the south wall during the sighting, its lower portion became partially transparent and observers saw humanoid beings silhouetted inside. These beings were looking down into the penitentiary, observing what was going on. The terrified guards reached for their machine guns, but Beck, the supervisor, ordered them not to shoot because there was no prison break attempt in progress and because the size of the flying saucer made machine-gun fire seem futile. After a few minutes the saucer left at such a high speed that it seemed to disappear.

* * *

In the spring of 1966, a UFO was sighted over an air defense missile base in Dillsboro, Indiana, 10 miles inland from the Ohio River along US Route 50, southwest of Cincinnati. Although the area is privately owned today, in the mid-1960s it was a key installation for the defense of Greater Cincinnati from a Soviet air attack or nuclear weapons. The base housed Nike-Hercules missiles that could be armed quickly either with high explosive or nuclear warheads. A primary witness was S. Blake (not his real name). Bill Jones and I interviewed him in 1998.

In 1966 Blake was in the Army, working in the assembly and test area of the base and assigned to Battery C, 56th Artillery. On the night of the sighting he was assigned to backup guard duty. At 12:30 a.m. Sergeant Grimes entered the guard office and told Blake and another enlisted man to relieve a guard at Post 4. The guard had called in and seemed to be "going crazy," Grimes said. When asked why this was happening, Grimes replied that there was a UFO over the assembly and test area near Post 4.

Blake and the other man left the guard office and headed toward Post 4. As they rounded a 20-foot-high pile of dirt by a construction area, they saw the UFO in the sky 200 yards away. It was disc-shaped and it seemed to be metallic. It emitted a pulsing orangish-red glow. When the pulsation reached its brightest, the outline of the object was barely visible. Blake could see round, blue-lighted outlines of what might have been portholes, but he wasn't sure what these really were.

What Blake called white "pieces of light" emanated from the bottom of the object and moved quickly to the ground where they disappeared; the "pieces of light" came out one at a time, with the following light not appearing until the previous one disappeared. The "pieces of light" seemed to Blake to be going down into the assembly and test area, although they might have been falling into a location between the assembly and test area and the missile storage facility that was also near Post 4.

When Jones and I asked how big the UFO was, how far away and how high, but Blake said he couldn't say because he had no way to judge.

Blake and his companion decided they were in danger. The companion ran back to the guard office and Blake entered a nearby communications trailer. From here he listened on the radio as officials at the base reacted to the sighting.

A warrant officer on duty raised a missile from its underground hangar and prepared it to fire on the aerial intruder from the launcher-control facility 1,900 yards from the base. Permission to fire was requested up the chain of command and in each instance the request was denied. The final request was made to NORAD in Colorado Springs and the final denial came from there. This denial included the comment that NORAD knew of the object and had tracked it for some time over the US. Blake, in the communications trailer, heard all of this on the radio.

The incident was now over and Blake vacated the trailer. He didn't see the UFO leave and he later said he didn't remember anyone describing the object's departure. He thought the incident lasted about 10 to 15 minutes.

Blake recalled that the next day seven to ten officers from WPAFB came to the missile base in two or three automobiles. He said he thought the group consisted of one "full bird colonel," several lieutenant colonels and a couple of lower-ranking officers. Blake thought two of these were Army and the rest were Air Force. These officials questioned everyone on the base regarding what they'd seen and heard about the incident. Blake was handed a blank piece of paper and asked to write down everything that happened.

Blake was interrogated by an officer particularly interested in the blue color of the round, porthole-like shapes. He was given a color chart and asked to identify the exact shade of blue he'd observed. After he made his selection from the chart, Blake asked the officer why he was so interested in the color. The officer replied that blue is associated with nuclear energy (Cherenkov radiation is electromagnetic radiation emitted when a charged particle passes through an insulator at a speed greater than the speed of light for that medium).

The officer asked Blake if he'd seen anyone looking out of the portholes; Blake chuckled and replied he had not. At the end of the interview Blake was told never to discuss the incident: "It did not take place." From what his friends on the base later said, Blake surmised that everyone there received the same order. Little was said about the incident after that.

When we asked if the base had lost power during this incident, Blake said that no, he'd seen no evidence of power loss and that nothing ever contradicted this observation.

Both Blake and his companion were subsequently disciplined for not following the order to continue to Post 4, but the discipline was not serious. Blake remained assigned to the air defense missile base until December 1966, when he was transferred to Europe.

This southern Indiana missile base incident is also similar to an event reported by Lawrence Fawcett and Barry Greenwood in their 1984 *Clear Intent: The Government Cover-up of the UFO Experience* (this incident is discussed in Chapter Six).

In a related investigation, Bill Jones and I discussed a similar UFO encounter over a military base with UFO abduction investigator Budd Hopkins. Hopkins, author of *Missing Time* (1983) and a world authority on abductions, has investigated memory lapses that occur in association with UFO abductions. Hopkins told us that numerous witnesses of this other military base encounter either forgot the episode or were warned not to discuss it.[33] He thought this UFO event might have psychologically affected the entire base.

* * *

During the 1960s, many reports included humanoid sightings. One such occurrence took place in an area bounded by Agler, Purdue, Paul and Aberdeen Roads on the outskirts of Columbus, Ohio.

On a September evening in the late sixties, Rick (not his real name), a central Ohio teenager, saw a large glowing figure standing by a woods in a dark alley near his home. Rick was frozen in fear throughout the sighting and couldn't move or scream.

He said he was about 70 feet from the figure at the closest point and could see it clearly, although he didn't think it saw him. The alley was unlit, but the light diffusing from the city was sufficient for him to observe details and he distinctly remembered seeing the form of the figure. As he observed the shape of the figure's body, his first thought was that it was a person in a costume. However, he decided it was too tall and thin to be human.

He said it was about seven feet high with very thin arms and legs that were about an inch in diameter. The head was large and egg-shaped and it glowed as if with a neon light. In the place of eyes it simply had indentations and these glowed also. He couldn't remember seeing a mouth or nose. Rick said the being's glowing head seemed to have streaks across it and he assumed these streaks were the branches of a nearby willow tree viewed against the illumination. It wore a silvery metallic belt that contained some kind of "instrument panel," but he couldn't remember any details about this. He said he thought its feet were cubical in shape and they made a sound when hitting the pavement. The figure walked away toward the woods, turned at a stream and disappeared into the forest.

When asked whether he thought the being was alive or mechanical, he emphatically said it was alive. Yet he described it as having no brain and said the head seemed transparent. This head turned from side to side as the creature walked, as if it were looking around. Its walking was stiff rather than flexible and its joints appeared not to bend. He couldn't remember whether it swung its arms as it walked.

Asked if the sighting took place on Halloween, he said the month was September; he was sure it wasn't Halloween.

When interviewed later, Rick said that he stood there shocked. He ran to the house as fast as he ever ran before and swung open the door screaming "Mom, Dad!" As soon as they found out what had happened the whole family jumped into the car and they went out hunting for it. His parents said that it was probably someone dressed up and told him to keep the story to himself.

Rick filled out a UFO sighting questionnaire in 1984 and he added that the next morning a neighbor girl came to the door asking if we had seen strange lights in the field the night before. Both sets of parents went to the field and found a large oval place where the grass and small trees had been pressed down.

The "large oval place" was about an eighth of a mile from where Rick saw the figure enter the woods. Rick said it was unusual for anyone to be in these woods at night and this was probably why Joyce's parents were concerned.

In the 1980s Rick's family still remembered the incident, although not in great detail. His mother recalled that on that September night, his father doubted Rick's story at first. But because Rick had always been truthful, he eventually decided Rick was telling the truth. Neither Joyce nor her family remembered the incident, however.

By the time of the interview in the 1980s, Rick had attended Mount Vernon Nazarene College and was finishing his master's degree in special education at OSU. He had served as a missionary in Africa, had worked in public speaking and public relations for his church and was teaching the mentally handicapped.

Rick concluded that he wished he could offer more detail, but the incident occurred at least 15 years ago. Many, many times he said he had gazed up at the heavens taking in the vast beauty of the Milky Way and the untold number of far-off alien suns and wondered what it was that he saw and heard walking through the dark alley so many years ago.

* * *

A similar-looking being was seen in Savannah, Illinois, in the summer of 1968 by another teenaged boy, Sam (not his real name), aged 15.

Sam's family was spending the evening at a campground at the end of a valley. After dark, when his family was asleep, Sam reported to me that he saw a red and green light moving slowly to the east and north of the family campsite. The light stopped moving and Sam later said it looked like an airplane coming in for a landing at a small airport. However, Sam later learned there were no airports in that vicinity.

Ten minutes later Sam was frightened to see the outline of a being he estimated

US abductee Travis Walton, whose experience was made into the movie 'Fire in the Sky'

to be more than six or seven feet tall. At first he thought it was a ghost, although he later thought it might be some kind of machine. Its form was fuzzy, like a cloud and it glowed with a pale bluish-white light. It was wearing no clothes and had an emaciated body with long limbs. Its legs joined its feet in the middle of the foot rather than at the end above a heel. The size of its head was, in proportion to its body, the same as a human's head. As in Rick's Alum Creek sighting described above, this creature had indentations where its eyes should have been. Sam said these indentations were perhaps darker than the rest of its face.

It ran toward him down the valley from the east with long strides and it stopped to the west of him. Its joints seemed to move like those of humans and it moved both its arms and legs as it ran. But it ran in a unique way, very smoothly, seeming to float. It made no sound.

When it stopped, it looked at him and he thought it was trying to get his attention. But he was too afraid to continue staring at it, so he turned away. For a moment he thought something had come up behind him. But after it looked at him, it turned and ran back up the valley. Then he went to sleep.

The next morning Sam inspected the area and saw large footprints where the being had been: these footprints were nearly square, with each side being about 16 inches long. He climbed the hill to where he had seen the spacecraft descend and discovered a "large circular patch," 30 yards in diameter, on the ground. The grass there was brown, as if dried up. He didn't go inside the circular area. Downhill from the area he noticed a power cable, a normal feed-type power line that went underground from the last pole. He later thought this suggested some kind of underground facility in the area.

At first Sam didn't tell his parents what he'd seen. His father was an Army unit commander (Sam suspected his father might be involved in a secret military operation) and Sam thought that because of his father's military connections, his parents would not respond well to his story.[34]

Sam couldn't remember whether this sighting took place in June or July of 1968. He did recall a mention of missiles in the area—possibly nuclear missiles—and he said he'd also heard there was a top-secret military base nearby.

* * *

Sam and Rick's sightings are particularly interesting because of the similarities. The two teens didn't know each other, but they saw similar beings in the same part of the country at around the same time and at about the same age. In addition, both saw ground evidence suggesting that something unusual had been in the area.

Of course, these are not the only sightings of thin glowing beings. UFO researcher Jenny Randles presented several such reports in *The UFO Conspiracy*, including the description of a 10-foot humanoid figure that glowed a phosphorescent green, had no visible legs and had a body formed by small points of light. Randles thinks these figures might be either some sort of holograms, which glow with reflected light, or a form of plasma. She also theorizes that fuzzy outlines such as the one Sam described suggest electrical forces at work.

* * *

I may have had my own smoking gun experience while working for the DIA, as Timothy Good reported in *Need to Know: UFOs, the Military and Intelligence*.

In 1968 and 1969, I worked with satellite photography for the DIA under code word security clearances that were above Top Secret and some of which were the most highly classified in the government. Two of these code words were "Keyhole" and "Talent" (TK). This work was done in a vault in a windowless building, where we had to work a safe combination, pass before a one-way mirror and through a security check just to enter the workplace. The work involved identifying all flying objects over certain airspaces.

This work was very secure and vital because the 1960s were a time of intense vigilance by the US in the face of a perceived Soviet threat. The US maintained reconnaissance operations via satellite technology and aircraft overflights of the Soviet Union and elsewhere. Jeffrey Richelson's *America's Secret Eyes in Space: The U.S. Keyhole Satellite Program* (1990) describes the Keyhole Program as one of the most significant military technological developments of the last century and perhaps in all history. The photoreconnaissance satellite played an enormous role in stabilizing superpower relationships because it helped dampen fears of weapons that the other superpowers had available and because it showed whether military action was imminent. Much information about photoreconnaissance satellites and similar technology is still classified. Photoreconnaissance satellites are crucial to the military and satellite and aircraft imagery also can provide new and valuable intelligence about UFOs. This work remains some of the highly secured in the government and according to Ashcroft also takes place in the highly secured WPAFB NASIC, building 856 that we visited.

Today it is still exceptionally classified and recently has been in the news because of e-mail news. Its current status the "TOP SECRET//SI//TK//NOFORN" level must be handled with great care under penalty of serious consequences for mishandling. Every person who is cleared and "read on" for access to such information signs reams of paperwork and receives detailed training about how it is to be handled, no exceptions—and what the consequences will be if the rules are not followed. In the real world, people with high-level clearances are severely punished for willfully violating such rules."[35] So I didn't carry away any of this information.

In 1968, I was working in a section called Air Order of Battle in the Soviet/ East Europe Division, Eastern USSR Branch. Our duties included identifying and recording all flying objects viewed via this satellite photography in this area, such as aircraft and missiles. I think the CIA was the recipient of our reports.

In July 1968, I mentioned the subject of UFOs to my colleagues. As I recall they included Mr. Reams, a high ranking civilian, William Carlisle, an Air Force Major and Rick Shackelford, a civilian. I think Mr. Reams may have had a high position, such as GS-14. To my surprise, no one ridiculed me. This was because in early 1968 (before I'd begun working in that section), they had observed a UFO on their TK photography. I looked at these photographs and made copies for use at the facility, but because they were classified, I could not take them home or record any identifying information.

The object in the pictures was photographed over water and I could tell by the water's wave pattern that the object was above the water and not in it. As I recall, the object was over the Black Sea. It was to the west of a mountain range that had a Soviet military installation on its other side. The object was photographed on at least two missions (a mission was one 90-minute satellite pass around the earth). It was in a slightly different place during each of the two passes, but it was in the same general area in both.

I made enlargements of the photographs and manipulated the object's size until I had two photos that showed the object from two different viewpoints with the object the same size in each. Thus, I could examine the object's shape stereoscopically. It was saucer-shaped, with a dome. This dome was tall in comparison to the brim— almost like that of a top hat. However, the shape may have been distorted by my method of reproducing and enlarging the photos.

The protocol required us to report the results of our photographic analysis to the CIA and the supervisors of my area said they'd reported the object as a UFO. I am unaware of any time that our supervisor's professional opinion about the identity of objects in the photos was questioned because they were the government's own top authorities. However, the CIA did not accept this report. The CIA insisted the object was an illusion caused by an imperfection in the film. The DIA analysts protested that because the object had been photographed on two different missions, there couldn't be such a photographic imperfection.[36] The CIA, however, was adamant.

To determine whether the object might indeed be an illusion caused by an imperfection in the film, the analysts sent the film to sensitometer and densitometer specialists. These experts analyzed it and reported that there was no imperfection and that a real object had, in fact, been photographed. My supervisors reported these results to the CIA, but the CIA continued to insist the object did not exist and was an illusion caused by flaws in the film. The specialists who analyzed the film thought this was highly unusual behavior on the part of the CIA. As far as I know, the Air Order of Battle section was the DIA's top organization for analyzing overflight information and I know of no other time that the section's professional opinion was questioned.

In this case, what should have happened is that the CIA should discuss the material with the experts in a courteous professional manner. If the experts were wrong, the reasons why should have been pointed out. This would improve the country's proficiency in photointerpretation.

But what did happen is interesting–instead the CIA gave an explanation that was weirder than the UFO–almost as if it were taunting the professionals. The images were very, very definitely not film flaws. If the CIA experts knew what caused them, they should have given us constructive information, rather than ridiculous replies.

Moreover a misidentification in the government's Photographic Interpretation Office could potentially start WWIII. This was highly classified and significant work. Because our work could easily involve UFO phenomena, I think we should have been informed in some way about it. We had a need to know, but we did not. Instead, we experienced something that could be seen as harassment from the government. This suggests that a much higher government agency can interfere with and maybe actively harass even people working in the government in areas that should be concerned about UFO phenomena.

In addition, I later discovered that the DIA has a significant, maybe vital, role in both UFO investigation and its cover-up. For one, many suspect that it might the agency that collected UFO reports after Project Blue Book was terminated on December 17, 1969. For example, John Greenewald, of the Black Vault in "The Defense Intelligence Agency's UFO Files" said:

> The Defense Intelligence Agency, their mission is to provide timely, objective and cogent military intelligence to. . . .the decision makers and policymakers of the U.S. Department of Defense and the U.S. Government. Did they take an interest in UFO sightings? They sure did and The Defense Intelligence Agency has hundreds upon hundreds of blacked out investigations into the UFO phenomenon.

Moreover, some of his released documents show that in 1968, when this occurred, the DIA was actually actively investigating UFOs, thus, some department likely was aware of our report.

In other documents, he said that the Central Intelligence Agency and Defense Intelligence Agency have conducted UFO investigations that have not been publicly released. This might be the majority of their documents on the subject.

And these agencies have been involved for a long time; the CIA sponsored the 1953 Scientific Advisory Panel on Unidentified Flying Objects, also known as the "Robertson Panel."

Our experience with this DIA behavior suggests that a department monitors UFOs along with other flying objects. Because their response to our report was ridiculous and insulting to the reporter's professional expertise, it may also cover-up and debunk UFO reports. These activities also reminded me of the Arnold events, where it appeared that a higher government echelon acted independently of the rest of the government (in addition, the reason I mentioned the UFO subject was because a few days before that people had nearly been killed during a UFO observation).

Many investigators, such as Timothy Good, have backed up this DIA inform-

This photograph was taken in Orrville, Ohio, of a disc-shaped UFO over a cornfield. It appeared to be metallic, about 30 to 40 feet in diameter, and an estimated 2500 feet from the camera. It was analyzed by professional photographers, Donald Brill and George Shuba and others, who thought it was of a real object. The photographer never came forward. (Credit: Rick Hilberg)

ation. This experience suggests to me that somewhere in the government is or was a group with knowledge of UFO activity. Moreover, it's likely that our Air Order of Battle section would have been monitored because it possessed widespread and the most recent coverage of the earth's surface and air space. And we should have been the agents to find the UFOs.

This inside the DIA experience certainly made me think that the government was involved in cover-up activities. In fact, it even made me slightly wonder if aliens were running the government.

This program is likely vital for UFO study, for as Stanton Friedman has observed, the government probably knows the most about the UFO subject and its best evidence might be its photo-reconnaissance programs. He mentions that the best equipment for monitoring UFOs is satellite or ground-based radar or high performance cameras and these are operated by government agencies.

He added that much of the data generated by spy satellites is born classified. Government agencies are always on the lookout for equipment coming in from orbit and recovery teams are instantly alerted when information comes in.

Because of the technical expertise exposed through this photography, it is among the most classified material in the country and this is regardless of whether UFOs are involved.

Moreover, as more information becomes known about DIA overseas investigation, UFOs associated with water and UFO activity in the Black Sea area of the world, perhaps this information might help to shed light on our DIA experience or our experience might help in the examination of additional little-known UFO events there. For example, why did a Russian airplane crash in the Black Sea in December 2016?

In addition to observing these mysterious photos and gaining insight into the CIA, while working for the DIA in Washington, D.C., I learned about the area's network of tunnels and vaults.

UFO literature contains many references to secret underground tunnels in Nevada, Area 51, WPAFB and other places, but there appears to be a tunnel system under Washington, as well.

I learned that the network of tunnels and vaults in Washington exists so that in an emergency, key personnel can be evacuated via tunnels to underground facilities. Because of the huge number of people and the enormous amount of classified information and equipment that would require very quick evacuation, these tunnels and vaults must be enormous. Perhaps this is the undisclosed location where Vice President Richard Cheney was evacuated during 9/11.

In the employee briefings and written information I received, I learned that the emergency evacuation or relocation headquarters for Washington's civilian employees includes facilities at Camp Pickett in Blackstone, Virginia. Other emergency evacuation stations are at the Naval Academy at Annapolis, the Naval Air Station at Patuxent, Fort Detrick at Frederick and the Marine School at Quantico, Virginia. Evacuation stations also exist at the Naval Weapons Laboratory at Dahlgren, Virginia, at the Vint Hill Farms in Maryland and at other military installations, as well. I gained the impression that people can quickly be transported to other locations in the tunnels. Such vaults could also be important to the storage of UFO material, as mentioned in the Hull family interviews.

* * *

The decade covered in this chapter—the 1960s—was the height of the Cold War. Perhaps this is why a number of sightings during the era were associated with government officials, both military and civilian. The cultural influence of UFOS included best-selling books and popular films, such as Close Encounters of the Third Kind, The Mothman Prophecies and Men in Black. Through such media presentations, people became more aware of UFO phenomena and of the possibility of government cover-up.

In an effort to examine UFO phenomena in relation to cultural (for example, the psychological impact of Cold War) and environmental events, I made a statistical study of both factors. The results, called "Examination of Social and Environmental Factors in Relation to Unidentified Aerial Phenomena," were published in 1987 edition of the American Association for the Advancement of Science (AAAS). This examination of the information from 1947 to 1969 showed that both cultural and environmental factors had significant correlations with UFO phenomena. For example, I found correlations between UFO activity and environmental factors such as sun spot cycles and correlations between UFO activity and historical events such as the wars in Israel.

The next chapter includes the examination of an historical event. This was a sudden increase in UFO reports that was concurrent with the Yom Kippur war, an event that nearly produced a military confrontation between the US and the Soviet Union.

CHAPTER SIX

The Early Seventies – The Great UFO Wave of 1973, a Mystery Roar and the Aftermath

AN abrupt series of events beginning on October 11, 1973, which included a strange booming sound, UFO sightings and entity encounters, may have been the most widely experienced ever to have been associated with UFO phenomena.

Police switchboards lit up with calls. Reports of a thunderous boom, close encounters, alien abductions, mutilations and similar events swarmed in and this activity continued over several weeks. Central Ohio law enforcement agencies received 150 UFO reports on October 17, six days after the initial activity and this is the largest number of UFO sightings ever recorded in a 24-hour period. In Wheeling, West Virginia, nearly 100 UFOs were reported on October 17, causing alarm in the city of 60,000 inhabitants. This wave and the nature of the sightings were so extensive that some referred to it as an invasion.

The precipitous increase of multi-state sightings has come to be known as the UFO Wave of 1973 and unlike most UFO events that leave behind little proof; the 1973 events included an unprecedented abundance of evidence. This included Dr. Harley Rutledge's study, which may be the best UFO research ever done. Additional smoking gun evidence includes seismograms of the boom.

At the time of the 1973 events, the Yom Kippur War between Israel and a coalition of Arab states was underway. This conflict led to an international crisis that included a nuclear alert and the threat of a nuclear confrontation between the US and the Soviet Union. This was a world-class DEFCON alert on October 6, 1973. Egypt and Syria launched a joint attack on Israel resulting in the Yom Kippur War and according to documents, just declassified in 2016, the move to DEFCON 3 was motivated by the Central Intelligence Agency. Only four such alerts have ever been made. At this time, Americans also were dealing with oil shortages and the Watergate scandal, as well as with the impeachment and resignation of the President. However, such tensions existed before and after the October 11 sightings, so there is no reason to think public anxiety or mass hysteria was related to them.

* * *

I discovered that this sound blast had been so enormous that it could be a smoking gun by itself and it also left hard evidence.

I became aware of the sound because my parents having heard a strange sound in Ohio called me in Missouri to ask if I heard it. This seemed so strange that I asked them if they just developed dementia (jokingly). Later I became curious and collected numerous newspaper accounts of this 1973 UFO wave and a thunderous roar that accompanied it. Several individuals, including geologist and State of Ohio seismologist Mike Hansen, Ph.D., helped me analyze and investigate the events. I accessed Freedom of Information Act (FOIA) material, collected and examined seismograph recordings from different locations and sought information from additional sources. Eventually I published information about the sightings and the mysterious sound. My "Investigation of a Sound Heard over a Wide Area," was published in a peer-reviewed scientific journal, *Ohio Journal of Science*,[37] and in a *MUFON UFO Journal* article

With the exception of the Krakatoa volcanic eruption of 1883, the 1973 boom could be the most widespread audible sound on record. The deafening boom roared through a multi-state area in the Midwest on October 11, 1973, at around 9:00 p.m. The sound was accompanied by a sudden increase in UFO sightings, reports of alien abductions and other unexplainable events–some at the exact time of the blast.

The boom was felt in 10 states including Ohio, Pennsylvania, Virginia, Maryland and West Virginia. It was first reported about 8:30 p.m. It first became evident over Indiana and western Ohio and traveled east to the coast. The sound covered a circular-shaped area, extending northward from Kentucky possibly to Canada and eastward from Illinois to Maryland.

A seismograph at the Pennsylvania State University's Seismic Observatory provided smoking gun evidence of this event when it recorded a five-second burst of very high frequency at 8:53 p.m., simultaneously with the window-breaking boom. The sound and vibrations could not be attributed to earthquake tremors, nor did the widespread pattern of the boom match that of a sonic boom.[38, 39, 40, 41]

Through seismograms, scientists can find clues to what caused a tremor. Earthquakes and mining blasts can be distinguished through their seismographs—earthquakes begin with relatively weak primary waves when compared to mining blasts. The recording made of the 1973 tremor was reported to have been lost (or possibly in possession of the government) and thus cannot be examined in detail.

Various agencies insisted there were no known aircraft that could have caused such a widespread sonic boom; hence, many concluded a minor earthquake had hit the East. But seismographic information showed no evidence of this.

Shelton Alexander, Penn State geophysics and seismology expert said the only other possibility is that it could have been a meteorite coming into the area. It appeared that the boom represented a physical object entering the earth's atmosphere at a high speed. This was probably an object similar to a meteorite or a craft. However, the expected meteorite wasn't seen. But concurrent with the sound, people began to see low-altitude flying objects that fit neither the pattern of falling debris, nor of a high-altitude cloud.

The Goddard Space Flight Center in Beltsville, Maryland and the National Aeronautics and Space Administration in Washington said they knew of nothing that could have caused the shock. Air Force officials in Pennsylvania and officers at the Naval Observatory in Washington said they had sighted nothing that could have caused a sonic boom or an explosion.

Information about sonic booms can show how unusual this sound was. I found that the width of the boom "carpet" beneath an aircraft is about one mile for each 1000 feet of altitude. For example, an aircraft flying supersonically at 50,000 feet can produce a sonic boom cone of about 50 miles wide. Thus, this 1973 boom was many times wider than that.

Joseph Tester has explained this boom as possibly that of an SR-71 supersonic plane in the area around that time.[42] Tester's article showed a graph someone made that showed an expanding sonic boom cone that began near Galesburg, Illinois and traveled directly eastward such that its eastern center was around Philadelphia, Pennsylvania; its lower eastern edge appeared to be in North Carolina; and its upper eastern edge was south of the Finger Lake region of New York. He attributed this to the sonic boom cone of the SR-71. However, the SR-71's sonic boom would have looked much different than this. The SR-71 traveled south of Chicago, north of Indianapolis and then to Griffiss AFB, near Rome, New York. This would have taken it near Cleveland and Buffalo and north of the Finger Lakes, rather than south of them as shown in the graph. It traveled at about 80,000 feet. Thus, its boom carpet would be 40 miles on either side and it would end up farther north of and very much smaller than the boom area he showed for it in his diagram. Tester's diagram is strange however, because it appeared to show the location of the mystery boom, not the trajectory of the sonic boom carpet of the SR-71.

The mystery boom might have been around 600 miles wide and would differ vastly from a SR-71's carpet. Tester's diagram also showed a cone-shaped area that became wider as it traveled eastward, rather than an 80-mile carpet of two parallel lines that would follow the ST-71's trajectory.

Thus, this boom was truly unusual not only for it size, but because it has never been explained.[43] I also wondered why my parents had the strange mental reaction to it and wondered if others did also.

* * *

Not only was there an unusual sound, but beginning around 9:00 p.m. on October 11, police switchboards were swamped with UFO reports and the sightings continued over the next weeks. There's no evidence this wave of sightings was caused by media coverage of the unusual activity. The sightings weren't reported until a day or two after October 11 and accounts appeared even later in weekly and monthly media such as magazines. These reports didn't seem to fit the pattern of a military test, where possibly a test cloud might be dispersed high in the sky and over a wide area. The UFO's reported seemed to be localized. Not only UFOs were reported, but also abductions.

Right at time of the sound, the Pascagoula Abduction, considered one of the world's most credible abduction cases, took place in Mississippi on October 11, 1973, at about 9:00 p.m. The two witnesses, Charles Hickson and Calvin Parker, began their report to the sheriff's office by saying they had seen a strange object land while they were fishing.

They sensed something behind them and turned to see an oval-shaped aircraft that was illuminated by a blue light and making a buzzing noise. Its hatchway

Charles Hickson and Calvin Parker – US abductees at Pascagoula

opened and three naked beings floated out. These beings were ghostlike and pale, with wrinkled skin, wide blinking eyes and conical projections where their noses and ears should have been. Instead of hands, they had claws—crab-like pincers— and instead of two legs, each had a round pedestal.

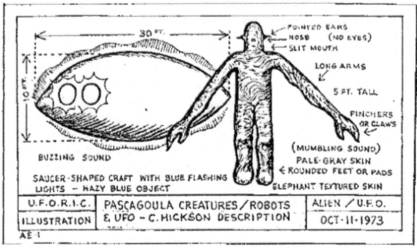

Drawing of the UFO and entity as witnessed by Charles Hickson & Calvin Parker

The beings somehow caused Hickson to float into the aircraft and they did the same to Parker, who fainted. Hickson could not move his body while he was in the craft. For 30 minutes, a large, eye-like device physically examined the men.

After the abduction, fearing they wouldn't be believed, neither wanted to report what had happened. Finally, however, they did report the event. At first they telephoned the Keesler Air Force Base, but a sergeant told them that the Air Force no longer investigated UFO reports. Next they called the Jackson County sheriff's office. The abduction occurred on Thursday and by the following Monday, Charles Hickson and Calvin Parker were famous throughout the country. Authorities believed them for several reasons, including the fact that even when they thought they were alone together, Hickson and Parker discussed the encounter as a real event and continued to show fear as they spoke of it.

* * *

On October 17 (also a day of an unusually high number of sightings), the Utah Roach Abduction took place. This was a landmark case because it was the first time anyone reported space aliens coming into a private home for an abduction and it was also one of the first group abduction reports.

Pat Roach awakened in the middle of the night feeling that something strange had just happened to her, but she was unable to recall what it was. Her two daughters told of an encounter with space aliens, but she couldn't remember this and refused to believe it. Because the daughters said the creatures had been inside the house, Roach called the police and had them check for prowlers.

For two years the family did not discuss the incident, but Roach finally wrote a letter to *Saga* magazine about the event. UFOlogists Kevin Randle and James Harder, Ph.D., investigated. Two of Roach's daughters still remembered the event and one daughter claimed the family had waited outside a UFO in a line that included several neighbors whom they recognized. But Roach could recall nothing. Under hypnosis, however, Roach reported she and some of her children were taken from their house by strange-looking beings with pasty-white faces, big eyes and small, narrow slits where their mouths should have been. The UFO had landed in a field near Roach's home. Inside the spacecraft, she underwent a gynecological exam, was shown some alien technology and was hypnotized and requested to relive certain experiences. Roach and one daughter both said a human-looking male was with the alien beings.

* * *

Another dramatic case from this period was the Coyne UFO Incident, one of best-documented and best-investigated UFO sightings. It took place near

Mansfield, Ohio, a week after the October 11 events, when an Army Reserve helicopter crew of four men encountered a metallic-looking, grey, cigar-shaped object. During the incident, a light beam lit up the cockpit, the helicopter made a quick ascent and witnesses both in the aircraft and on the ground described the object. Jennie Zeidman, Bill Jones and Warren Nicholson intensively investigated and gave me additional information. The government involvement in this was strange and intriguing. [44]

Captain Lawrence Coyne

On a clear, calm, starry night, when the moon was in its last quarter and just rising, a UH-1H helicopter left Port Columbus International Airport flying northeast toward its home base of Cleveland Hopkins International Airport. In command in the right front seat was Captain Lawrence J. Coyne, a 36-year-old pilot with 19 years of flying experience. The other crewmembers were John Healey, a Cleveland police officer who was the flight medic; Robert Yanacsek, a computer technician; and Arrigo Jezzi, a chemical engineer.

The helicopter was cruising at 2,500 feet above sea level at an airspeed of 90 knots when, 10 miles south of Mansfield, Healey saw a single red light to the west, flying south. Two minutes later at 11:02 p.m., Yanacsek noticed a red light on the southern horizon. He watched it for about a minute and called it to Coyne's attention. Coyne assumed it was distant air traffic and told Yanacsek to keep an eye on it. After another half minute, Yanacsek announced the light had turned toward the helicopter and seemed to be on a converging path.

Coyne verified Yanacsek's assessment. Thinking the light was an Air National Guard F-100 from Mansfield, he put the UH-1H into a powered descent of 500 feet per minute. He established radio contact with Mansfield control tower, 10

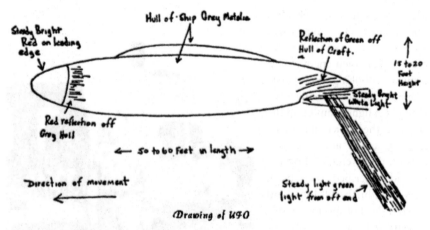

Drawing of the UFO as witnessed by helicopter pilot Captain Lawrence Coyne

miles northwest, but the radio contact failed. Jezzi attempted UHF and VHF transmissions without success. Coyne later learned that the Mansfield airport had no tape of their transmissions and that the last F-100 in the vicinity had landed at 10:47 p.m.

Meanwhile the mysterious red light continued its bearing and increased in intensity, so Coyne boosted his rate of descent to 2,000 feet per minute and his airspeed to 100 knots. The last altitude he noted was 1,700 feet. Just as a collision appeared imminent, the object abruptly halted in its course and hovered above and in front of the helicopter for 10 seconds.

The object was a featureless gray metallic structure, cigar-shaped and domed, with windows along the dome. To the witnesses it covered a space nearly equal to the width of the front windshield. The red light observed by the four men was coming from its bow and a white light became visible at its slightly indented stern. As the men watched, a green pyramid-shaped beam, like a directional spotlight, became visible from the lower rear section. This green beam of light passed over the helicopter's nose, swung up through the windshield and bathed the cockpit in green light.

The object then flew off to the west. Only its white taillight was visible and this light maintained its intensity even as its distance increased. Finally the UFO made a sharp turn to the right, heading toward Lake Erie. The men watched it move away and Jezzi later said it traveled faster than the 250-knot limit for aircraft below 10,000 feet. There had been neither noise, nor any turbulence from the object, except for a bump as it moved west.

When the object had stopped hovering, the men noticed their magnetic compass disc was making four rotations per minute and their altimeter read 3,500 feet: a 1,000 foot-per-minute climb was in progress. Coyne insists the collective lever (one of three flight control inputs) was still bottomed from his evasive dive. Because it could not be lowered, he had no alternative but to lift it. After gingerly maneuvering the controls as the helicopter reached nearly 3,800 feet, he regained control of the helicopter.

All four men had been aware of the dive, but only Coyne was aware of the climb. The helicopter was brought back to the flight-plan altitude of 2,500 feet, radio contact was achieved with Akron-Canton Regional Airport and the flight proceeded uneventfully. The duration of the sighting was longer than that for a typical meteor. In addition, the object hovered, changed course and emitted light strong enough to illuminate the ground.

UFOlogists Bill Jones and Warren Nicholson later investigated and found there were ground witnesses for this event.

These witnesses were a woman and four teenagers. Driving south from Mansfield at 11:00 p.m., they saw a single, steady, bright red light flying south through the sky. They watched for half a minute until it disappeared. Five minutes later, as they drove east on Route 430 approaching the Charles Mill Reservoir, they became aware of two bright lights—one green and one red—descending toward them from the southeast. The red light appeared to be in front. As Conley pulled onto the shoulder of the road, the lights slowed and moved to the right of the car. The family noticed another group of lights, some flashing and they heard a beating sound—the helicopter—approaching from the southwest. Two of the teens jumped from the car and watched both the helicopter and the object, which they described as like a blimp, as large as a school bus and pear-shaped. The object covered an area (subtended an angle) equal to a cigarette box held at arm's length and it hovered over the helicopter, now around 500 feet above the road and the trees.

The object's green light flared and the witnesses saw what looked like rays coming toward both the earth and the helicopter. Everything around them turned green: the helicopter, the trees, the road, the car and the ground. The two witnesses outside the car ran back to it and the driver accelerated to move the car. No one was sure when the object stopped hovering, but they agreed it crossed to the north side of the road, moved east briefly, then reversed direction and climbed northwest toward Mansfield, taking the same flight path reported by the helicopter crew.

Some Ohio UFO investigators reported that Mansfield residents thought there had been a power failure that night in the area of the helicopter encounter. One witness looked out a window and saw the UFO, the helicopter and the green light at the same time. This person also said the power went out in the area at that time.

Unlike many UFO witnesses, Coyne was never harassed. On the contrary, he was promoted several times. However, government personnel later made inquiries about the dreams of the helicopter crew.

A strange government interest in this is shown by the fact that three weeks after the event Coyne received a call from a man who identified himself as being from the Office of the Surgeon General of the US Army Medical Department. This caller asked if Coyne or other crewmembers had had any unusual dreams since the UFO experience. Coyne had had two.

In one, he was outside his body. In the second, he was holding a bluish white sphere in his hand and he heard a voice say, "The answer is in the circle."

Coyne said that every two months he was telephoned and asked a series of questions about whether certain things had happened to him or if he had dreamed of them since his UFO experience. He was told to question the rest of the crew as well and to mail their answers to the Pentagon.

Crewmember Healey said the Pentagon contacted him with similar questions; in particular, he was asked if he ever dreamed of body separation. He had. He was also asked if he had dreamed of anything with a spherical shape. He hadn't.

In his 1991 book, *The Watchers: The Secret Design behind UFO Abduction*, author Ray Fowler says the CIA has an interest in extra-sensory perception (ESP). He thinks the agency is investigating whether a link exists between UFOs and ESP and whether UFO witnesses might have ESP abilities. Fowler thinks the questions asked of the helicopter crew were based on investigations of abductions within the ranks of the military and NASA. He asserts that this crack in government secrecy lends credibility to abduction cases. The Coyne event was not thought to involve abduction, but perhaps the government felt that because a green light was shined on the witnesses the incident was abduction-like. Or perhaps the helicopter's inexplicable climb suggested abduction.

Either way it is evidence that some government component is studying the mind control/telepathic/psychic aspects of UFO phenomena.

The green light has been a matter of interest in this case. Both the helicopter crew and the ground witnesses saw the light and the crew associated it with magnetic anomalies in the

US author and researcher Ray Fowler

148

helicopter. However, debunker Phil Klass, a member of the Committee for the Scientific Investigation of Claims of the Paranormal (CSICOP—now called the Committee for Skeptical Inquiry), believed the green light the crew saw was actually the effect of a green-tinted windshield in the helicopter. On the other hand, it is known that the green windshield tint is very subtle and not even as dark as the tinted windows of many cars. In bright sunlight, there was a faint and barely noticeable tint of green in the cockpit, but this was not strong enough to cause a light shining through the windshield to appear green or to give the effect of the cockpit turning green.

UFO sceptic and author Philip Klass

However such green lights are very interesting, because they have been reported numerous times in association with UFO phenomena and because they can have strange effects. For example in the Schirmer abduction, a green light seemed to be a sort of tractor beam. And in the case of the Soviet Aeroflot airliner flying over Minsk, in an effect somewhat like the Coyne case, it shot out a blob-like object that cast a greenish tint over the landscape. When one of the beams projected into the cabin, it caused weird effects including multiple lights of different colors and fiery zigzags. The beams outside changed shape to mimic the plane. Walter Webb once said that beams of light focused on UFO witnesses often precede impressions of missing time and abduction scenarios and perhaps there is an association to this also.

I discussed Klass's comments with Zeidman, who investigated the event and she recalled that when she and Klass were interviewed for a WOSU radio broadcast in Columbus, Ohio, Klass said the UFO had been in sight for only a second or less and had been a meteor. Zeidman, however, affirmed that the object was in sight for longer than this and thus, it could not have been a meteor.

* * *

On October 11 at around 9:00 p.m., hundreds or even thousands of people throughout the eastern US suddenly and independently began to report strange events. A sampling of information about these sightings, taken from Kevin Randle's 1989 *The UFO Casebook*, local interviews and newspapers, is included here.

In Ohio, at around 8:00 p.m. on October 11, in Dayton (home of the by-then defunct Project Blue Book), many persons reported low-flying objects. Law officers in other parts of Ohio were swamped with UFO reports. In October, a Montgomery

County officer reported photographing a UFO hovering over the village of Union. On October 17, UFOs were reported in Chillicothe and Greenfield, where the police department received so many calls that they stopped keeping track of them. From October 16 through October 22, authorities in Franklin County received 40 to 50 UFO reports a day in several locations around the city. One of these involved an Air National Guard flight controller in Columbus who said a UFO landed in a field near his house. UFO-related fires were reported.

In nearby Indiana, UFOs were reported above the area of the Naval Ammunition Depot in Crane. On October 21 in Hartford City, two disembarked human-looking beings were seen.

On October 15 and 16, residents of Hart and Hardin Counties in Kentucky observed a huge object launching small red and white lights. The mayor of Munfordville, Kentucky, saw a smaller aircraft.

In Tennessee, an enormous object escorted Franklin County Police Chief James Park's patrol car on October 16. In Berea, Tennessee, barking dogs awakened farmer James Cline, who saw a UFO with blinking lights in the woods and a being with a glowing white head. Traces of both the being and the UFO were found the next day. On October 17 in Watauga, Tennessee, a copper-colored UFO hovered near the ground while a tall alien being reached out and tried to grab two children. Like the being in the Pascagoula Abduction, this one had claw-like hands and wide, blinking eyes.

In Pennsylvania during the last two weeks of October, 103 different humanoid sightings occurred. A single being was observed by 13 witnesses, including a police officer and members of a UFO study group.

Perhaps the most credible of these sightings took place in Michigan, when Ohio's vacationing Governor, John Gilligan and his wife watched a vertical-shaped, amber-colored object for more than 30 minutes in Manistee County.

Reports flooded switchboards in the southern states, as well. On October 16, a UFO was seen over Madison, Jefferson, Hancock and Highland counties in Louisiana.

Not far away in Mississippi, an object the size of a two-bedroom house appeared at 1,000 feet and drifted over Jackson on October 12.

Two days later, in Columbia, Mississippi, a retired Air Force officer, meteorologist and director of civil defense, James Thornhill, reported that a mysterious blimp in the air had jammed his radar for 20 minutes. Another UFO landed on a highway, blocking traffic. A car approached but its lights went out and the engine died. The car's occupants saw a human-looking being.

In Alabama, a police chief in Falkville, Morgan County, photographed a "space robot" 17 miles from the Huntsville Redstone Arsenal in Huntsville in Madison County. Objects acted as if they might have been inspecting the Redstone Arsenal and the George C. Marshall Space Flight Center.

Meanwhile on October 17 in s Georgia, a cone-shaped object landed on a highway in front of a car driven by Paul Brown. Two four-foot-tall being dressed in silvery suits emerged. The landing forced Brown to stop his car and he fired several shots at the being. Two days later in Tifton, a spacecraft landed and human-looking beings disembarked. Near Loxley, a witness named Clarence Patterson said his pickup truck was sucked into a huge, cigar-shaped craft and he was jerked out of the cab by robot-like beings. He thought they could read his mind.

Sightings in the New England states included many in New Hampshire. The local papers reported on November 5 that 17 police officers, from Farmington to Exeter, had spotted a UFO the day before. Police radios were subsequently inundated with UFO reports and with humanoid sightings. A thunderous boom preceded these sightings.

Randle noted that UFO reports came from the American Southwest, as well. On October 16 William and Donna Hatchett were driving a pickup truck on an Oklahoma county road when they saw a bright light. The UFO turned toward their truck and as it descended Donna begged her husband to stop. William stopped the truck and an enormous object the size of a jet hovered at the front of the pickup giving off a blinding white light. The Hatchetts detected a penetrating, low-pitched hum.

On October 15 a cab driver saw a blue UFO land in front of him and his cab stalled. He heard tapping on his windshield and turned to see a crab-like claw, resembling the one seen in the Pascagoula Abduction. A weather service specialist named Howard Moneypenny saw a bright light glowing in the distance on October 16. A private pilot chased an object but gave up after several minutes because he was not catching up to it. As he returned to the airport, he observed the object following him. The UFO finally disappeared.

This flap did not only affect people. It extended to animals. For example, Stringfield notes that on October 14, 1973, the Greenfield, Ohio, police responded to a hysterical call from a woman who said a UFO had landed on her farm. This report was one of 80 UFO sightings by residents of west central Ohio that night. It was unique, however, because her cow was missing. Another missing cow account came from Dayton, Ohio, where a UFO was reported to have killed two cows. Another dead cow was concurrent with a UFO sighting in Louisiana. These events foreshadowed the cattle mutilations that today are sometimes reported in rural UFO cases.

Cows weren't the only animal casualties. Stringfield notes in *Situation Red* that at 9:00 p.m. in Lynchburg, Ohio, as a Mrs. Long pulled into a driveway, an orange-colored object hovered over her car. Her lights dimmed, she screamed and the object disappeared. Her pet cat, which had been in the car with her with the windows up, had also disappeared.

The UFO events were not confined to the US; the increase in sightings took place around the world. For example, in Argentina on October 27, Dionisio Llanca reported that a series of examinations had been performed on him aboard a UFO. In Canada in October and November, UFOs, humanoid beings and electromagnetic effects on cars were reported.

* * *

In 1975, another wave of UFO sightings began and this one included UFO events at numerous military bases. Although the government had presented itself as no longer investigating UFOs when it shut down Project Blue Book, it maintained documentation about these sightings, but the documents were not available to the public until the Freedom of Information Act (FOIA) became law. However, several investigators discovered this wave independently.

Lawrence Fawcett and Barry Greenwood reported in *Clear Intent* that using the FOIA, they gained access to information proving that in the 1970s many missile sites in the US experienced low-flying UFOs and that at some of these sites the military computers were affected with changed targeting coordinates.

For example on November 7, 1975, remote electronic sensors triggered an alarm at Malmstrom Air Force Base in Montana where Minuteman missiles were housed. Members of Sabotage Alert Teams investigating this alarm saw an orange glowing object of tremendous size that illuminated the missile site. Launch-control personnel ordered these teams to proceed to the site, but the members refused to go further because of their fear of the object. As two F-106 jet interceptors were launched from Great Falls, Minnesota and approached the area, the object rose and disappeared from North American Aerospace Defense Command radar. When targeting teams and computer specialists later examined the warhead computer that targets the missiles, they found that the target numbers on the computer tape had mysteriously changed.

FOIA documents suggest that shots were fired during a sighting at Grand Forks Air Force Base in North Dakota, but details are lacking.

In Maine on October 27, a UFO flew at low altitude over Loring Air Force Base. The object resembled a helicopter and had a red light and a white strobe light but no doors, windows, propellers, or engines. As it closely circled a nuclear weapons storage area, a state of high alert was declared on the base. That same day, as two young men were driving nearby they encountered a UFO that took control of their car. They blacked out during the encounter, but they later reported what they remembered of the incident. No one believed them, but the authorities might have if the Loring encounter had been reported in the media. The following day the UFO returned to Loring and hovered five feet above the weapons storage area.

Two weeks later on November 10, 1975, a bright object flew at low altitude over Minot Air Force Base, also in North Dakota.

Reports of UFOs at military installations during this period were not confined to the US In November 1975 in Ontario, Canada, UFOs approached the Canadian Falconbridge missile site. Another military base encounter occurred at a NATO missile installation on a Mediterranean island in 1975. And it is thought that salvos of Russian ground-to-air-missiles were fired at a group of UFOs; these missiles exploded harmlessly at a distance from the targets.

In *Situation Red* Stringfield wrote of UFO encounters in Arizona, Colorado, Pennsylvania and Ohio during October and November 1975. These were concurrent with reports of cattle mutilations. The Ohio flap that he reported ended as quickly as it began. After November 20, southwest Ohio went into a lull. Stringfield was one of several investigators who learned about certain UFO events without the benefit of FOIA access to documents (the information was still classified when Stringfield did his research). Thus, he independently reported a wave that occurred at the same time as the one reported in *Clear Intent*.

Such activity is something the government should certainly investigate and would be quite negligent not to.

* * *

Another 1970s event is the reception of what might be an actual signal from extraterrestrials. It is still considered the most promising of all candidate signals from extraterrestrial intelligence. On August 15, 1977, Jerry R. Ehman, Ph.D., was working on a Search for Extra-Terrestrial Intelligence (SETI) project at the "Big Ear" radio telescope of OSU in Delaware County, Ohio. He detected what is now called the "WOW! Signal," a strong narrowband radio signal that bore expected hallmarks of a potential non-terrestrial and non-solar-system origin. In discussions of SETI results, considerable media attention has been focused on this signal.

During the 1980s and 1990s, I worked as a volunteer at Big Ear and had the opportunity to ask several scientists why they thought no one had ever received understandable communications from intelligent extraterrestrial beings. Robert Dixon, Ph.D., (who is now Chief Research Engineer, Ohio Academic Resources

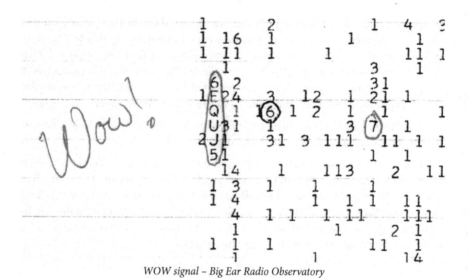

WOW signal – Big Ear Radio Observatory

Network and OSU, Office of the Chief Information Officer) theorized that communication by radio signal might be a method that civilizations use only for a short window of time before moving on to more advanced methods of communication.[45] In the 1990s, Big Ear was taken down to make way for a golf course, but many of the researchers continue their SETI work.[46] They now use a 24-element Argus array located on the OSU campus. Dixon says he knows of no researchers who have used methods other than radio or optical SETI.[47]

* * *

Dr Harley Rutledge

The 1970s events were included in one of if not the best scientific study of UFO phenomena. Between 1973 and 1980 a team of researchers led by Harley Rutledge, Ph.D., (a solid-state physicist and chairperson of the Physics Department at Southeast Missouri State University) examined UFO activity in Missouri. Called *Project Identification*, this study is unique because the team observed UFOs in real time, during the events, rather than after the fact. Monitoring in real-time meant the scientists could determine a UFO's velocity, course, position, distance and size. The high number of sightings during that period made such a study possible. UFO interactivity, a highly important but little studied

154

aspect of the UFO phenomena, could also be examined under controlled conditions.

He set up the experiment using the scientific methodology used in field research, which involves a range of well-defined, but variable, methods and can be characterized as qualitative research. Many well-established methods have been developed for analyzing data gathered in the field. Thus, his results were compatible with standard scientific methodology and would be acceptable to peer-reviewed scientific reportage and statistical analysis.

The study also provided an important comparison of the 1973 events with activity during the following years. Rutledge and his team logged a maximum number of sightings in 1973; after that, the number of sightings sharply declined, as reported by Rutledge in his 1981 *Project Identification: The First Scientific Field Study Of UFO Phenomena*. During my discussions with Rutledge, he seemed extremely precise, knowledgeable and honest.

Missouri lights – antennae's erected by Dr Harley Rutledge

Rutledge examined UFO activity in southern Missouri (generally near Piedmont) because of numerous reports of UFO-associated activities, including: car stops, beams of lights from the sky; interference with television and radio signals; frightened animals; objects on the ground; and flying objects that would turn their lights off and on, hover, streak away and exhibit other strange behaviors. These incidents in the small, out-of-the way region of Missouri seemed to presage the UFO Wave of 1973 and some UFOlogists have even speculated that alien intelligences studied a small area before engaging in worldwide activity.

Assembling a team of 40 scientists, Rutledge set off for Piedmont. He was confident that a few weekends with his team, utilizing scientific techniques and instrumentation, would solve the mystery of UFOs. As the study continued, he set up stations where trained observers used scientific instruments to study UFO activity. These instruments included: Celestron, Criterion and Questar telescopes; sophisticated cameras; infrared-sensitive film; radios; spectrum analyzers; magnetometers; a gravimeter; binoculars; and other electrical and optical devices. The scientists used triangulation data, photographic plates, plots, scans and many other methods to analyze their data. They made simultaneous observations from widely separated locations; this allowed them to plot the courses, positions and speeds of the objects. They eliminated IFOs such as satellites, aircraft, meteorites, headlights, refraction effects and similar objects and lights.

The scientists recorded a surprisingly high number of UFO sightings. Most people spend their entire lives without seeing a UFO, but in this study, several sightings often occurred during a single observation period. The team investigated 178 anomalous objects. Over a seven-year period, they logged 158 viewing station set-ups and watched the sky for 427 hours. They recorded 157 sightings, of which 34 UFOs were Class A (the best sightings—ones that had physical properties that defied conventional explanation). The scientists distinguished UFOs from normal air traffic by several means, such as identifying lighting that was not Federal Aviation Administration (FAA) compliant and identifying maneuvers such as quick starts, instantaneous stops, sharp turns, very high speeds and accelerations, hovering, turning off and on, scintillation and matching the appearances of stars. Other anomalies included noise in the absence of verified sonic booms and the abilities of the UFOs to merge with or discharge other UFOs. Additional behaviors, such as an object engaging in a jet chase or beaming a blue light at a witness, were also described.

The scientists discovered numerous reasons why studying UFO phenomena is difficult. Normally a field study of the phenomena is impossible because UFOs do not make regular and predictable appearances. In Project Identification, although scientists spotted numerous unidentified flying objects, they often were unable to photograph such subjects as Class A UFOs because the UFOs would disappear, would appear when cameras could not be brought to bear on them, or would not show up on film after being photographed.

Rutledge did not publish a report of the observed incidents until seven years after the conclusion of the study. This was because the data was so unexpected. One aspect of the UFOs' behavior was particularly puzzling: when certain UFOs came within the range of measurement, they would move, change course, or halt. The most significant observations of Rutledge's team were of 30 recorded occasions when the movements of the objects synchronized with the actions of the observers. Objects sometimes responded to observers who switched lights off and on, to verbal or radio messages, pointing or aiming, flashlight beams, aiming of cameras or telescopes—and even the scientists' thoughts. Rutledge had actual experiments showing this. He interpreted this behavior to mean the UFOs were detecting the investigators' intentions, voices, or thinking. He speculated that the objects were telepathic and were able to react to thoughts. In other words, the objects seemed to show a form of consciousness (although skeptics argue that this conclusion is false and based on illusion). One might also wonder whether such actions showed telepathy or mind control of or from the objects.

The UFOs seemed to have capabilities beyond that period's prevailing technology and they did not behave as a human would when visiting another planet, such as by landing and saying, "Take me to your leader."

The scientists' most astonishing discovery was that the intelligence controlling UFOs was aware of their presence, that the UFOs may have purposely attracted their attention and that they may have reacted to them. The UFOs reacted to human presence by turning lights off and on, by moving away and by changing course or brightness.

Rutledge described many instances when an object would approach as if to pass overhead, but would go around the scientists' position. When scientists changed their position, the UFOs would change course. In addition, the objects changed appearances. For example, Rutledge described an instance in which a man encountered a landed disc. When the man stepped back two paces the disc was invisible and he could see the trees behind it, but when he stepped forward two paces it became visible again. In other cases, one observer could see an object but another nearby person would be unable to see it. During the study, Rutledge's scientists sometimes even wondered if the UFO events were being staged for their benefit. He added that unless one has actually been in the field studying the phenomena, one cannot begin to comprehend it.

Rutledge ultimately concluded that UFO phenomena result from a non-human intelligence and stated that a possibility exists that a great deal of UFO activity is subliminal–which could have very serious ramifications.[48]

He had the courage to report observations of a nature that would have been rejected by many in the scientific community. Rutledge told me that by 1987 he'd personally had 160 UFO sightings, many of which he hadn't reported. Unlike most UFO witnesses, however, he had additional witnesses and instrument recordings to confirm many of his observations. He said people would often ask him, as a scientist, why he had so many UFO experiences. He viewed this as an indictment rather than a question. He said the answer was that he went where UFOs were found and that eventually they seemed to get to know him. And after spending many hours in observation and analysis, he was better able to detect them than the average person. He also was much better able to examine the data.

Rutledge was sensitive to the skepticism of those researchers who thought that any sighting is suspect and that multiple sightings by the same person (called "repeater phenomena") may even indicate a mental disorder. He noted that a debunking article in *Omni Magazine* said Rutledge should be in the *Guinness Book of World Records* for his high number of UFO sightings. He called it an insensitive, inaccurate and insipid little piece of writing.

Rutledge continued his work long after his book was published and it appeared that government agencies took an interest in it. For example, in 1986 he wrote to me, "I had been to a meeting in Minneapolis with top NSF-officials [National Science Foundation] and many Project Directors. It was quite fruitful."[49] This suggests that the government continued to research the UFO phenomena and was interested in civilian work.

The data Rutledge presented in his book framed the UFO Wave of 1973. In the first sentence of his study, he said that beginning in late February 1973, strange events were reported in the Piedmont area of Missouri. He began his investigation on April 6 when he and an associate traveled to do their first feasibility study and, at the same time, made their first UFO observation.

Although Rutledge's team began the study before October 1973, because of the scientific community's anti-UFO bias (Rutledge thought he was jeopardizing his career), information about his research was not released before the UFO wave and the UFO Wave of 1973 became nationwide news. Therefore, other scientists were unaware of the characteristics he observed in UFO phenomena—information that might have spurred similar investigations.

* * *

The UFO wave that occurred in 1973 was so intense that it caused massive cultural effects, such as apprehension in the general population. In *Situation Red* Stringfield notes that during this period the people of his city, Cincinnati, like others, maintained an outward air of nonchalance—but each night as the sun went down, anxiety grew over the increasing number of UFOs reports. He added that those on isolated farms were fearful each night when their daily routines ceased for the evening.

The 1970s were a time of enormous cultural changes and scandalous political events, such as Watergate, which led to the impeachment and resignation of the President and a major military conflict that brought about a severe international crisis including the threat of a nuclear conflict between the US and the USSR.

However, no evidence existed to show that these events brought on the UFO events, although some hypothesized that such events were staged to prevent such a war.

The October 1973 events are still unexplained and this points out a problem with the scientific study of UFOs. Scientific investigation of the phenomena is often presented as a process of simply collecting more and better data. However, the research presented here draws attention to a more fundamental problem: there was much physical evidence of an event and much observational data, but people had no idea what it meant.

Even though Rutledge had made possibly the best study ever of the phenomena that addressed such problems, because of its strange nature and because of scientific prejudice this information had not been widely disseminated.

An analysis of these events indicates that new methods for studying UFO phenomena are needed. A related issue is that today's scientific paradigms are based on the idea of controlled experimentation—with the basic assumption that humans are in control. In the case of UFOs, that may not be true. Methods need to be developed to study phenomena that may not be under our control–phenomena that may even be more intelligent than us.

CHAPTER SEVEN

The Late Seventies And The Eighties – Close Encounters of All Three Kinds

IN the early 1970s, authorities were inundated with UFO reports, but in contrast, the era between 1976 and 1990 seems comparatively inactive.

However, an important advance in the study of UFOs took place in the early 1970s when J. Allen Hynek introduced the "close encounters" (CE) classification method for UFO incidents (J. Allen Hynek, *The UFO Experience: A Scientific Inquiry*). In Hynek's system, in general, a "close encounter of the first kind" (CE1) refers to a UFO that is observed but leaves no evidence. In a "close encounter of the second kind" (CE2), the UFO leaves behind physical evidence such as a burn mark. A "close encounter of the third kind" (CE3) refers to human contact with an animate being. A category not used by Hynek that UFOlogist Jacques Vallée added later, is a "close encounter of the fourth kind" (CE4), where an alien abducts a human. UFOlogists and others now use this general system; perhaps the best-known

Dr Jacques Vallee – UFO researcher and author

example is the title of Steven Spielberg's 1977 film, *Close Encounters of the Third Kind.*

Another advance taking place in the 1980s was the application of the computer to studies of UFO phenomena. For example, Dr. Hynek told me about setting up the pioneering UNICAT PROJECT, a computer study to catalogue and investigate UFO activity.[50]

* * *

Many important observations and CE episodes took place in the 1980s and many show the interactive, observer-dependent and sometimes mind controlling nature of the phenomena that was observed initially by Arnold and in the Rutledge and Skinwalker studies that makes the phenomena so mysterious and difficult to examine.

For example, in September 1981 at 11:30 p.m., Jones and I interviewed two teenaged sisters, Iris and Della Brighton (not their real names), who observed a UFO in a 15-acre pasture. This event showed that witnesses in the same place could experience different versions of the same event.

The two girls were returning from a high-school football game to the home they shared with their parents in rural Delaware, Ohio. Both saw the object as they pulled in their driveway. Iris thought the UFO was dark, but Della thought it looked like a fireball. Both were scared as they sat in the car and watched.

Iris saw two objects, one behind the other. As she watched, a ramp was lowered from one of the UFOs; Della, however, did not see this. Both ran to the house to get their mother and the three of them watched as one object flew away.

Iris later said one object was behind the other as the UFOs left and this is why the second was not visible to her mother and sister. She thought that she saw the ramp and Della didn't because she had been prepared for a more intensive experience.

This preparation may have involved earlier UFO events the family experienced. Several family members had previously observed a car-sized ball made of a pink plasma-like material hovering 10 feet over their front porch. Several months later, family members observed a similar ball behind their house.

West of the Brighton house was a pond and woods. This area was outside the bedroom window of one of the Brighton sons who was younger than Iris and Della and who lived in the house longer than they did. The son said he had seen several UFOs over this area.

As witnesses, the Brightons were considered very credible and were from an influential family. The sisters' father founded a computer company known throughout central Ohio. One of the children's grandfathers helped invent xerography and an uncle, who still designs satellites, participated in the design of the F-14 Tomcat. The sister who made the report is a fashion model.

* * *

A sighting occurred that was similar to the well-known sighting over the O'Hare International Airport (November 7, 2006), but several years earlier. The *Chicago Tribune* had filed an FOIA request and Jon Hilkevitch investigated in a story that climbed atop the paper's list of most-viewed stories on its Web site.

This sighting occurred about 4 P.M. on February 23, 1984, at Hamilton Hall on the Ohio State University (OSU) campus and lasted about 25 minutes. The object was over the approach slope for Port Columbus International Airport, Columbus, Ohio's principal airport.

It would fit the criteria of an excellent sighting because (1) it was observed for a long period of time; (2) it involved an object of large enough angular diameter that structured surface features were visible; (3) it was observed by very high caliper witnesses, who provided signed reports and drawings; (4) it was investigated while the sighting was taking place; (5) it was a daytime sighting; (5) it was in the glide slope of a major airport.

When MS first saw it, he had glanced up out an east-facing window. The object appeared to be in or above the approach slope of the Port Columbus airport to the east and a low jet plane that was landing appeared to pass under it as he watched.

During most of the sighting, the object looked like either a solid rectangle or a rectangle on top of a light. It would appear to very smoothly rotate, or change appearance, in a regularly timed cycle (~ 60 seconds), not in the random pattern of a windblown object.

But it appeared different when he first spotted it. This might have been because he was closer to it and looking up. Later they saw it from a more sidewise angle. At first, it had an incomprehensible appearance like a construction made of beams/girders just floating in the sky. This "girder" appearance had a fog surrounding it. The fog wasn't a cloud; it was small and traveled with the object. The object changed appearance in a regular fashion. At first, there would be a shape he couldn't understand that looked somewhat like a rectangle–constructed of metallic beams

163

like a building framework. Then, a real clear and obvious rectangle would appear that lasted for a while. Then, it would either look like a thin line, or disappear, or go toward its large shape (He can't remember which). It had a white light and made a complete cycle of shape change at totally regular intervals of perhaps once a minute. It didn't just twist randomly in the wind.

He went to the third floor and asked doctoral student MC to look at it with him. He asked her if it looked like a balloon and she didn't know. They went to the physiology department office (room 312), where more people began to watch it.

They opened the window to get a clearer view. They asked Dr. C, a professor, to watch. He watched briefly and said maybe it was a box kite. They then asked Dr. B, another professor, who watched it for a while and asked if it were a balloon. There was no balloon shape above or below it and a balloon shouldn't be in a landing slope. After several more minutes he said, "Maybe it's a UFO." Doctoral student JD watched and discussed it with them.

When MS first watched the object, it seemed to be headed straight east. Near the end of the time, it was to the northeast and looked as it had traveled quite a distance (its apparent size was smaller). It then appeared to be a little north of Port Columbus.

During this time, for the most part it looked like a rectangle that would undergo a very regular appearance change (probably rotation) about once a minute. During this rotation, it would look like a clear rectangle with its long axis up and down, then disappear and then reappear as a rectangle. It continued this appearance for some time.

By then, he could clearly see it traveling and was sure it wasn't a box kite. There were buildings, trees and electric lines in the way and no wind. It would have been impossible to fly a kite on a string around these obstacles.

MC and MS asked several of the people that were watching if there were a telescope in the building. They were unable to find one. While they watched he called Warren Nicholson, a scientist at the nearby Battelle Memorial Institute (holds several U.S. Patents, etc.) that was also an experienced UFO investigator (e.g. investigated the classic Coyne Helicopter incident, was head of a UFO group and others), to tell him what they were witnessing. He didn't know how the object disappeared. After he talked to Nicholson, he looked again and couldn't see it.

Many people should have seen this object, especially some of the thousands of OSU students. It was one of the first warm days of spring and many people were outside.

Mr. Nicholson later told him that he had checked with Port Columbus immediately after he called him. They told him the wind velocity was 0, so the object shouldn't have been a box kite. They couldn't see it. That was strange because, it had been in the Port Columbus approach slope. Mr. Nicholson also had climbed to the Battelle roof to look (on the opposite side of Hamilton Hall from the airport), but had been unable to see it. Mr. Nicholson called MS that night to say there had been other sightings that day–he had received a report from a very credible family that reported seeing a UFO that looked like four teardrop-shaped lines in the sky. All four then flew away in different directions. They photographed it using advanced equipment–a 1200 power telephoto lens with ASA 400 color film. Mr. Nicholson described the day as having a 'flurry' of activity.

All witnesses were highly credible. All OSU witnesses were in the medical school and all now have Ph.D.s and have been, or currently are, university professors. The reports were collected from five of the witnesses within a few days of the sighting. Each witness was asked to independently write a description and make a drawing of the object. All did and no one knew what the object was. They signed and dated the reports and he sent them to CUFOS.

The sighting was quite odd. It's unknown how the object remained suspended in the air. No witness saw or drew a balloon shape and should have if it were a balloon. During one part of its rotation/phases, it would completely disappear, also indicating that it wasn't a balloon. It had no visible wings or propellers. It had a strange appearance–its shape seemed fluid, or changeable.

Also, it rotated in a regular pattern the entire time. The other witnesses commented on this in their reports. Its rotation was smooth and regular, unlike random twisting in the wind. It would need some kind of power plant and maybe a computer to keep this rotation going, regular and stabilize it. Another indication that the object might have been powered is that it appeared to travel against the wind. The official Port Columbus weather report on that day showed that the Wind Speed was 5 mph (North). This means that the wind was traveling from North to South. Thus, the object should have traveled in that direction, rather than its observed direction toward the Northeast. (At 4:00 PM, the visibility was 10 miles and the wind was 5.8 mph from the East with scattered clouds).

It seemed extremely strange that the airport was unaware of it. It could have been a very dangerous obstacle to aircraft. It was in the landing slope, well within their radar and visual range during the entire sighting and remained for a considerable time. Mr. Nicholson said he called the airport immediately and they hadn't seen anything visually or with radar. However, they should have. For example, even small objects (geese) over an airport can cause a disaster, such as when Chesley Sullenberger saved his passengers and airplane when it hit geese. When MS first saw it, it was lined up with the glide slope.

The airplane pilots should have seen it. It was comparatively large with an extended apparent diameter–not a point source. It was large enough to be visible for nearly half an hour. All witnesses drew an object of extended area containing features.

Unlike a balloon, it had a very bright light; balloons usually don't carry lights or reflectors and hot air balloon gas jets don't look like that. He assumed at first this was a reflection. However, as the object traveled, it was at different angles to the sun, but the bright light was still there, thus, this might have been a real light, or some sort of directional beacon. Although it was daylight, the light was strong enough to be visible most or all the time the object was observed and seemed much brighter than an aircraft navigation light. It was stable, in phase with the objects rotation and didn't fluctuate in brightness when it was visible (not like a dangling piece of metal or mirror twisting in the air). The witnesses watched it for shorter periods than he did, but reported the bright light at different stages. It wasn't a Chinese lantern and no ad plane was seen towing it.

It was in the path of airplanes swooping low over OSU and Columbus. This was so close that his sensitive instruments would sometimes pick up airplane–tower communication, thus, it could have been a security breach.

It is still unidentified; there was no evidence that it was a balloon–no balloon was visible, it rotated regularly, it could completely disappear, it appeared to be powered and there was no evidence that anything had been released at that time.

Although this probably has nothing to do with UFOs, that night the electricity went off in his house. The lights wouldn't come on for about an hour. He checked the circuit breaker box. None of the neighbors had electrical trouble then.

The location of the sighting is an interesting historic site, because the object's trajectory would have been over Battelle right before they saw it. Battelle and sightings over it have played a crucial role in UFOlogy. Battelle's scientists had conducted the massive study, *Project Blue Book Special Report No. 14 (SR-14)* and several of its participants still worked there. A Battelle physicist named Howard Cross is thought to have reported viewing a UFO over Battelle, is thought to be the author of the *Pentacle Memorandum* and may have had substantial input into analysis for *SR-14*. Battelle also has been reported to hold UFO debris, such as that from a 1954 Marysville, Ohio, event. OSU had been Dr. Hynek's home ground.

Another aspect that seemed strange is that although MS had paid little attention to the subject previously, the reason he had decided to report the earlier sightings at that time, was that he had suddenly developed a fear of the phenomena, such that he didn't want to leave the house–even when the dog disappeared. In addition, some of his earlier sightings suggested that UFOs might be dangerous (hadn't reported earlier because of and work-related reasons and public ridicule). Hence, he had decided to report that he and other witnesses had seen some possible UFOs. And as he filled out the report, he not only had the sighting but it a 25-minute daytime sighting over a populated area and airport with no one noticing, which seemed unreal. He was certainly glad that he had witnesses.

* * *

What was called a "City in the Sky" UFO event occurred in Columbus, Ohio.

This impossible sighing occurred on June 22, 1985. Scott Barkley was visiting his brother Jeff and their friend Ralph (not their real names) in the 800 block of Harvest Lane Court on the far east side of Columbus, Ohio. Scott said that around midnight he and his brother had stepped outside. Scott cannot remember if the moon was out, but to the east they saw something he later described as "fragments falling down."

Suddenly the area of the sky they were looking at "blacked out." This startled them, particularly when they realized that an enormous dark UFO was the cause of the "blackout." An unknown object, moving north to south, had entered the air space between them and the falling "fragments" in the distance. It moved slowly and took several minutes to pass overhead.

The object was metallic, highly polished and rectangular in shape with rounded corners and edges rather like a cigar. Protrusions and engravings covered it and circular constructs were seen on one side. Four openings on the back end glowed white and as the object moved further south, it tilted upward and the openings became brighter. Lights of various colors, mostly blue, appeared on the object; these lights were diffuse and didn't seem to originate from single sources. The object briefly emitted a "blaring sound" that stopped after a few seconds. Then a light beam shined on the ground, lighting up the back yard of the Harvest Lane residence. The light went out and the blaring noise was replaced by 30 seconds of a "banging sound" like that of heavy machinery. After this there was silence. The object picked up speed as it ascended into the night sky before disappearing several minutes after beginning its upward climb.

The object flew at a low altitude: "If I had a .22 rifle I could have bounced bullets off of it easily," he said. He added that the object reminded him of a "city in the sky."

Two neighbors, Ken and Linda Tomkins (not their real names), also witnessed this UFO. Ken remembers that the sky was "crystal clear." On the way home as they neared their residence, Linda saw the object and said to Ken, "What is that in the sky?" Ken turned down a side road and the two got out of their car.

Looking to the east-southeast, they saw a huge silent UFO—an "inverted city in the sky," Ken called it. It was so big and so low it blotted out the sky above them. Ken estimated that the object was 200 to 300 feet wide and 500 feet long and that its altitude was 200 to 300 feet above the houses.

Ken and Linda got back in their car and headed home. When Ken pulled in his driveway, he didn't notice Scott, Jeff and Ralph in the yard next door. Ken said Scott scared him by banging on the roof of Ken's car asking, "Did you see that? Did you see that?" As soon as Ken's heart slowed from Scott's sudden noisy arrival, Ken replied he had.

Ken went in his house and called Port Columbus International Airport, about a mile west, to ask what the people in the control tower had seen. He was astonished to learn that control tower personnel had neither seen the object nor detected it on radar. Ken phoned the Franklin County Sheriff's office and the Columbus Police Department to ask if anyone else had reported the UFO. No one had.

Ken said a newspaper later noted that the Soviet Cosmos 1530 satellite had re-entered the earth's atmosphere that night. Its point of impact was in the Atlantic Ocean.

But Ken never forgot his sighting. He was so impressed by what he saw that he went outside every night for three weeks to see if the object would return. It never did.

UFOlogists considered Ken and Linda to be reliable witnesses. They were respected business people and they were stable, still residing in the same house when interviewed 11 years later. Ken remained adamant that what he saw was not the burning re-entry of a satellite; it was something huge and not of this world. He thought he remembered news reports from that night of sightings in Michigan, Ohio, West Virginia and North Carolina.

Scott later showed UFOlogists two newspaper articles from the Columbus *Citizen-Journal* in which he was quoted describing the object as looking like a "giant aircraft carrier" and "a city in the sky." He noted that it was a solid object; therefore, it's unlikely that it was some aspect of satellite re-entry.

Meanwhile nine miles to the west in Columbus, Ohio, a similar incident may have been an independent sighting of Scott's UFO. Paul Burrell investigated this sighting.

The primary witness, John Darrell (not his real name), did not report the sighting for several years and although he knew it took place on a summer evening, he was unsure of the exact year. He thought it occurred between 1982 and 1986. He was certain that on that evening a Russian satellite was reported to have broken up.

In addition, he and another witness described the UFO as a city in the sky.

* * *

Yet another similar report in Columbus, Ohio, possibly involved the same UFO.

Kevin McCoy (not his real name) became aware of this event through a newsbreak that interrupted regular television programming: newscasters reported an object hovering over Port Columbus International Airport. Kevin and his family could see it from their Sagamore Road home on Columbus's east side.

He noted that sightings occurred throughout central Ohio that night as people called to report the object hovering over Port Columbus. These witnesses said it emitted a bright white light. It moved up and down or back and forth and it hovered for quite a while. Witnesses said they could see planes circle it at a distance to avoid it. Radio and TV announcements warned people to stay away from the road into the airport; nevertheless, the McCoy family jumped into their Chevrolet and drove out to view the UFO. Near the airport, police had set up a roadblock with a cruiser in the middle of the road. The police were busy and didn't immediately notice when Kevin's father pulled off the road near the Morning-Side trailer court at Cleveland and Joyce Avenues.

From this location, the family could see the UFO clearly. It was enormous and was right above them. Kevin thought it was about 100 yards wide and 50 yards deep and it hung right over the streetlights.

A police officer noticed them speaking to Kevin's father, the officer said, "Sir, would you kindly leave," and threatened him with jail if he refused. Kevin's father asked what the object was and the officer replied, "Look, I don't know what it is. They don't tell me anything." The father turned the car around.

The McCoy family left the scene, but they followed the object in their car and then stopped to watch it with other witnesses in an A&P grocery store parking lot. Because police were still cruising the neighborhood, the group soon dispersed. Kevin's father returned home via side roads.

This sighting was the talk of the community for many days afterward and Kevin and his brothers and father remembered the event many years later. In addition, a close friend of investigator Bill Jones lived in the area around Port Columbus and he, too, remembered this event. He also recalled that there had been a newspaper report about it, but he doesn't remember the date of the sighting.

The police monitoring indicates not only government knowledge or the event, but an apparent inability to do anything about it.

* * *

Peculiar and unexplained physical marks on the earth, such as crop circles and "mystery burns," have recently garnered interest among UFOlogists and are considered CE2 events. Crop circles are probably the best known and most common phenomena of this kind. Mystery burns, however, are also difficult to explain or reproduce and they deserve further study.

A classic event from this period was a series of abductions and a mysterious burn seen by an Indiana family. Budd Hopkins investigated the mystery burn and reported on it in *Intruders: The Incredible Visitations at Copley Woods*. Meanwhile in June of 1984, a similar burn

US alien abduction researcher and author Budd Hopkins

was found near Columbus, Ohio. My sister, Sue Postle and I discussed the Ohio burn with Budd Hopkins when he was writing *Intruders* and again several years later. Hopkins thought the Ohio and Indiana burns had a number of similarities.[51]

For the Ohio mystery burn, as in many such reports, no one witnessed the source; however, during the month preceding its discovery, UFOs had been observed within a mile of its location.

Farmer Thomas McKey (not his real name) discovered the burn in a field of knee-high green alfalfa hay. His two workers also saw the burn before the hay was cut. Plants at the burn site were standing but were blackened and charred to the roots. No other vegetation was affected. The burn was sharply defined; plants next to it were undamaged. McKey —who along with his wife had no interest in UFOs— reported it to the fire department.

McKey and his workers affirmed that no fertilizers, pesticides, or similar substances had been applied to any part of the alfalfa field. A fence enclosed the area and it could be entered only through a gate secured with a heavy chain and a lock to which McKey had the only key. The burn site was on the other side of a steep hill from an Interstate freeway, but not visible from the freeway. Thick prickly vegetation grew between the freeway and a tall barbed wire fence that stood at the top of the hill.

The mark was quite large: approximately 130 feet long and 6 feet wide. It consisted of a central circular area (McKey called this the "blast area") and a second

A photograph of the June 1984 trace taken in Delaware, Ohio, about two months after it was found. It originally consisted of standing alfalfa plants burned into black cinders from their tops into their roots. The surrounding area was undisturbed and plants did not grow back. Analysis showed no trace of unusual chemicals, such as pesticides or gasoline

smaller circular area beside it about 7 feet in diameter. Extending from it to the south was a swath of burned vegetation that ran straight for approximately 25 feet. A strip of unburned vegetation extended down the center of this swath. From the north, another swath curved over a hillside and became gradually less distinct. Similar to the Indiana incident recounted in *Intruders*, deep cracks were visible in the ground at the center of the Ohio burn.

Samples from the burn area and nearby control areas were taken. The local fire chief, a senior industrial chemist named Art Sill, Ph.D. and several US Department of Agriculture scientists were contacted for the analysis. Sill's examination of some of the samples via spectrometry yielded charts showing mass spectrum and electron impact results. To determine whether gasoline might have caused the burn, Sill tested for gasoline residue. He found no trace of gasoline in the sample. Several agricultural experts further checked his results and found no trace of pesticide or herbicide products or degradation of such products.[52] Most of what was found was common organic substances from farm plants and weeds. The scientists thought two of the chromatograms might have been from DMSO (dimethyl sulfoxide), which would not normally be found in an alfalfa field. These analyses indicated that neither gasoline, pesticides, nor similar chemicals had made the burn. The results confirmed what the farmer and his employees said: no such chemicals had been applied to the ground.

The test results suggested the burn had been caused by the application of heat, microwaves, or something similar. There was no evidence that the burn was caused by a blast from a hot air balloon, by dumped gasoline, by pesticide, or by lightning. It appeared that seeds had been destroyed in the burn area. I took a sample of the soil and of nearby soil from an undamaged area. Seeds grew in both samples. Thus, there was nothing in the soil that interfered with plant growth. However, algae grew back only in the sample of nearby soil. Later on, as a few dandelions began to grow in the area of the mark, an unusual number looked deformed. Not much else grew there; no alfalfa grew back. Several years later, some of the rocks in the area were red.

* * *

The area along Interstate 75 from Lexington, Kentucky, to Dayton, Ohio, has been the site of a number of UFO events. One of these—a CE3 event, a "close encounter of the third kind"—took place on January 6, 1976.

Louise Smith, Mona Stafford and Elaine Thomas were driving home to Liberty, Kentucky, from a late dinner at a Stanford, Kentucky, restaurant when, about a mile south of them, they saw a UFO as big as a football field. It was disk-shaped and metallic grey, with a white glowing dome. A row of red lights rotated around its middle. On the underside three or four red and yellow lights glowed and a bluish beam emanated from the bottom.

The object rocked gently for several seconds, moved across the road, circled behind and above some nearby houses and returned to the highway.

The inside of the women's car lit up with a bluish light. Smith and Stafford panicked. The car pulled to the left and Smith screamed at Stafford to help her control it. The speedometer registered 85 miles an hour, but Smith wasn't accelerating; she even raised her foot in the air to prove this to her companions. The three women had the sensation that the car was speeding along, but a red light on the instrument panel indicated the engine had stalled. As Smith and Stafford wrestled with the steering wheel, all three experienced a sudden burning sensation in their eyes. Smith later described an additional pain that radiated through the top of her head.

They felt the car being pulled backward and it bounced along as if traveling over speed bumps. Thomas glimpsed the UFO behind them. It was beautiful, she said; she had never seen such a gorgeous shade of red.

The women then saw a strange, well-lit road stretching as far ahead of them as they could see and the next thing they knew they were coming into Hustonville, eight miles beyond where they'd encountered the UFO.

They continued home to Liberty, where Smith went into her bathroom. Removing her watch to wash her hands, she was startled to see the minute and hour hands spinning on the dial. She took off her glasses and splashed water on her face and with this exposure to water, her hands and face burned in pain. Moreover, on the back of her neck Smith had a red mark that looked like a new burn before it blisters. The two other women had similar marks on their necks and all three reported burning and watering eyes.

The three immediately contacted a neighbor who ushered them into separate rooms and had each draw the object she'd seen. The sketches were nearly identical.

After the incident, Smith's pet parakeet refused to have anything to do with her. Each of the women lost weight. Stafford had severe conjunctivitis and sought medical help.

The three witnesses were interviewed by UFO investigators and were hypnotized. Under hypnosis Smith remembered that her face had been covered with a fluid. Stafford, also under hypnosis, described being on a white table where a large eye observed her. Thomas, when hypnotized, recalled a contraption around her neck that had tightened and choked her when she tried to speak or think.

Several UFOlogists, including Len Stringfield and Bryan Thompson, Ph.D., investigated this incident. Thompson told me the women experienced headaches and nausea and he thought these could be symptoms or after-effects of abduction. He speculated that during abduction, the women might have been immersed in fluid to enable them to withstand a possible rapid acceleration and this might have caused some of their symptoms.[53]

* * *

Although fewer UFO reports were made during the late 1970s and the 1980s, this fact may have been the result of relatively sparse media coverage. People are bolder about reporting strange events when others are making similar reports.

To further examine the effects of media coverage and the ratio of reported and non-reported events, I hypothesized that many more UFO observations are made than are reported. To study the ratio of reported to unreported observations, I surveyed people living in Delaware County, Ohio, near the site of a reported UFO observation. Of 62 respondents, 31 percent reported UFO observations and 17 percent reported knowing someone who'd made an observation. These results, showing that many people will report observations of possible UFOs after a publicized sighting, were published in the peer-reviewed *Ohio Journal of Science* and in the *MUFON UFO Journal*.[54] Although skeptics suspect UFOs are widely reported by publicity seekers, the data suggests that many UFO observers are hesitant to report them. For example, David Jacobs reported that in the early 1950s the Air Force estimated that only 10 percent of people who had sighted objects actually reported them.

By the end of the 1980s the term "close encounters" was firmly entrenched in the vernacular and the idea of—if not the belief in—alien UFOs had become part of popular culture and the individual psyche.

As the decade of the 1980s ended, opinion surveys showed a clear cultural shift: many people now thought (or at least entertained the thought) that if the earth is home to living things, other worlds might hold life, too. The idea that UFOs might represent alien life became increasingly widespread. This cultural awareness of UFOs was evident when Jon Hilkevitch's *Chicago Tribune* story about the O'Hare sighting became the most read story in the history of the *Chicago Tribune*'s Web site, with almost a million hits.

Meanwhile, Americans became painfully aware that government cover-ups were a reality. People earlier had believed in the US government with a nearly religious faith. However, by the end of the 1980s, not only had Americans experienced Watergate, they'd also become aware that the government had authorized secret harmful tests on US citizens and had concealed data about these and other activities.

As such, information became public knowledge, people felt bolder and less reticence about reporting UFOs—and this new sense of honesty led to the intriguing UFO accounts revealed in the next chapter.

CHAPTER EIGHT

The Nineties and The New Millennium – Cornucopia

A VARIETY of UFO forms and activities characterized sightings in the 1990s and the new millennium. Increasingly commonplace were reports of dancing lights, multiple types of aliens, sightings of strange merges and separations, possible mutilations and abductions, mind control, force fields, action at a distance, new informants and their information and many impossible events.

The government showed new methods of involvement and some possible interaction with the phenomena.

As in the past, UFO phenomena presented themselves in complex ways. And although sophisticated investigation techniques were now available, researchers encountered the problems those that plagued Harley Rutledge of Project Identification in the 1970s: UFOs seemed to interact with people and often to outsmart researchers. Such reports were not accepted because they did not fit into science's common nuts and bolts physics paradigms.

* * *

One such event took place on October 24 and November 4, 1995, when multiple small, flashing red lights were seen "dancing" for nearly five hours above a cornfield outside Logan, Ohio. The witnesses included three deputy sheriffs and other government observers. This was an excellent sighting case because today's technology allowed it to be investigated at the time it occurred, it was a close encounter and it had multiple real-time witnesses and contacts and government investigators. The phenomena also may have showed interactive behavior with witnesses, some of the investigators and possibly Jones and I. Evidence of strange government involvement included no direct interaction with the witnesses, but direct investigation.

The two primary witnesses, Mark and Cindy (not their real names) lived across Route 93 from the cornfield. Mark was walking his dog on a cloudless night at 7:45 p.m. on October 24 when he noticed 10 or 20 red lights the apparent size of stars in the cornfield. The lights hovered and moved erratically from right to left or up and down, brightening and dimming, sometimes accompanied by a short, white, funnel-shaped or fan-shaped object below them. The lights were spread out 15 to 30 degrees up from the horizon. Mark said some were as close as 100 to 200 yards from him and they flew no more than one-quarter to one-half mile above the field. None touched the ground and they were silent. Mark recalled, that they were close enough that if they had been something that he understood, he would have been able to hear them.

Mark told Cindy and her teenage daughter about the lights. The two came out and stood on the porch; they watched the red lights flashing and blinking in the sky. Sometimes there were only two or three, Cindy said, but at times she counted at least ten visible at the same time.

Mark said, that there were times when we would watch one and have another appear next to it. One of the lights left the rest of the group and briefly followed a southbound car traveling around 55 miles per hour. As Mark put it, there had been a car coming in the distance from the direction of town and he'd been watching one over the cornfield and it actually went to the left and hovered above this car and then followed it down the road above it. It then stopped short of the house by 100 or 150 yards, hovered and let the car pass.

Cindy said the light followed the car around a bend in the road near their home and then it shot up the side of a hill beside the road. This spooked a group of deer. The deer ran down the hill, but instead of crossing the road into the cornfield as they usually did, they went off in another direction.

Cindy noted that at times the lights would create a half-moon formation over the field. At other times she would stare into an area where there were no stars and suddenly a red light would appear in that area. She described the lights as ball-like and said they made no sound.

Mark had been watching the lights for half an hour when he phoned the Hocking County Sheriff's Office. The office treated the call seriously and dispatched a cruiser and two deputies, who arrived 20 minutes later. The deputies said they didn't know what the lights were.

As the officers stood in the driveway watching the lights with Mark, Cindy and her daughter, a wheezing noise came from the cornfield. Cindy said it sounded like a cow with a bad cold or a person with severe asthma. One deputy said a deer was making the noise; however, Mark, an avid deer hunter, replied that he'd heard hundreds of deer snort and grunt and this was no deer. Cindy had also heard deer before and it didn't sound like a deer to her. The sound continued for five minutes. The deputies stayed 15 minutes then filed their report and left.

A short time later, two family friends arrived to view the lights.

Mark went in the house and called his father to tell him about the incident. By now, it was 9:00 p.m. As Mark spoke on the phone, he heard a loud noise outside. He ran out and saw a white 'life flight like' low-flying helicopter coming from the south. It passed over the house and left. Five minutes later, two small, propeller-driven planes arrived, flying slowly and at low altitude. They moved in a grid-like pattern as if surveying the area. This activity continued until past midnight and the lights remained in the field the entire time. At one point a light left the group in the field and followed one of the airplanes.

A second cruiser arrived at 10:00 p.m. The deputy said he'd been in another county when he'd heard about the sighting on the police radio and he wanted to see the lights for himself. He watched the lights and the planes. The lights continued blinking on and off, appearing and disappearing in different numbers and the planes continued in their grid-like pattern.

Cindy was later asked if any witnesses went into the field while the lights were there and she said no, everyone was afraid to. A UFO investigator examined the cornfield after the event but found nothing unusual.

A local television station covered the incident. On October 25, reporter Marcy Fleisher of WBNS-TV in Columbus revealed in a newscast that the Federal Aviation Administration, WPAFB and the Ohio National Guard had all been contacted about a UFO sighting outside Logan, but that none knew of any aircraft in the area at that time. The local sheriff's radio log was included in the broadcast, noting Mark's report and other radio traffic about the UFOs. The sheriff's personnel had no comment beyond saying they'd received calls about UFOs the previous night.

On November 4, the lights returned. At 11:30 p.m. Mark and Cindy were watching television with the same family friends who'd witnessed the October 24 sighting, when someone noticed lights outside. This time Mark and Cindy filmed the lights with a video camera they'd borrowed after the previous sighting.

In the three-minute video, the lights weren't as numerous nor as active as previously, but the video clearly shows five red flashing lights that vary in intensity and rate of strobing. The video also shows three dimmer lights that blink on and off at different rates, then blink on and off in unison.

Sometime after the October 24 sighting, Mark alone observed a UFO with a row of square, red, sequentially blinking lights. It passed silently overhead and left.

Paul Burrell and Dilbert Anderson investigated this sighting initially. Bill Jones and I made a second visit to the site on November 4 and again interviewed the witnesses and reenacted the events. Interestingly enough, the second sighting occurred on the very night of our visit.

This event showed interaction in several ways: when an object followed one of the airplanes, when one followed a car, when they would appear when a witness stared into the air and another was possibly when a visitation occurred right after Jones and I were there.

Many government agencies were contacted and some witnessed the event. Some agency sent the helicopters and airplanes. This agency had the financing to afford these assets and to plan a method to survey the activity. However, the witnesses were not interviewed and the results of the investigation and even the agency were secret. This appeared to be a new phase of government involvement.

* * *

A similar event occurred on an autumn night, October 13, 1992, at around 8:00 p.m., near the Columbus, Ohio, intersection of Interstates 270 and 7, as a pair of mothers and their two sons drove home from a movie they looked up in the sky to see a UFO.

This resulted in an excellent UFO report for the reasons given above. As in the previous sighting, there were multiple witnesses and they reported the sighting as it occurred, enabling a real-time investigation of the event. They contacted several government authorities during the sighting, allowing their responses to be examined. They experienced strange physical effects, were willing to be interviewed by researchers and one witness reenacted the event for UFOlogists. Bill Jones, Bill Mumma and I interviewed the two adult witnesses separately. We traveled with Ellen Carmindy as she reenacted her sighting at its location at nearly same time in the evening as when it took place. We noticed that at that time of the evening, just after dark, the area outside the apartment complex was almost deserted.

The four witnesses—Nadine and Alex Nordstrom and Ellen and Stuart Carmindy (not their real names)—were near their home when they saw the object hovering in the west, about 200 or 300 feet away, over trees at the edge of the large apartment complex where they all lived. Nadine, the driver, stopped the car to observe the UFO and at first, they thought they might be watching a plane crash.

The witnesses generally gave the same account, although when interviewed separately, some discrepancies occurred (which is normal in individual accounts). For example, when interviewed separately Nadine said that when she first saw it the hovering object resembled a circular orange-yellow glow surrounded by lights. Ellen, also interviewed separately, described the object when she first saw it as dark, oblong and surrounded by white light and with three to five white lights around it. It covered an area (subtended an angle) of about 8" at arms' length.

As they watched, the UFO sped north and stopped over another part of the apartment complex. The two adult witnesses said the object now appeared to be triangular. They drove into the complex and parked in a space near the building, intending to exit the car for a better view. But none of them could open the car doors or lower the windows. Moments later, however, they could easily do so. As they left the car, the UFO appeared to split into several smaller objects.

The witnesses lived near the flight paths of two airports and so were familiar with low-flying aircraft. However, the object or objects were probably not standard aircraft, because local agencies were unaware of them. For example, while the object was still in view Nadine rushed into her apartment and phoned the nearby Port Columbus Airport. The control tower said no aircraft was in that area (airport personnel subsequently notified the National UFO Reporting Center in Washington state). Nadine also called the Columbus police and Don Scott Airport, northwest of Columbus. The officers said no police helicopter was in the area and Don Scott employees reported seeing nothing unusual.

Meanwhile the object shot up into the sky, came back down and changed into multiple balls of light. As Ellen stood outside, one ball of light swooped to within 20 feet of her. Other lights resembled searchlights shining down from above, Ellen said.

The two boys ran through Nadine's apartment from the back door and out the front to the apartment of a neighbor who lived across the street to the north. This neighbor might also have seen some of the balls of light. The balls of light finally lined up in a row and three of them joined together. Nadine said all the lights then flashed, accelerated and disappeared. Both adult witnesses said the sighting lasted about 45 minutes.

The two boys were frightened by the experience and had lasting reactions (as did Nadine's dog). One boy had intermittent insomnia and strange dreams and he constantly wanted his mother's company. One consulted a school counselor for help, but the counselor was dismissive, denying that UFOs exist. One boy had friends who teased him about the sighting. Both mothers felt the boys became "sensitive" about the experience and about UFOs in general and neither allowed investigators to interview her son.

Because the events in this sighting, such as their inability to open the car doors and the events seemingly being invisible to government contacts are common and provide a reason why such reports should not be rejected, although they generally are.

* * *

A 1995 Missouri incident also included dancing lights and alien sightings and showed evidence of new physics paradigms.

On July 9, 1995, at 11:00 p.m. two couples in their early twenties—Janet and Michael and Thomas and Lori (not their real names)—went to pay a late-night visit to a friend. On the way they saw, hovering above trees near a field, a UFO made up of a large lower disc and a small higher disc connected by a rectangular shaft. Four beams of light shone down from the bottom and white balls of light descended through the beams to the ground.

Janet was afraid and wanted to leave. Michael saw the object but was neither fearful nor interested in it; he fell asleep in the back of the car and stayed there for the rest of the incident. Thomas and Lori wanted to see what would happen next; they drove Janet to her car so she could leave and they returned to the site.

The UFO was still there—along with a multitude of alien beings.

Lori could see the aliens but not the spacecraft and Thomas could see the craft but not the creatures.

According to Lori, the aliens were on the ground and varied in shape, size, color and attire. Some were emaciated and tall with brown skin and bald heads. Some were big and muscular; these wore capes. Some were cream-colored and wore robes. Others were small, muscular and purple; these alternately appeared and disappeared. Some were transparent human-shaped outlines containing flecks of light. One was dressed in white and was digging in the ground.

Several creatures milled around, as if looking for something, while others were running very fast. The different types stayed in clusters with their own kinds.

One of the transparent light-flecked beings ran toward Lori and Thomas. Terrified, the two jumped in their car and the creature ran past them into the woods leaving behind a trail of flecks of light. These lights gathered around their car and

180

somehow they entered the vehicle. This was the last thing about the incident that Thomas and Lori remembered.

Meanwhile Janet was waiting for them to meet her at their friend's home. At 2:30 a.m. she left to look for them. Driving alone in her car, she was halfway to the site when she was overcome with fear. As she turned her car around in a parking lot to head back to the friend's home, four blue lights, each about two feet wide, appeared in front of her. These were attached to an enormous UFO hovering six feet above the trees. The object appeared to be six stories high and two acres wide. Its top and bottom were triangular and it had three flat vertical sides. The blue lights were attached to each bottom corner, with a fourth light in the center of the back. Terrified, Janet sped away.

About 10 or 15 minutes later she arrived at the home of her friend Donald (not his real name). When she related what she'd seen, Donald said he'd also seen unusual things in the past and knew how she felt. He promised to stay awake with her until sunrise. Nevertheless he fell off into a deep sleep and she couldn't wake him.

While he slept, she saw several creatures outside his home. One was a tall, blond, male human-looking form, but with translucent, bluish skin. Another male, shorter and with glowing skin, was with him. Janet described a third, also shorter, as seeming to be made of energy.

She noticed more beings in the yard, about 20 or 30 of them, of the latter two types. The 'energy' beings were walking from north to south, or from her right to her left. As they disappeared from her view to the left, more replaced them on the right. Periodically a glowing, lavender, troll-like being would also appear; it had messy brown hair sticking out all over its head. When the aliens tried to look through the window at her, the tall blond one pushed them away so they couldn't see her.

As she watched these beings, she was overcome with sleepiness. She tried to fight this, but she dozed off. She awoke to see a large black box above her head that closed into itself and disappeared. This was the last thing she remembered about that night.

From then on, however, Janet, Thomas and Lori continued to see UFOs. These included a 'flying saucer,' an egg-shaped object and another object of undetermined shape. They saw them both at a distance and at close range. The three frequently saw white balls of light during the day and at night. The sightings took place whether the witnesses were together or alone. At last report, the sightings were still occurring.[55]

This event almost spells out what is unusual about the UFO phenomena. The ability of the balls of light to take different forms suggests that they are alive, intelligent, can take on different characteristics and influence people's minds. They show a property noted in quantum physics studies of being able to pass through solid walls. They showed mind control in many ways, such as the ability to allow terrified witnesses to suddenly fall asleep and could cause witnesses to see different things. The observation indicates that the individual balls are intelligent beings taking different forms, but that these can merge. Such events suggest that this data should be investigated using different paradigms than our nuts and bolts ideas of space ships.

* * *

Many dancing-light sightings have been reported during the past two decades. For example, on the evening of June 28, 2009, as Anna Dean (not her real name) called her dog outside her home in Indiana, she saw numerous white globes of light ranging from golf-ball-sized to basketball-sized. A larger red globe, approximately 10 feet in diameter, accompanied these. She watched the lights in the woods near her home for half an hour, but when they moved toward her, she and her dog went inside. Once in the house, she couldn't move from the door. Several globes approached the door and she felt the temperature drop. Small amounts of liquid fell from the globes.

The dog, which had been closer to the balls than she, suffered lasting effects. Its eyes swelled shut, it began to tremble repeatedly and it refused to go outside after dark.

A Columbus College of Art and Design student in Ohio reported a similar sighting to MORA investigators. She said that she sometimes saw small balls of light travel through her bedroom. One time when this occurred, a friend tried to enter the apartment and was unable to open the door. When the globes left, the door could be easily opened.

* * *

Many sightings involving balls of light associated with UFO-related or supernatural events have occurred during the past decade. Some are similar to the events reported above and to incidents encountered by Rutledge's researchers. In fact, in what some consider a continuation of Rutledge's work, the National Institute for Discovery Science (NIDS), a privately funded scientific group, conducted an on-going investigation that has come to be called the Skinwalker Study. This was a field analysis of UFO phenomena. It was described by NIDS investigator Colm Kelleher, Ph.D. and investigative journalist George Knapp in *Hunt for the Skinwalker: Science Confronts the Unexplained at a Remote Ranch in Utah* (2005).

The Skinwalker events began in the mid-1990s when a cattle-ranching family purchased and moved to an isolated ranch in northeast Utah. Here they encountered UFOs, poltergeists, mutilated cattle, disembodied voices, teleported objects, invisible creatures and so on. The family loved their home but because of the mysterious events, they left. Las Vegas billionaire and space entrepreneur Robert Bigelow, who brought in a team of senior research scientists to investigate the activity, purchased the so-called Skinwalker ranch.

Week ending Friday, November 29, ▇▇

Ranch family terrorized by unknown forces

A LOCAL farming family has been reporting mysterious incidents occurring on their farm recently, but many think this a cry-wolf situation.

After the disappearance of their 10-year-old boy last week, the boys father has made calls to the police almost daily reporting strange incidents such as wolf tracks all over his property, and

By ▇▇▇▇▇▇▇

bright lights flashing in his field. "I'm sure it's just vandals trying to spook him because of what happened to his son," said the sheriff. "There have been cattle disappearing all over the state, which explains the wolf tracks.

As for the bright lights, they're just flashlights."

With further reports of footsteps being heard of his roof and scratching on his door, the rancher has been granted police-surveillance on the property to ensure his safety.

Police are continuing their search for the rancher's 10-year-old son.

Press coverage of the sightings at the Skin Walker ranch

As Rutledge's group had done, the scientists set up observation stations, but they were unable to collect the desired data because the phenomena seemed to respond to them. For example, although researchers could see moving balls of light, they would be unable to photograph them. The lights would merge, or split apart, or disgorge other objects; this inconsistent activity made it difficult for researchers to collect the data needed for scientific study. Many of the scientists felt the phenomena had a kind of intelligence, could read minds and could even exert mind control. For example, one researcher reported that he experienced what seemed to be an "unnatural" or artificially induced fear when some of the objects were near him.

Another researcher reported that as he changed positions, certain orange objects would disappear then reappear. (Rutledge described a similar phenomenon.) At another time, when researchers set up viewing equipment to look directly at the orange objects, some reported they could see a window into somewhere else and that it sometimes appeared to be into the blue sky of another world. The rancher's homestead was the only vantage point from which the orange structure was perfectly visible. It was like a three-dimensional orange tunnel that receded

183

Brutal Texas Cattle Mutilations Examined in at Least 10 Counties

Press coverage of the cattle mutilations

away from them, with three sides of the tunnel perfectly camouflaged with the sky, so from a side view an observer could see nothing at all. The only perspective that gave a good view into the interior was directly opposite the mouth of the tunnel.

And this mouth pointed straight at the homestead.

Rather than simply seeing an orange UFO, the researchers seemed to be look-ing into what they described as a torn place or a rent in the sky. For this reason they conjectured that the UFO might be a pathway into a different dimension or alternate reality, a doorway through which an object could enter and exit this world.

To watch one dull-yellow-colored flying object, researchers used night-vision binoculars and cameras loaded with infrared film. As one scientist positioned his binoculars, he saw not just a light, but a tunnel and he suddenly exclaimed, Jesus Christ! Something is in the tunnel. The tunnel seemed suspended two feet above ground. In it, a large, black, human-like figure with no face was using its elbows to move forward. When it reached the end of the tunnel, it lowered itself to the ground and walked away. The researchers then explored the site where this occurred; there they detected a pungent, sulfur-like odor that made them nauseous. However, their instruments revealed nothing unusual. A Nardalert counter, which detects alpha, beta, gamma and X-rays, registered background levels only. A Trifield meter, which detects magnetic spikes, registered nothing. No footprints were visible on the hard ground. And photography disclosed only a single faint blurry light in one photograph and nothing on the rest of the film roll.

The phenomena seemed able to read the minds of researchers and others on-site. In one earlier incident, the ranch's previous owners had driven past their bull enclosure and glanced proudly at their four beautiful bulls. The wife remarked how awful it would be if any of the animals were lost and 45 minutes later the couple returned to find the enclosure empty. As they searched for the animals, which weighed approximately a ton each, they looked in a small trailer with a tightly locked door. Inside, crammed into the tiny space, were the four huge bulls and they appeared paralyzed, hypnotized and barely conscious. When the ranchers finely woke them, the bulls scrambled outside and stampeded.

Another incident further illustrates the difficulty of studying the phenomena. Six surveillance cameras were set up where cattle mutilations had occurred. The cameras could record images in darkness and copies of the recordings were regularly made and monitored. One morning an observer saw that three cameras, each mounted 15 feet above the ground, had stopped working. Researchers examined the cameras

Photo of one of the many so-called cattle mutilations

and found the wiring of all three was ripped out. The wiring for each was anchored to a pole by sturdy plastic tubing and heavy-duty duct tape, with the wires for each camera wrapped separately. All of the duct tape had been unwound.

A fourth camera happened to include the three disabled cameras in its view and the scientists eagerly replayed this tape. However, in spite of much digital enhancement, the tape showed only the red lights of the cameras suddenly stopping. It did not show what had happened to the wiring.

Because of numerous problems, researchers were not only unable to study the UFO activity on the ranch, but even to develop the means to study it. They discussed the possibility that they were investigating entities more advanced than humans and that therefore, they lacked the necessary tools for investigation. They speculated that the methodology of counterintelligence might provide a more effective model—better than the traditional scientific methods used to investigate physical processes—for UFO study.

* * *

In the 1990s, interest grew in UFO-linked animal mutilations, child abductions and genetic experimentation upon people by aliens. Stringfield was probably the first to mention the subject of mutilations; in *Situation Red* he described livestock mutilations that occurred in 1975 in tandem with UFO sightings in states including Pennsylvania and Ohio.[56]

I happened to learn of one set of cattle mutilations in November 1993 when the Triad Research Conference of UFOlogists was held in Indianapolis and coincided with an auto show. At that event, I videotaped a conversation between UFOlogist

Michael Lindemann and American racing car driver Bobby Unser. Unser had won the Indianapolis 500 races in 1968, 1975 and 1981, as well as numerous other national championship races. He is the brother of Al Unser, another prominent racecar driver. Unser approached Lindemann's display and said he was experiencing both UFO activity and cattle mutilations on his ranch. According to Lindemann, Unser said, "We go outside, we look out at the back forty, we see flying saucers all the time." Lindemann discussed this conversation in his November 20 presentation. I videotaped the conversation and published a photograph of Unser talking to Lindemann.

More disturbing than livestock mutilations is the possibility that extraterrestrials, our government, or both are behind some child abductions. MORA and Ohio's Mutual UFO Network, Inc. (Ohio MUFON) members have interviewed informants about human abductions and received different opinions.

For example, one informant said to Bill Jones, that he supposed Jones had heard about the missing children. He went on to claim that children were being taken away to secret locations such as one near Nellis Air Force Base in Nevada. (It was unclear whether he meant the kidnappings were done by space aliens, or by the American government, or by both working together.) Some secret locations were underground, he asserted and were used for genetic studies. He said most of the children would never be returned. He also said 'liquidation lists' were being maintained and that these contained the names of officials who had worked on space-alien cases and had revealed secret information to others. He added that a government exists at a higher level than the US president and that it is worldwide.

Jones is investigating the subject of missing children to learn more. He has hypothesized that some missing children may have been abducted by aliens or by the government and will not be returned.

Informants have proposed reasons behind such government cover-ups of UFO information. Some have told us that if officials high in the government do know about UFO phenomena, but can't do anything about it, they may not tell the public. Another common reason given is the fear of inciting panic. (A 1938 radio drama, *The War of the Worlds* presented by Orson Welles, did this.) Of course, the most common reason behind cover-ups may be the desire to keep ahead of other countries, or to make it appear that the US has the use of alien technology, or to hide this knowledge if they do.

Another event related to both abduction and genetic manipulation involved the abduction of an Indiana family reported by Budd Hopkins in *Intruders: The Incredible Visitations at Copley Wood*. The incident includes one of the first reports of genetic experimentation on humans by extraterrestrials. According to Hopkins, Kathy Davis (not her real name) and members of her Indiana family

Abductee Debbie Jordan & US researcher and author Budd Hopkins

were not only abducted, but genetic experiments were conducted on them and alien-human hybrid children were produced as a result.

When I interviewed Hopkins about this issue, I asked how aliens could impregnate human females, considering that human and alien chromosomes and other genetic material are probably incompatible. He replied that such reproductive activities take place artificially and that the incompatibility is offset via advanced alien technology. However, he thought sexual contact between aliens and humans is rare.

* * *

Additional studies conducted during this time period shed light on the UFO phenomena. For example, Kenneth Ring, Ph.D., a professor of psychology at the University of Connecticut and author of *The Omega Project; Near-Death Experiences, UFO Encounters and Mind at Large* (1992), found similarities between the experiences of UFO abductees and those of individuals who'd had near-death out-of-body experi3ences.[57]

Researcher Kenneth Ring, Ph.D.

* * *

Many high-level people, such as US presidents and astronauts, have expressed interest or concern about UFO phenomena. For example astronaut Buzz Aldrin, the second to walk on the moon, has openly disclosed his interest in UFO phenomena. Additional astronaut informants, including Edgar Mitchell, Ph.D., Gordon Cooper and Donald Kent "Deke" Slayton, have spoken out about UFO phenomena, as have Presidents Jimmy Carter, Gerald Ford and Ronald Reagan.

Such accounts are also significant because they support the idea that government officials are prohibited from speaking out about UFO phenomena. For example,

Astronaut Edgar Mitchell who was a big supporter of the UFO community

Astronaut Gordon Cooper who made his own UFO sighting

Mercury astronaut and retired Air Force Colonel Gordon Cooper has described a 1951 incident where he and others observed UFO flights over a two-day period in Germany. In May 1957 at Edwards Air Force Base, some of Cooper's crew filmed a metallic-looking craft with tripod landing gear as it landed and took off within 50 yards of them. Stringfield told Bill Jones and Beckie Minshall that one day he received a call from Cooper. Cooper told Stringfield he'd soon no longer be able

Astronaut Buzz Aldrin, the second man to walk on the Moon is alleged to have witnessed a UFO during his flight in Apollo 11 when heading towards the Moon

These three former US presidents, Ronald Reagan, Gerald Ford and Jimmy Carter have all made positive comments regarding the UFO subject

to talk about UFOs because he had been advised that he was about to be visited by a certain person whom he didn't name. Cooper later confirmed that the visit had occurred. Because Stringfield and Cooper both had been involved in a UN initiative to establish some sort of UFO agency at the UN, they had become friends.

* * *

In the 1990s, Bill Jones and I investigated a number of informant reports with some amazing results. One man provided an especially credible report because he was highly placed in the CIA. Jones and I had been employed in organizations through which we knew background information about this man thus we could confirm his credentials.

On impulse one day, we made a surprise visit to this person at home. He welcomed us and had much to say about UFO phenomena. He told us about a Roswell-like situation that had occurred in Australia a few years ago. Debris from a crashed UFO was flown in a C-141 Starlifter military aircraft under strict secrecy and the informant traveled with the debris to the US. While he was in the plane a green ray from the debris hit him in the face and he later developed cancer at this spot. The informant suggested that this Starlifter may have been attacked en route, but it arrived in the US with its cargo.

To our surprise, he confirmed that major UFOlogy groups are monitored, sometimes from within by government agencies. The agencies track civilian UFO discoveries, watching how the UFOlogy community functions, observing who's working together, what each group of UFOlogists is studying and what various elements of the UFO community think about each discovery. The informant said the agencies want to know how the UFOlogy community communicates, processes information and distributes its findings to others. He asserted that government agencies use UFOlogy organizations to distribute the agencies' own information and disinformation to the public at large (such behavior was initially observed by Arnold).

We began to think this was possible, because to our surprise, even though he had not attended any of the meetings of an Ohio group to which we belonged, he knew all about us personally, including our addresses and other details. Although I had never met him, he knew much about me.

In addition, UFOlogists also suspect that the government may monitor private residences. When I interviewed Stringfield in his home, he mentioned that private residences have been monitored by agencies of the American government and had us walk outside during some discussions. Other UFOlogists also suspect the government may monitor their homes. I observed this first hand at other times. In one case Jones and I dropped in unannounced to an operative's home and had a long discussion about UFOs, but Jones suddenly decided to leave. He said this was because he feared that the house might be bugged and we would get the operative in trouble. Although this idea at first seemed preposterous, when I asked others about it they thought it was quite possible. In other instances, when I interviewed government employees and contractors in their homes, it was not uncommon for them to indicate that the conversations might be monitored (such monitoring was also observed by Arnold) . Similar private-home-monitoring activities were in the news in late June 2010 in connection with a Russian spy case in which the FBI arrested eleven people.[58]

Government officials also monitor civilian responses to Internet information. For example, on April 10, 2010, at an Ohio Academy of Science meeting, I presented a paper on my study of responses to Internet information, "Comparison of YouTube Viewers' Comments on Channels with Male vs. Female Labels." Colonel Linda Steel-Goodwin, deputy director of the Human Effectiveness Directorate at WPAFB, later contacted me. She said she was interested in my results because her laboratory studied human responses to material on Internet sites.

* * *

'Black helicopters'—mysterious and often silent helicopters seen periodically in the areas of recent UFO sightings—are another icon of the 1990s. Although this is presented as urban legend, we had direct experience with this activity. They were reportedly used to harass UFO witnesses and groups and they were sometimes seen in areas where cattle mutilations have been reported. Even many UFOlogists typically dismiss black helicopters as the stuff of urban legend.

However, a smoking gun kind of black helicopter incident took place on June 15, 1993. UFOlogists Frank Reams, Joe Stets and Bill Jones were featured between 7:00 and 8:00 p.m. on a local central Ohio call-in TV talk show, Phyllis Ransom's *Profiles*. The show aired on Channel 62, a low-powered station that is rarely advertised and has a tiny audience. Its signal is beamed north of Columbus and viewers in Columbus receive it poorly if at all. Reams' phone number was flashed on the screen at the end of the show.

Around 20 minutes later the Reams family saw a 'Huey' military helicopter approach, from the west, their rural home north of New Albany, Ohio. It appeared to be black and they were unable to see any markings. The family heard the slow whish-whish-whish sound typical of this type of military helicopter. The chopper hovered at 100 feet and pointed its front end down at the house. With its front end in this position, it circled the house three times. This maneuver frightened the family because it meant the helicopter was in a position to open fire on the house. Then it departed.

Reams is a corporate pilot, his daughter is a commercial pilot and the rest of the family is familiar with aircraft. They were sure this was a military Huey, but Reams never determined where the helicopter came from. Ohio National Guard Huey helicopters were stationed at Rickenbacker International Airport south of Columbus and at Springfield-Beckley Municipal Airport in Springfield, Ohio, east of Dayton. Rickenbacker is 20 miles from the Reams house and the Springfield airport is 60 miles from the house. The signal for the Channel 62 broadcast would not have been received in either area, so if the helicopters had been dispatched from either location in response to the TV program, someone north of Columbus and within reach of the Channel 62 signal must have notified someone at Rickenbacker or Springfield-Beckley, or notified an intermediary.

It's expensive to operate these helicopters, which are sometimes used by Special Forces military groups. Including ground maintenance, the cost can exceed $1500 per hour of flying time. Moreover, the flights must be cleared with authorities—one can't just grab a Huey and fly away on a whim or for a prank.

And this response was hostile and threatening, for the helicopter was in a firing position.

This immediate response to the call-in show suggests that a special hot line may link some UFO reporters to government agencies. Additional reports from other researchers claim that some agencies have direct telephone lines to WPAFB for reporting unusual events.

For example, in an investigation of how police react to UFO incidents, Ohio UFOlogist Kenny Young told about 'Signal 50,' the code used by the Ohio State Highway Patrol (OSHP) during radio communications to announce the observation of 'unknown aircraft.' He also noted that after a UFO sighting at the Lebanon Correctional Institute, dispatchers at the OSHP and the Warren County Sheriff's Office used a special, confidential and direct-access phone number to call WPAFB and confirm that they were aware of the sighting. Both the OSHP and the Warren County Sheriff's Office refused to disclose the number to Young, saying it was for a restricted line and was not releasable to the public. This story is believable because WPAFB is thought to test experimental aircraft. Authorities at the base would want to be informed as soon as possible in the event of a crash or another problem.

In another example, at a 1987 MUFON meeting in Columbus, Ohio, Shirley and George Coyne, directors of MUFON in Michigan (no relation to the Coyne of the Coyne Incident discussed in Chapter Six), told of being followed by a helicopter that stopped and turned back when they stopped their car under an overpass.

* * *

Another vital question concerning UFO investigation by the government is whether the government has continued to research the topic after the Condon Committee came to its negative conclusions in 1969 and discontinued its collection of reports from the public. I asked Beverly Trout, a long-time UFO investigator who had been the MUFON State Director in Iowa and who had been invited into the MUFON Board of Directors, about this. Her reply was as follows:

> I've seen two sources that quote Brigadier C. H. Bolender's memo of October 20, 1969. It's in the *UFO Cover-up* by Fawcett & Greenwood, Page xvii of the Preface and on Page 3 in the first chapter. Also, it's covered in Timothy Good's book, *Above Top Secret* on Page 443.

> Bolender made it clear that "Reports of unidentified flying objects which could affect national security are made in accordance with JANAP 146 or Air Force Manual 55-11 and are not part of the Blue Book system." That quote is on Page xvii of the Preface. Then on Page 3 there's an explanation of JANAP 146 E.[59]

She added that she thought that it's safe to assume that collection of UFO sightings has gone on ever since and that she would be shocked if the intelligence and military community were not trying to control or retrieve information from civilian groups. She had been told about the Cloud data storage system. She said James Clarkson (the former State Director of state of Washington) mentioned on a Jerry Pippin interview that MUFON was using it. A friend in St. Louis who keeps up on privacy issues, told her that there are security issues with it and it'd be easy for government agencies to gain access to that information.

I had also asked her about NICAP, which I had heard had been infiltrated by government agents. She replied that from what she had read, it smacks of some kind of undermining influence. And that it is also important to pay attention to whether there's some kind of implosive effort behind the scenes with MUFON.

Because some UFOlogists have been confused by the role of Robert Bigelow, whose association with the government is unclear, I asked her about his role. Bigelow is an aerospace and real estate entrepreneur. He created Bigelow Aerospace to revolutionize space commerce via affordable and

Robert Bigelow

Nuclear physicist and UFO researcher and author, Stanton T. Friedmann

expandable space habitats. The Bigelow Aerospace Mission Control Center in Nevada operates the company's spacecraft (Genesis I and Genesis II) and plans to control Bigelow Aerospace's future space facilities.

Bigelow funded the National Institute for Discovery Science (NIDS), which was involved with the Skinwalker study. In 2009, Bigelow signed a contract with MUFON and undisclosed backers put up the money for this contract. The contract may have allowed Bigelow to purchase and control the MUFON database of sightings and other data and controversy still exists regarding it. However, the contract is no longer in effect. Trout said that she did not know whether Bigelow was/is part of that, or not, but that is wise to raise that question.

To check on the current status of Bigelow, I called the Columbus, Ohio, airport in November 2016 and asked about how to report an unidentified object. They gave me information about the Bigelow Aerospace Advanced Space Studies and a phone number.

I also asked nuclear physicist Stanton Friedman, one of the original Roswell investigators who has also intensively researched government cover-ups, whether the government has continued its UFO research. He replied:

> Couple of thoughts come to mind. First try reading the 3 part article on Government UFO Lies at my website www.stantonfriedman.com (I think the direct URL is http://www.stantonfriedman.com/index. php?ptp=articles&fdt=2005.05.15.) Very important is the Bolender

(USAF General Carroll Bolender) memo saying that reports of UFOs which could affect national security are not part of the Blue Book system, but are reported using JANAP 146 or air force manual 55-11. . . . John Greenwald's Black Vault website has instructions for today's military pilots telling them what to do if they see an unidentified surface ship, unidentified submarine, unidentified aircraft, or Unidentified Flying Object. Also available are 156 TOP SECRET UMBRA National Security Agency UFO documents on which one can read about one sentence per page (Everything else whited out) and about 57 TSU CIA UFO documents. all blacked out except for 5-10 words. There is also a chapter on the Cosmic Watergate in my 2008 book "Flying Saucers and Science."[60]

These replies were similar to those of many researchers whom I questioned and indicate that many UFOlogists think that the government still collects information on UFO phenomena.

* * *

During this era, UFOlogists and others increased their ability to gather archive and disperse UFO information. This occurred largely because of the ubiquity of the Internet. Indexing and retrieval methods for Internet data continue to improve and the accessibility of the databases of UFO groups is increasing. Growing amounts of information can be found in these databases and elsewhere on the Internet. However, such items as individual news reports, case studies and additional local information—especially those from the pre-Internet era—generally have not been recorded and are difficult to find and access. To preserve some of this UFO history, several collections of regional UFO-related material from Ohio MUFON and MORA are housed in areas such as the Rare Books and Manuscripts Room at OSU's main library, in the Ohio Historical Society's Archives and in the Archives for UFO Research. The Archives for UFO Research, founded in Sweden in 1973, is perhaps the world's most complete repository of UFO data. Detailed descriptions of many UFO events can be found there.

Moreover, in the second decade of the new millennium UFOlogists have access to a variety of sophisticated techniques for recording and investigating UFO activity. Examples include MUFON's developing of the ability to respond rapidly to a UFO event and collect quality evidence through its STAR Impact Project (SIP), which began as a collaborative effort between MUFON and the Bigelow Aerospace Advanced Space Studies. When a UFO report was received it could immediately be evaluated via a defined set of criteria and if it merits further investigation, a specially trained rapid-response team is dispatched to the scene to investigate. Widespread public awareness, better information access and improved investigative methods might eventually yield irrefutable evidence that extraterrestrial UFOs are real.

By the millennium the cultural influence of UFOlogy was massive, as shown by such blockbuster films as *Men in Black, Independence Day, E.T. the Extraterrestrial* and the *Star Wars* and *Star Trek* movies, as well as Art Bell's *Coast to Coast AM* radio show. People around the world were now familiar with stories of UFO sightings, abductions and related phenomena.

* * *

This investigation has provided much evidence for a government cover-up of the UFO phenomena. This evidence shows that some form of possible cover-up, or at least knowledge of the phenomena, existed before the first public knowledge of UFO activity. At first the government began an examination of UFO phenomena with results to indicate it represented something real, but very soon it began a debunking campaign. This has been used for seventy years, but it has been ineffective, for the public continues to be interested and many think it represents something real. Perhaps the government should stop its cover-up, release the information and allow everyone else to examine it.

UFO Flying Saucers comic - Hickson case - splash page

CHAPTER NINE

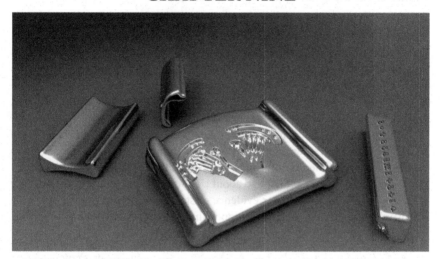

Recent UFOlogy – A New Millennia, Government Cover-Ups and Smoking Guns

AS humanity entered a new millennia, the UFO phenomena continued. For example, the examination of government documents became a crucial portion of UFOlogy, because this could provide further "smoking gun" evidence for the reality of the phenomena.

Few verified serious government studies of UFO phenomena exist. These include the WPAFB projects, research done at Ohio's Battelle Memorial Institute discussed in Chapter Two and the Condon Committee and Robertson Panel reports discussed in this chapter.

Of these, only one study appears to be a truly scientific examination of UFO phenomena, *SR-14*. Portions of the work of agencies such as Project Sign and Blue Book also appeared to examine the phenomena in a serious manner. And findings of both Sign and Battelle were that a UFO phenomenon was real and possibly extraterrestrial.

After these studies, the government began to present opposing views. These government-sponsored UFO research projects, such as the Condon and Robertson studies, were undertaken, but they generally seem to have been done as debunking activity (discussed below). In addition, although papers such as the Majestic-12 (MJ-12) documents (also discussed below) have been discovered, these lack the authenticity of the WPAFB and Battelle documents.

Hence, an important part of current research involves not only examination of sightings, but finding documents suggesting authentic UFO study and investigation and searching for evidence that physical material was collected. Because WPAFB and Battelle were known to have been involved in UFO research, UFOlogists seeking these forms of evidence have focused on these institutions. I have worked at Battelle and been stationed at WPAFB and my colleague Bill Jones worked at Battelle for many years, thus, we've had unique opportunities to investigate, both formally and informally, some activities associated with these organizations. We have talked to interesting informants, researchers and even some of UFOs top hoaxers who spread lies, disinformation and sometimes used our material in this (we took no part in this). We learned about UFOlogy from all sources. And because Battelle is where the only major evidence exists of serious government study, we intensively investigated it in conjunction with additional events, such as Roswell.

* * *

And we found and reported the first smoking gun evidence that UFO material may have been studied at Battelle:

Roswell is probably the world's best-known UFO case. Unlike other researchers, we could investigate from the inside to see what reliable information exists about it, what studies were done and who did them, whether material was taken from the Roswell debris field, whether it was extraterrestrial in origin, whether it represented anything beyond state-of-the art science and whether government-sponsored research was affected by any knowledge gained from retrieved Roswell material.[61] Hence, part of our research involved determining whether Battelle or WPAFB ever housed UFO artifacts. In the 1990s, WPAFB historian Bruce Ashcroft was involved in the search for materials or documents at WPAFB associated with the Roswell events and so we questioned him. He reported that he'd spent considerable time studying reports from the "hottest" materials research projects undertaken by the Air Force during the 1947-1951 time period and could find no evidence of new directions in research that might have resulted from the Roswell material.

Nevertheless, we continued these investigations and discovered "smoking-gun" results suggestive that they did examine something.

Although Roswell was generally unknown before 1980, there is evidence that some kind of material was studied. The general assumption today is that it is Roswell debris, but its source is unknown. However much evidence exists that Battelle employees, long before anyone had heard of Roswell, thought that some substance was being examined there. Thus, regardless of what they examined, they would not have been influenced by the Roswell legend at that time. And today people should not assume that it was Roswell debris.

Our smoking gun was the account we reported of a former Battelle employee, Elroy John Center, who left Battelle in 1957.[62] Center said that while working at Battelle, he was responsible for a project that required him to study 'parts' that were represented as retrieved from a flying saucer. These parts had a sort of writing on them and it was his job was to "find out what the characters meant." He said that there was "lots more I can't go into..." Because some of the material, which was described as small "I beams" retrieved from the pre-crash debris field near Roswell, New Mexico in July 1947, has been described as having some sort of writing on it, the obvious question is did the "parts" Mr. Center study come from this crash event? Given that Mr. Center's story was told long before the details of the Roswell debris were known publicly, the possible confirmation of his story by the later descriptions of that debris cannot be ignored. To our knowledge, this is the only smoking-gun evidence in which a Battelle employee claimed to have worked with UFO artifacts.

This disclosure is especially credible because Center, who is listed in *American Men of Science*, had excellent credentials–a preeminent materials scientist, chemical engineer and research chemist. He made major and breakthrough contributions in materials and alloys research. His work had centered on developing new techniques for the microanalysis of new titanium alloys. Surprisingly years after his mention of the material, it was discovered that he co-authored the Battelle reports that were suspected as linking to the Roswell crash.

Center's information is important to ongoing studies of physical UFO evidence. An example of the importance of and interest in Roswell research is the fact that the first edition of Thomas J. Carey and Donald R. Schmitt's *Witness to Roswell: Unmasking the Government's Biggest Cover-Up* was the best-selling UFO book of 2007/2008. In the 2009 edition of *Witness to Roswell: Unmasking the Government's Biggest Cover-Up*, Carey and Schmitt summarized our discussions:

> In 1992, Dr. Irena Scott, herself a former Battelle employee, interviewed a close friend of Elroy Center, who had told him a very intriguing story in 1960. The story related to a science and engineering project involving "unique materials" that Center had worked on at Battelle

199

years before. Center told the friend that he had assisted on a baffling science assignment that involved the evaluation of a very unusual material. He was required to study a "piece of unknown nature" that he understood was resultant from the crash of a UFO that had earlier been retrieved by the US government. Center indicated to the friend that the "piece" had some sort of indecipherable "writing" impressed upon its surface. Center had been asked for his input on the "glyphics" and performed various types of technical analysis on the part. He spoke sparingly to his friend and did not provide any more details. (283)

* * *

The above information about Battelle's role in UFO research is an example that fits into a paper trail documenting a larger, long-term pattern of government investigation and cover-up of UFO information.

This trail began with the first institutional studies at WPAFB such as Project Blue Book and its predecessors. The fact that these initial studies were classified and unavailable to the public shows that the cover-up was in place immediately. Eventually, as part of the upgrading of Project Blue Book, Ruppelt (then head of Project Blue Book), contracted with Battelle for consultants in fields such as astronomy, physics, mathematics and psychology. This research at Battelle was also classified. For example, according to Hynek and others, such Projects as Stork and White Stork were top secret. Indeed, the first four status reports on Project Stork were classified as "secret," and the fifth and sixth were marked "Restricted Security Information." (Although Jones did not have the needed clearances, he and others heard through the grapevine about it. He said that once at Battelle he said, "Project Stork," and was strongly hushed.)

Beginning under Project Stork, Battelle was contracted to produce an improved sighting questionnaire and to carry out a statistical study of UFO reports, in addition to providing the consultation services. The questionnaire explored how much a witness would see and remember from a UFO incident. This information would be used to improve the government's own UFO sighting questionnaire, or "interrogation form," for UFO witnesses. It is curious that the Air Force would choose Battelle, an organization with considerable expertise in metallurgy, to design a UFO questionnaire, so one wonders if this was a camouflage project for other UFO-related activities. Nevertheless, Battelle scientists worked closely with academic psychologists to draft a simple and effective UFO reporting form.

For the statistical study of UFO reports, the government's agenda was to show that UFO phenomena were not real. The results of the study were precisely the opposite, however (as mentioned in Chapter Two). But rather than accept these results analysts ignored them; moreover, they massaged the summary of the data to support the opposite conclusion.

In May 1955, ATIC issued this modified version of Battelle's results in *SR-14*. This report contained both the questionnaire and the statistical analysis. With this version of the Battelle study's conclusions, the Air Force claimed it had disproved the existence of UFOs, although the results of the actual study showed just the opposite. And one would wonder why they developed the questionnaire if UFOs didn't exist.

One problem surrounding the discovery of such information is the fact that, like WPAFB, Battelle is considered a "place of secrets." Through my own familiarity with Battelle, I decided to research several aspects of these stories.

* * *

Because the information we had uncovered about Center provided smoking gun results, I continued this investigation with Carey, Schmitt and Anthony Bragalia in an attempt to find additional evidence about UFO debris.

I also found that they had been involved in some of Ufology's top recent hoaxes, for example, in producing a show with great fanfare and a large audience, the "Roswell Slides." However, after the opening it was quickly labeled a hoax. In this, audiences were told that they had "smoking gun" evidence that extraterrestrials have been here, which were Kodachrome slides dated 1947 showing an alien. The event took place May 5, 2015 and was done by researchers including Donald Schmitt, Tom Carey and Bragalia. However, other investigators almost immediately found that the alien in the photographs was actually a human mummy. Some sources have described Schmitt as a con–a hack writer who had been discredited years ago for lying about his qualifications, lying about his education, making false statements in books co-written with Kevin Randle and misrepresenting his research. He also was behind a deceptive "affidavit" of Walter Haut. Schmitt admitted that he wrote it, not Haut (who was suffering from dementia/Alzheimer's when it was written). This was said to be an attempt to make money by including the document in their sensationalistic book mentioned above.[63]

Besides this, Bragalia has been involved a number of similar activities. Some of these seemed to sully some of the previous UFO observations for which the best evidence existed. For example, the Trent photographs taken in 1950 by Paul Trent, who lived near McMinnville, Oregon. These were two world famous UFO photos published in *Life* magazine that had been subjected to intense scrutiny for more than sixty years and have never been shown to have been hoaxed. In this Bragalia claimed that there were other photographs showing that the Trent photographs

Police officer Lonnie Zamora – witness to the UFO landing at Socorro, New Mexico

had been hoaxed. However, researchers found that the photographs that Bragalia claimed to show this hoax had actually been taken later by the magazine and were not the originals.[64]

He used similar techniques on the Socorro case, which is often viewed as one of the best-documented UFO reports. It was immediately investigated by government sources– the U.S. Army, U.S. Air Force and FBI and it received considerable coverage in the mass media. It was one of the events that helped to persuade astronomer Dr. Hynek, one of the Air Force's primary investigators, that some UFO reports may represent an intriguing mystery. Even after such an extensive investigation, Project Blue Book was unable to come up with a conventional explanation.

Artist's impression of the UFO observed by Police Officer Lonnie Zamora – courtesy of Jose Antonio Caravaca

4/28

Defensor ☠ Chieftain

PRICE 10¢

d Since 1540 — Home of the Famed New Mexico Institute of Mining & Technology

Published Tuesdays & Thursdays in Socorro, N. M. 87801   TUESDAY, APRIL 28, 1964

Of UFO Landing Here Observed

City Policeman Zamora Reports Sighting Egg-Shaped Object and Views Take-Off; Tourist Sees Craft Just Before Landing

Santa Fean Reports Seeing UFO Landed North of Espanola

An unidentified flying object was reported to have landed and taken off near La Madera, north of Espanola, two days following the stop of a UFO in Socorro.

The evidence that Orlando Gallegos of Santa Fe reported was similar to that found in Socorro. He and his family went to visit his father, just north of La Madera, arriving about 12:30 a.m. Sunday.

Gallegos later told State Police he saw the object sitting on the ground in a gravel area when he went outside to chase away horses. He did not approach closer than 200 feet. He noticed a (Continued on Page 4)

What appears to be substantial evidence of an unidentified flying object landing and taking off in Socorro has been observed.

City Policeman Lonnie Zamora, a highly reliable source, saw a four-legged, egg-shaped object, and two persons in a gully a mile south of the courthouse shortly before 6 p.m. Friday. He saw the object rise straight up and take off, and disappear beyond Six-Mile Canyon to the west. Some of the evidence of the landing and take-off remained in the gully. There were four shallow holes where the object apparently landed on its legs; there were burned greasewood and seared clumps of green grass; there were two round, very slight depressions. No footprints were found.

Zamora said he saw lettering on the side of the UFO, and he sketched the lettering on a paper sack after the object had taken off. He did not believe the lettering was in English and he observed no numerals as there are on known aircraft. Zamora said he was not at liberty to further describe the lettering.

Where UFO Landed in Socorro: State Police Sgt. Sam Chavez and Lewis A. Reddell, publisher of El Defensor-Chieftain, stand at one of the stone-circled depressions (arrow) made by a leg of an unidentified flying object which landed in a gully a mile from the courthouse last Friday. The arrow in left foreground points to another depression made by a leg. Near the center foreground are burned greasewood and clumps of grass. The person at the left also looks over the scene, which had not been trampled by the curious Saturday morning when his photo was taken.

Press coverage of the UFO landing at Socorro, New Mexico

Here Lonnie Zamora, a New Mexico State police officer, who was on duty, had a UFO close encounter on Friday, April 24, 1964, near Socorro, New Mexico. Several additional primary witnesses emerged to report stages and aspects of the event, including physical evidence, such as ground prints and burned places, left behind

Bragalia's hoax claim rested on a letter where Dr. Stirling Colgate, President at New Mexico Tech and a world-famous astrophysicist at Los Alamos National Laboratory, stated that he felt the Zamora sighting was a hoax created by a student. Bragalia pulled correspondence of noted scientist Linus Pauling, a multiple Nobel-Prize winner, into his story. However, Bragalia had uncovered no good evidence, such as students coming forward showing how they did it. And it would have been extremely difficult to do.

Although they did some excellent research, some portions were hoaxed. It is unclear whether such activities were simple mistakes, individual efforts, or could be government sponsored, however they muddy the waters. The effect is that when people search for information about UFOs, they will come across these bogus claims and view all UFO study as flim-flam.

* * *

Although some of Bragalia's work is controversial and viewed as a hoax, he used material from Jones and me that we had published many years before this. Thus, I will state what is my own research, will label anything he added as his and check his work using my own sources.[65]

Bragalia claimed he had additional evidence in his reports about Cross, Center and the Roswell artifacts.[66] He wrote under a section heading "A Scientist under Stress":

> In 1992, Center's friend "Nick" Nicholson (a holder of several US patents and a former Battelle engineer) confessed to MUFON Ohio State Director and Battelle employee Bill Jones and to former Battelle scientist Dr. Irena Scott that Elroy Center had told him something profoundly disturbing in 1957. Center had told Nicholson that while he was at Battelle he was directed by his superiors to evaluate pieces of unknown material that had "hieroglyphic like" markings on them. The metal debris was kept in a heavily secured safe at Battelle. Center had learned that the material came from a crashed UFO that was retrieved by military some years prior.[67]

Nicholson had told Jones and me that he had been romantically involved with Cathy Center, daughter of Elroy John Center, the Battelle metals tester.

Bragalia said that he contacted Center's family and said they told him that Center became UFO-obsessed. Center's daughter, Cathy, said that Center was aware of Battelle's UFO studies, brought home draft copies of UFO-related reports and pored over secret reports written for Project Blue Book by his bosses at Battelle. Center was visited at home by an FBI investigator she thought was named Jack and

Center and Jack frequently discussed UFOs. Cathy Center distinctly remembered overhearing her mother and father discussing UFOs and her father saying, that he don't know if they should mention this to Cathy at all. Bragalia said that Center was eventually fired by Battelle and was later diagnosed as an alcoholic.

Bragalia also contacted Nicholson, who then confirmed the details of what he had told me nearly two decades ago. Nicholson said Center told also him UFO crash debris was stored in a secure safe and that some of the material contained the element boron.

Nicholson had decided not to tell Cathy about his conversation with Center because she was very impressionable and excitable and because Center had told him about it in confidence. Bragalia said that Nicholson knew that Center was an alcoholic; however, he is certain Center was lucid when he spoke of the debris. Nicholson added that he was aware of other indications of Battelle having been contracted to study UFOs even into the 1970s. For example, Nicholson says a Battelle superior told him the CIA was still involved in secret UFO studies at that time, as was Battelle.

Although Nicholson was a young man when Center told him he'd been assigned to analyze UFO debris, he is a very credible witness. He was a Battelle scientist specializing in physics and electronics for nearly 20 years. He had top-secret clearances and he holds several patents for lasers and other designs. He also holds patents with Battelle and with the Medex medical device company and he has been recognized for his technical achievements.

He became interested in UFO study in part due to his talks with Center and he later associated himself as an investigator with the civilian research group NICAP. Moreover, Nicholson exposed a well-known UFO hoax—the Zanesville, Ohio, barber UFO photo—and obtained a confession from the barber that he had faked the pictures. Nicholson also reported that Battelle employee Gustavus Simpson, Jr., knew more than he ever divulged about UFO phenomena.

* * *

I then investigated additional information tying Center to UFO studies. For example, the researchers found documents showing that Center had an association with Howard C. Cross, Ph.D., a central figure involved in Battelle's UFO studies that our own investigations suggested actually headed these studies (see below).[68]

One pertinent report is "Second Progress Report Covering the Period September 1 to October 21, 1949 on Research and Development on Titanium Alloys Contract No. 33 (038)-3736." The report lists its authors as follows: "Simmons, C. W., Greenidge, C. T., Craighead, C. M. and others." Battelle completed this report for

Zainsville, Ohio UFO photograph in 1967

WPAFB's Air Materiel Command. John Center is one of the scientists responsible for a technical subsection of the report, "Analytical Methods for the Titanium Base-Alloy," which refers among other items to a nickel-titanium phase diagram that is required to make the substance nitinol.

This report is important for several reasons. First, its "and others" portion of the author list included researchers, such as L. W. Eastwood, who were important scientists working on titanium alloys and other metals. This is significant because Eastwood published with key Battelle researcher Howard Cross, a metallurgist and an expert in exotic metallurgy, for example, "Development of Cast Aluminum Alloys for Elevated-Temperature Service," by Webster Hodge. L. W. Eastwood. C. H. Lorig and H. C. Cross.

Given that Cross was the Battelle point person in metallurgy research, that he co-authored research results with the creators of the "Second Progress Report," and that Center wrote one of the report's technical subsections, it is likely that Cross and Center worked on some of the same projects. And if Center worked with retrieved UFO crash debris at Battelle, it's possible that Cross did, too–actually it is probable because as we discovered Cross was probably the head of Stork and thus Center's supervisor.

More importantly, Cross was the point person in Battelle's later UFO studies for Project Blue Book in the 1950s. Evidence also exists that Cross was Battelle's chief titanium metallurgist–he was the scientist who led Battelle's "memory metal" studies. Cross has been referred to as "Research Director."

Center's technical subsection is revealing. His portion of the report begins on page 97 and describes chemical analysis used to detect and quantify metal impurities. To be used for shape-memory metal applications, titanium must be of ultra-high purity. One-challenge researchers faced when creating the memory metal nitinol was the detection of oxygen in titanium and this was Center's area of concentration.

In addition, the information that Center had actually brought home draft copies of the Battelle UFO studies indicates that he participated in classified UFO research. This is because the UFO work was classified at that time.

* * *

Moreover, Cross was far more than merely a metallurgist; he had extraordinary "clout" and power for his position. His name appeared in unexpected places. For example, Cross interacted with the heads of the Office of Naval Research, the CIA and Air Force Intelligence. He had close relationships with those in the uppermost echelons of the American government on UFO matters. For example, Cross had a working relationship with the CIA and was visited by the CIA's Chief of Scientific Intelligence, H. Marshall Chadwell, Ph.D., on official matters.[69] Cross was closely associated with the National Advisory Committee on Aeronautics (NACA, the predecessor of NASA). Vannevar Bush, Ph.D., chaired NACA and Cross may have worked with him. According to another document uncovered, in 1952 Cross investigated debris from a crashed flying object in Virginia.

In the late 1940s, Cross helped direct Battelle's metals alloy research into such materials sciences areas as titanium, stainless steel and chromium. Yet he was also involved in directing Battelle's government-sponsored UFO research in the early 1950s. One would wonder why a materials engineer studying exotic alloys would later help lead Battelle's government-funded studies on UFOs, which involved making a questionnaire and statistical studies.

* * *

However, I discovered a probable reason why Cross held an important place in both metal and UFO research. I was told by a Battelle employee from that time that Cross likely headed Battelle's Project Stork under which *SR-14* was done.

The Robertson Panel

He authored the January 9, 1953, Pentacle Memorandum and possibly worked on the missing *Project Blue Book Report No. 13* (to be discussed).

Cross's Pentacle Memorandum may be the most significant existing documentation of the US government's approach to UFO phenomena. It was a crucial point along the paper trail documenting government UFO investigation and was discovered by French UFOlogist Jacques Vallée. The document was dated January 9, 1953, five days before the CIA-sponsored Robertson Panel convened. Vallée thought the American government had substantial UFO information and he speculated that some of this data was so highly protected that it was not supplied to Blue Book personnel or to the Robertson Panel. For example, he notes a passage in the Pentacle Memorandum about what can and cannot be discussed with Robertson panelists.

This once-classified memo began with a recommendation, based on analyses of several thousand UFO reports, to the Air Technical Intelligence Center (ATIC) regarding future methods of handling the UFO problem. This opening paragraph clearly established that prior to the 1953 Robertson Panel meeting in Washington, massive numbers of UFO reports had been analyzed on behalf of the US government—and that this information was classified. Cross then recommended that the Air Force should conduct a controlled experiment by which reliable physical data could be obtained (Cross's design is similar to that later used by Rutledge and with government funding, in general, it would make an excellent research project). In the memo, Cross recommended that test areas be set up, such that:

> This area, or areas, should have observation posts with complete visual sky watch, with radar and photographic coverage, plus all other instruments necessary or helpful in obtaining positive and reliable data on everything in the air over the area. A very complete record of the weather should also be kept during the time of the experiment. Coverage should be so complete that any object in the air could be tracked and information as to its altitude, velocity, size, shape, color, time of day, etc. could be recorded. All balloon releases or known balloon paths, aircraft flights and flights of rockets in the test area should be known to those in charge of the experiment. Many different types of aerial activity should be secretly and purposefully scheduled within the area. . . . This should make possible reasonably certain conclusions concerning the importance of the problem of "flying saucers."

The Pentacle Memorandum was addressed to WPAFB's Miles E. Goll, head of intelligence analysis for the Air Materiel Command. In the memo, Cross asserted that he had the authority to speak in an official capacity on behalf of Battelle about its UFO work for the government. Cross also insisted that WPAFB delay the work of the CIA's UFO study group, the Robertson Panel, until after Battelle completed *SR-14*, the statistical study of UFOs commissioned by the Air Force. Because Battelle wanted to keep secret its authorship of *SR-14*, it requested that the organization's name be withheld.

Even more interesting I also learned that on October 2, 1951, in Columbus, Ohio, a Battelle physicist named Howard Cross reported viewing a UFO. It appeared as a bright oval with a clipped tail and it flew straight and level before fading into the distance after one minute.[70] After uncovering this information and after discussions with Battelle employees, I suspect that this Howard Cross is the H. C. Cross of the Pentacle Memorandum (some told me that this sighting was over Battelle). I further speculated that if Cross made the UFO report, the Pentacle Memorandum, rather than stating a government opinion, represented the individual thinking of Howard Cross. Cross's sighting and the fact that he reported it suggest to me that he took the UFO phenomena seriously.

In addition, at a time when many scientists were skeptical about UFOs, in the

Pentacle Memorandum Cross seems sincerely concerned about valid analyses of UFO data. I think he may have been torn between his own thinking about UFO phenomena and the government's official stance to ridicule it. Thus, because of his own direct interest, he may have had substantial input into the excellent analysis that eventually was published as *SR-14*.[71]

Because of Cross's importance and because he seems to have made a UFO report himself, I asked Jennie Zeidman, who worked with these people, what she remembered about him. She thought he was the author of the Pentacle Memorandum. She said he was "all business." He was a gruff, physically imposing man who would often bang on tables to make a point. As a young woman, she found him frightening; thus, he was an ideal guardian of secret information.[72]

After these investigations in regard to Cross, I made several inferences. First, the Pentacle Memorandum and my own research indicate that Cross was in a supervisory position in relation to UFO studies. Thus, Cross had "clout." Second, Cross had insisted that WPAFB delay the work of the Robertson Panel until Battelle could complete its Air Force commissioned statistical study of UFOs (*SR-14*). Cross's insistence and probable reporting of a UFO sighting together imply to me that Cross was a scientist concerned with a true examination of the data. His suggestions for further study in his Pentacle Memorandum showed a concern for scientific truth. The CIA consulted with Cross and concurred with him on the need for delay; ultimately, however, both the CIA and Battelle were overruled by the Air Force.[73]

Hence, I think that Cross had a crucial impact upon UFO study, even though the government covered this up. Thus, evidence exists to suggest Battelle also participated in government-sponsored UFO metallurgical studies. Given the caliber of the Battelle staff (the world's top physicists and metallurgists), its security, its proximity to WPAFB and its state-of-the-art equipment, it is reasonable to think that if metallic debris from UFOs existed, it would have been studied at Battelle.

* * *

I also wondered where I might find information about whether this possible study of Roswell debris might have influenced Battelle research. Several long-term Battelle employees thought that the metals research documents would be proprietary and would belong to the organization that sponsored the research. The Battelle library was not, therefore, likely to have copies of the documents; the paperwork would have been returned to the contracting organization or have gone back to the Air Force. If reports were Air Force documents and now unclassified, they belong to the Air Force or to the area where the Air Force archives such information. However, if they were unclassified, they would be difficult to locate because the Air Force has many branches with numerous libraries and repositories. Nevertheless, I learned that some documentation might be housed at Battelle, but not in an area such as the library where a civilian researcher might find them. My sources thought that unlike WPAFB, where the offices of Project Blue Book and similar projects are thought to no longer exist, some areas of Battelle associated with these studies might still exist and might even be found in the same places as during the studies and I discovered that Battelle is protective of these areas.

* * *

Cross and Center weren't the only employees who fit this metallurgist/UFO profile. My interviewees from Battelle mentioned employees other than Center and Cross, who might have worked on or had knowledge of Battelle's metallurgical studies of possible alien artifacts. These individuals included Arthur Westerman, Gustavus (Gus) Simpson, Jr., Dr. Hynek, Jennie Zeidman and Mr. Livingston.[74]

Of all living sources, Zeidman may be the one with the broadest and most extensive knowledge of government UFO studies. Zeidman began as Hynek's research and teaching assistant at OSU's department of physics and astronomy. However, through her own detective work she soon discovered that although her paychecks seemed to be from OSU, Battelle was the organization that was paying her. She is perhaps the only living person who worked both for Project Stork at Battelle and for Project Blue Book at WPAFB. She told me her work for Hynek involved examining incoming UFO reports before he did. She had security clearances, served with some of the top people in UFOlogy and knew Cross, Westerman, Reid, Rieppel and others who may have worked with UFO debris. She was also acquainted with members of the Robertson Panel and the Condon Committee. She was employed in the Project Blue Book offices and she knew Captain Edward Ruppelt, former head of Project Blue Book; his temporary replacement, Lieutenant Robert Olsson and others. She was aware of the positions, the organizational structures and some of the politics of the government UFO studies. She was also well acquainted with the data on UFO sightings and with how this information was used by the authorities. She has been the principal investigator of many UFO cases and she has been on both the MUFON and the CUFOS boards of directors. Zeidman also investigated whether Battelle examined alien artifacts.

She had interviewed many knowledgeable people, such as Clyde Tombaugh (Pluto's discoverer) and Lincoln LaPaz. She knew the inner workings of Project Stork, which she and others said began before Battelle's UFO work. Zeidman told that the original mission of Stork was to ascertain the capability of the Soviet Union to engage in technological warfare.

Thus, the Stork projects were not necessarily tied to Battelle UFO work.[75]

UFOs were originally investigated by the organization already studying foreign technology in Battelle and in the ATIC/FTD divisions of WPAFB. This work was already highly classified and it is where the best reports would have gone. Blue Book and similar projects were likely set up to collect civilian information and influence public opinion about UFOs, but the main examination was done elsewhere.

Zeidman thought that because the Battelle study. *SR-14,* was top secret, it was organized as objective research. (However, she added that the government ensured that the *SR-14* analyses later presented to the public both met with government standards and showed the negative findings the government wanted.) Zeidman said that if WPAFB did have alien artifacts, they would probably have been analyzed at Battelle.

Zeidman and several others whom I interviewed thought Arthur Westerman, a metallurgist who had published scholarly research papers on alloys, might also have worked with alien artifacts. He co-authored studies with Cross and was listed as "H. C. Cross/A. D. Westerman" on the Pentacle Memorandum. Moreover, some UFOlogists thought Westerman might have been involved with the Robertson Panel. Zeidman told me she made a substantial effort to obtain information from him, but he for the most part "didn't crack" (he divulged nothing formally to her or to other investigators). However, she quoted him to me as once saying, "We were concerned." She interpreted his comment to mean that the Pentacle Group was open to the possibility that ET might well be involved. This in a way might be a smoking gun, because why would they be concerned if there were nothing to it? [76]

Bill Jones, who worked with Westerman at Battelle, said that he had questioned Westerman, but he had not disclosed anything suggesting that he worked with alien artifacts.[77]

Another person of interest is Gus Simpson, Jr. Several informants told me he was involved in UFO studies. My research showed that he was a manager on the Stork projects when Battelle researchers were investigating UFOs and that he told Jones he was the author of the first Battelle *Special Report,* a history of the first five years of Project Stork.[78] Simpson also seems to have been involved in Project Blue Book. When I saw a video taken of the Project Blue Book Alumni Day, which was held at WPAFB in 1994 on the 25th anniversary of the project's closure, Simpson and all three living Project Blue Book directors—Robert Friend, George Gregory and Hector Quintanilla—attended.

Simpson was considered a founder of the Battelle extracts system. He had an interest in metallurgical engineering. He was employed by the Air Force between 1946 and 1951 and later by Battelle in information research. In June 1947 he published work on the properties of R303 aluminum alloy sheet. Most of Simpson's

Battelle publications are from the 1960s and this later work appears to have focused on information processing (work that perhaps was also associated with the Ohio Chemical Abstracts Service, CS and the Ohio College Library Center, OCLC). However, several Battelle employees told me that Simpson and two others were supervisors with detailed knowledge of UFO projects.[79] As Bragalia told me, "Battelle employee Gus Simpson knew more than he ever had let on about the phenomena [of UFOs]." [80] Nicholson also had said this and it supports my own findings that Simpson knew about Battelle's UFO research and may have even worked on projects concerned with alien artifacts.

Yet another person of interest is Mr. Livingston (not sure how to spell his name). An Internet article discusses research by Jones and me into Elroy John Center and Battelle.[81] This further story has been told in rough terms with alteration so that it didn't mention the details. However a very important detail, the person's name is revealed here for the first time, Livingston.

Jones had a best friend whose father was a big wheel at Battelle, Robert Livingston. In fact, he got Jones and Warren Nicholson their jobs. The friend had told them that a man he had worked with had been happy because he had just gotten a new project testing some metal parts that had come from a Soviet device. This happened in the late 50s before anyone had heard of Roswell. Sometime later, the man was in a disturbed state of mind and when asked what was wrong, he would only say that the material was not part of any Soviet thing and could not have been made by anyone on this planet. When Jones was told this story several years later, he called Livingston (the Battelle big-wig) and asked about this. He received only a pleasant denial. But after he hung up, his friend told him that the father went in person to his son's, Bill's friend's, residence and gave him the riot act about talking ever again about matters such as this, especially to a UFO researcher even if it was Jones.

Thus, what may have happened is that possible WPAFB crashed disk project personnel heard of a new test procedure at Battelle–possibly to analyze orderly metallic crystal structure that was not possible previously. Some Battelle heavyweights accepted the task, knowing what this is about, but they assigned the actual testing to people, such as their top metallurgists, who could best do the actual technique–but did not tell them the truth (told them that it is a Soviet device). But some may have begun to realize that these supervisors lied and they were not dealing with anything even vaguely normal. Even with such a "leak," the whole thing remained classified because no authority figure ever released any information.

This evidence suggests that Livingston also either worked with UFO materials

213

or knew about such work. I found no evidence that he had published with any of the others, but his somewhat common name made it difficult to check.

I also investigated others listed on the Pentacle Memorandum: Bertram Thomas, L. R. Jackson, William Reid, Perry Rieppal, V. W. Ellsey and R. J. Lund. Along with Westerman, all of these individuals worked for Project Stork.

Thomas's field of specialization involved ways of concentrating chemicals. Jackson had published with Cross and Eastwood (one author of the "Second Progress Report," mentioned above) and he worked on titanium, ceramics, sheet metals, alloys and aircraft materials. Reid, a chief technology officer, often worked on power sources and fuel cells and had worked with boron, but there's no evidence that he co-authored any papers with the others; he was an engineer and may have been involved with the Robertson Panel. Rieppel, who was a welding specialist, may also have been involved with the Robertson Panel; one of his papers was titled "Welding Tantalum For High-Temperature Systems." I uncovered nothing by Ellsey, or by the two other authors of the "Second Progress Report," C. T. Greenidge and C. W. Simmons. However, I found that Lund worked with fuel cells.

It's strange that scientists, who appeared to have been predominantly metallurgists (rather than statisticians or others involved with information processing), were selected for the statistical work that lead to *SR-14,* Similarly designing a questionnaire would seem to be out of the field of expertise for these engineers. This suggests that the metallurgical analysis of artifacts may have been a component of the UFO research conducted at Battelle.

* * *

After investigating Battelle and WPAFB, I found smoking-gun evidence from two sources, Center's statements and those of Exon, suggesting that Battelle performed research on alien artifacts. Moreover, my findings indicate that Center represented the tip of the iceberg. For as I continued searching for more evidence about who else might have been researching Roswell artifacts at Battelle, I located several people who knew Cross, Simpson, or Livingston. I was told that Cross, Simpson, Westerman and Livingston were managers. Zeidman said she thought Cross was head of Project Stork and had been Simpson's supervisor. She added that, although she did not work in the same area as he did, Cross made his rounds frequently so that she saw him often. She said Simpson and a man named John Morehead worked directly under Cross. Another Battelle informant also said Cross was Simpson's supervisor.

Thus, I located additional persons, such as Westerman, who had career profiles that were quite similar to Center's. These people appear to have associated with

Cross and Center. Several Battelle employees (who I interviewed) suspected them of working with alien debris. Hence, they may also have worked with or had knowledge of Battelle's possible research into crash artifacts.

What is truly interesting here is that long before anyone had heard of Roswell, the idea that material UFO evidence was under examination at Battelle was well known and prominent. Battelle had a very powerful grapevine that even included people knowing who did the research and questioning some of them about artifacts. This was many years before Roswell became common knowledge and took place in spite of the security classification of the work. Such people as Jones and Zeidman talked about this as if it were just common knowledge and they didn't seem to pay much attention to the idea that no one would have even thought about such studies before the information about Roswell came out.

Because Battelle and WPAFB are the only two places where verified documentation exists about serious government study of UFO phenomena, the people mentioned above and Battelle itself are of considerable interest as an important part of the UFO story.

* * *

Moreover, Roswell witnesses described a lightweight, metallic looking, "morphing" material that returned perfectly to its original state after being crumpled. Bragalia suggested that government-funded studies were done in response to the retrieval of material from the 1947 crash. And although Ashcroft told Jones and me that he found no evidence of new directions in research after Roswell (see Chapter Two), some information suggests that research related to new materials may have been undertaken. This suggests that either no such studies had taken place as Ashcroft said, or he did not have the technical expertise to search in certain directions, or he lacked security clearances needed to view the material, or he knew about the research and was part of a cover-up, or he was exposing us to some information without making formal statements to let us draw our own conclusions.

Because WPAFB is where early reports of UFO phenomena were collected and investigated, some UFOlogists think that authorities from WPAFB had contacted Battelle and asked its scientists to study Roswell debris and to develop a similar material.

Many have speculated about this and some evidence might exist even in the WPAFB literature:

> [T]he Army also delivered a large amount of captured documents
> to Wright Field. By the end of 1947, Wright Field personnel had

processed over 1,500 tons of documents, adding over 100,000 new technical terms to the English language. The technical knowledge gained revolutionized American industry. Besides the aviation-related advances, new designs for vacuum tubes, the development of magnetic tapes, night vision devices, improvements in liquid and solid fuels and advances in textiles, drugs and food preservation were made available to American manufacturers.[82]

Bragalia thought that scientists did hands-on studies of debris and that one outcome of these studies might have been a substance called nitinol. Nitinol, an alloy of nickel and titanium, exhibits many properties of the reported Roswell debris. Nitinol is a "memory metal" that "remembers" its original shape, is very lightweight, possesses a high fatigue strength and is able to withstand extreme heat.

After 1947 laboratory interest in titanium (a nitinol component) rose dramatically; indeed, abstracts show that published work on titanium spiked after 1946. Moreover, Battelle began its titanium studies immediately after Roswell. Some footnotes cited military-sponsored studies into memory metal.

I interviewed employees, who had knowledge of Battelle's activities during the period or interest and I searched for documents about nitinol and "memory metal" research at Battelle.[83]

Several Battelle sources thought that Battelle did conduct materials research on UFOs. Indeed some even said this was common knowledge. This research, done as part of Project Stork (later renamed Project White Stork), was performed at the height of the Cold War and it was classified–even the project names were classified.[84] It's possible the researchers told family members about their work and investigations into this possibility are ongoing. One interviewee said it was routine to tease the metallurgists rumored to be working with alien artifacts about their research on UFOs. Sources at Battelle also said those selected to investigate alien artifacts were initially told they'd be working with Soviet materials.[85] This was before anyone had heard of Roswell. After they obtained their clearances, they learned the materials were not Soviet. Several informants said the research seemed to depress or even distress people. All of these accounts are consistent with the stories about Elroy John Center.[86]

I learned that one secured area at Battelle was reserved for work related to foreign or counter-insurgency technology and that this area included linguists who were among the world's top translators and cryptologists. If this is true and if the Roswell debris was inscribed with written symbols as some witnesses reported, these people would likely be the ones the Air Force would call on for translations.

Many other mysteries about this Battelle research are still being discussed today. One classic mystery associated with Blue Book and *SR-14* involves *Project Blue Book Report No. 13*. Between 1951 and 1953, the Air Force prepared 12 status reports about the progress of Project Grudge, later named Project Blue Book. When the summary report was published, it was "No. 14," causing many to ask, whether there was a thirteenth report and, if so, what happened to it?

Bill Jones has investigated this question. He found that the Air Force released 13 reports prior to *SR-14*. Of these, 12 were "status reports" and one was a "special report."[87] Jones told me that he contacted Gus Simpson, who said Projects Stork and White Stork issued special reports about specific studies. Simpson guessed that the number 14 just happened to come up when the report about the UFO studies was issued and that the numbering of this special report had no connection to the status report numbers. The only special report he remembered was the first, which he wrote. On another occasion, Simpson said 12 or 13 other special reports were done under Project White Stork. These reports were classified but were not the same as the Project Blue Book status reports.

Jones thought that *Project Blue Book Report No. 13* dealt not with UFOs but with some other aerospace subject. Hoping to settle the matter, on August 8, 1995, Jones submitted a Freedom of Information Act request to the NAIC for the first 13 Battelle reports. His request is still pending.[88] Jones and I asked Bruce Ashcroft, the WPAFB historian, if he had ever seen *Project Blue Book Report No. 13* in the NAIC archives and Ashcroft had not.

* * *

A further point of interest along this paper trail involves the "Robertson Panel," which had been commissioned by the CIA in 1952 to respond to UFO reports, particularly those of sightings in the Washington, D.C. area. Howard Percy Robertson, Ph.D.—a physicist, CIA employee and director of the Defense Department Weapons Evaluation Group—was instructed by the CIA's Office of Scientific Intelligence to assemble prominent scientists to review the Air Force's UFO files. As preparation, Robertson reviewed Air Force files and procedures and he found the Air Force had commissioned Battelle to study all UFO reports collected by Projects Sign, Grudge and Blue Book.

The panel's first formal meeting took place on January 14, 1953, under the direction of Robertson.[89] Panel members were briefed on US military activities and intelligence. Despite the impressive credentials of the members, some of those most knowledgeable about the UFO phenomena were excluded from the panel or

Dr. Hynek's Center for UFO Studies UFOlogists: Mike Swords, Stuart Appelle, David Pritchard, Mark Rodeghier, Don Johnson. and Jennie Zeidman. (Credit: Jennie Zeidman, 1995)

Dr. Hynek's Center for UFO Studies staff: Mark Rodeghier; Dr. Stuart Appelle, George Eberhart, Jennie Zeidman; Dr. Ed Bullard, Dr. Don Johnson, and Dr. Mike Swords. (Credit: Jennie Zeidman, 1995)

from some meetings. For example, Zeidman reports that although Hynek was a member of the panel and despite his considerable background in aerospace studies, he was excluded from the Robertson Panel's inner circle and was even made to leave the room during some meetings. This speaks for itself about the intent of and true investigative purpose of the Panel.

Robertson wanted to access the statistical results Battelle had put together for the Air Force, but Battelle refused access, saying scientists had not yet had sufficient time for a proper study.

The report produced by the panel was at first classified as secret. In it, the panel revealed its conclusions that UFOs were not a direct threat to national security, but it did not say that the phenomena didn't exist. The panel also suggested a public relations campaign be undertaken to debunk UFOs and to reduce public interest in the subject. It further recommended that civilian UFO groups be monitored.

This portion of the Robertson Panel's recommendation—to monitor civilian UFO groups—has been highly significant to investigators of government cover-ups because it is suggestive of counter-evidence to the idea that the government would not infiltrate UFO groups. For example, according to Richard Dolan in *UFOs and the National Security State* (2000), a public relations officer named Al Chop told Edward Ruppelt that the panel planned to work up a debunking campaign to plant outlandish UFO claims in magazines and media broadcasts; the goal would be to make UFO reports sound ridiculous. Dolan also reported that several weeks after the Robertson meeting, the Air Force issued Regulation 200-2. This directive ordered Air Force officers not to publicly discuss UFO incidents unless the cases were considered solved. In addition, it ordered that all unsolved cases be considered classified. The 4602nd Air Intelligence Squadron of the Air Defense Command investigated the most important UFO cases; these cases did not go to Blue Book, as Hynek said and we have discovered. Dolan added that four military studies had concluded the UFOs were interplanetary; these included the 1948 Project Sign "Estimate of the Situation" and a 1952 Project Blue Book engineering analysis of UFO motion.

The Robertson Panel's overall conclusions—that UFOs were not a direct threat to national security— reverberated throughout the US government. Agencies seemed to interpret that as meaning that the phenomena didn't exist. The CIA abandoned a major UFO investigation. Pentagon UFO research projects were halted. A scientific advisory board that Project Blue Book's leaders had hoped to establish never materialized.

However, many observers thought the panel's investigation was not conducted in a scientific manner. For example, Zeidman reported that Hynek said, that they are not going to have a scientific investigation. For some strange motive they voted it down. This panel didn't even take a decent look at the data, but they decided to discredit them. Jacobs commented, that these men, apparently ignorant of the phenomenon, were designated to decide on the future of a subject of grave concern. They would spend less than twelve working hours listening to experts like Ruppelt, Hynek and Fournet and reviewing reports.

Meanwhile Hynek had acquired the Pentacle Memorandum. He was outraged to learn that some of Battelle's UFO information was being withheld from the panel. Hynek, a mild-mannered professor, even took the memo to and confronted Cross, a man with a reputation for anger. Cross responded by lunging and grabbing back the memo, demanding to know how Hynek had gotten it and insisting that Hynek was not supposed to have it.

* * *

The next point along the paper trail documenting government cover-ups came in 1966 when the Air Force turned its UFO problem over to the University of Colorado and nuclear physicist Edward Condon, Ph.D. In so doing, the Air Force failed to choose the most experienced or knowledgeable UFO experts. Zeidman says the fact that the Air Force turned to Colorado and Condon was an insult to Hynek, an Air Force consultant, Chairman of the Astronomy Department at Northwestern University and the American scientist with the most extensive UFO background. Hynek characterized the appointment of Condon as analogous to appointing a non-cook as head chef at Maxim's.

Condon directed a study of UFOs for the government and in 1969 the University of Colorado released his 1465-page report, *Scientific Study of Unidentified Flying Objects*, which has come to be called the *Condon Report*. Condon, along with project coordinator Robert Low, allegedly conducted an independent, objective study. However, the two arrived at the negative conclusions the Air Force wanted.

According to Jacobs, in *UFOs and Abductions: Challenging the Borders of Knowledge and* Story, in *The Encyclopedia Of UFOs,* both Condon and Low were contemptuous of their subject. For example, Condon expressed disdain about UFOs before any research took place and this attitude casts doubt on the study's objectivity. Moreover, neither Condon nor Low conducted field investigations, but the project's researchers who did investigate the sightings found them worthy of further attention. Condon later ousted those who took a scientific approach.

Approximately thirty percent of the cases used in the study were unsolved. Despite this, the study concluded, that nothing should be done with them in the expectation that they would not contribute to the advancement of science. Even more astonishing was their response to the question of a national defense issue of the reports, they claimed that the history of the past 21 years has repeatedly led Air Force officers to conclude that none of the things seen, or thought to have been seen that pass by the name of UFO reports, constituted any hazard or threat to national security. How would they know that if they couldn't explain nearly one third of their data? They added, that they know of no reason to question the finding of the Air Force that the whole class of UFO reports does not pose any defense problem.

UFO researchers Bill Moore, Jaime Shandera & Stanton Friedmann

These conclusions are amazing because this was the height of the Cold War. A UFO might be an incoming nuclear missile or other advanced weapon; or manned, but off-course airplanes, such as those used in the September 11 attacks; or a drone; or spy plane. Such UFO's could touch off a nuclear war, or even destroy humanity. They should certainly be brought to government attention, recorded and studied. The last portion of the Condon Report summary cautioned teachers to discourage any interest of pupils in UFOs, because such study would be harmful to their development. (If UFOs do not exist, how would an interest in them harm pupils and why should pupils be brainwashed?)

Story added that some of the reports had left some of the Condon Report authors very puzzled and practically admitting the physical reality of unconventional UFOs, contrary to the report's conclusions. Jacobs noted that shortly after the report's release, a minority report in book form argued that Condon was biased and had not really considered the data.

Because of the negative conclusions in the summery, the Air Force and the media presented the *Condon Report* as scientific evidence that alien UFOs were nonexistent. However several scientists gave scathing reviews of the report. In short, the investigations behind the *Condon Report* revealed that UFOs were significant phenomena worthy of study, but the published conclusion was that nothing significant was found.

In addition, the Air Force regulations were still in effect for reporting unidentified flying objects that could affect national security. These reports were to be made in accordance with JANAP 146 or Air Force Manual 55-11. (See Chapter Eight.)

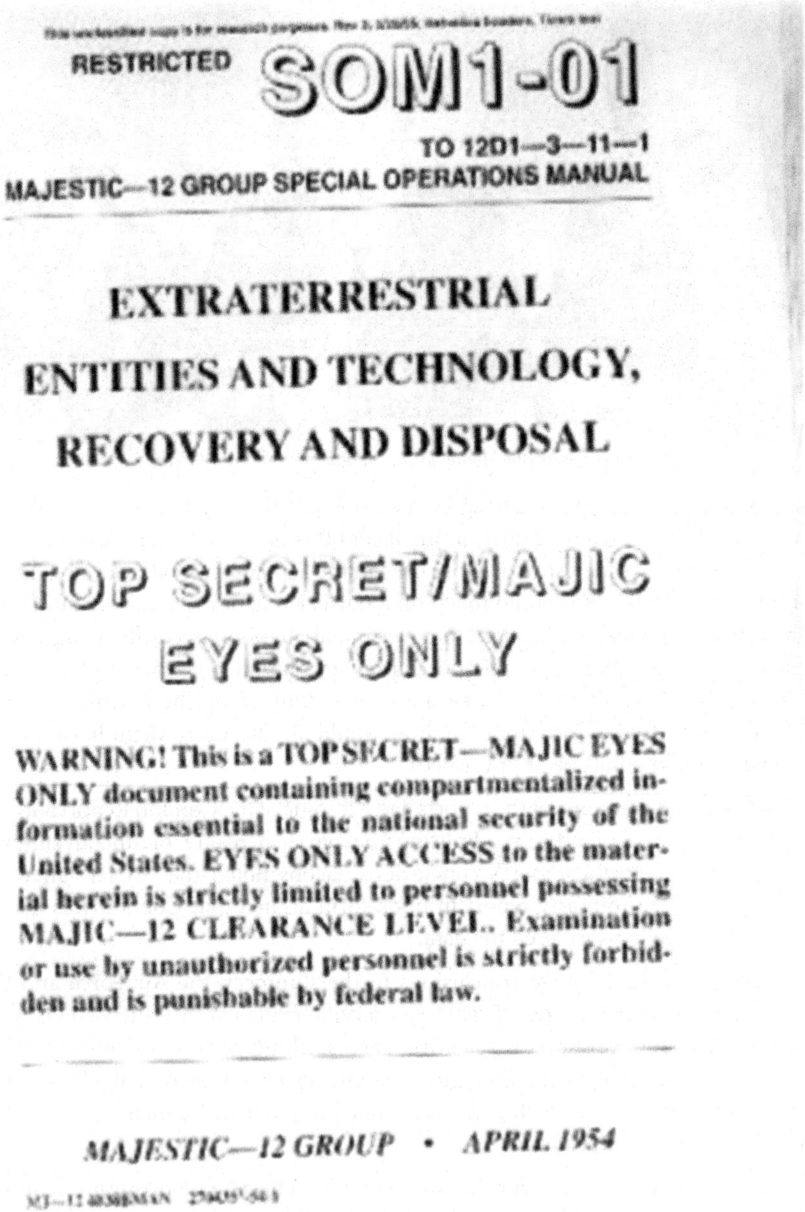

RESTRICTED

SOM1-01

TO 12D1—3—11—1

MAJESTIC—12 GROUP SPECIAL OPERATIONS MANUAL

EXTRATERRESTRIAL
ENTITIES AND TECHNOLOGY,
RECOVERY AND DISPOSAL

TOP SECRET/MAJIC
EYES ONLY

WARNING! This is a TOP SECRET—MAJIC EYES ONLY document containing compartmentalized information essential to the national security of the United States. EYES ONLY ACCESS to the material herein is strictly limited to personnel possessing MAJIC—12 CLEARANCE LEVEL. Examination or use by unauthorized personnel is strictly forbidden and is punishable by federal law.

MAJESTIC—12 GROUP • APRIL 1954

MJ—12 4838BMAN 2S6O5'-54 I

One of the so-called MJ12 documents

222

Paul Bennewitz

The government might not be too concerned about civilian sightings, because they had already been infiltrating civilian groups and with today's Internet they can find much of this information on-line.

* * *

Much additional evidence documented the paper trail of government cover-ups–including the Majestic 12, Bennewitz and related affairs–as Jones and I found out first hand. In the first instance, a desire to lay hands on documents related to government UFO projects led to the ostracism of one UFOlogist and the physical and mental deterioration of another in what has come to be called the Bennewitz Affair.

In 1980 UFOlogist William Moore co-authored with Charles Berlitz the first book about Roswell, *The Roswell Incident*. That same year Moore received a call from a mysterious individual who gave his code name as "Falcon" and whom Moore thought was a high-ranking government official. Falcon said he represented "The Aviary," a secret group of military intelligence insiders, scientists and government officials, all of whom were opposed to the government's policy of secrecy about UFOs. Moore was told that this group not only investigated UFOs, but that its members were actually in contact with extraterrestrials. (Falcon was later shown to be Richard C. Doty, who worked closely with Bob Collins, who we met later. Although to make matters more complicated, Doty also was thought to be a stand in for a real Falcon, who was a high ranking DIA official.)

Falcon brought Moore into contact with other members of the intelligence community, including Richard C. Doty, counterintelligence officer with the Air Force Office of Special Investigations. In return for divulging information, the Aviary wanted Moore to provide them with details about UFO researchers and organizations and to work with Doty to influence an Albuquerque UFO investigator, Paul Bennewitz. Moore, hungry to gain insight into the government's knowledge of UFOs, obliged.[90]

Paul Bennewitz had nearly completed a Ph.D. in physics and had founded the Thunder Scientific Corporation, a manufacturer of high-altitude testing equipment for

Alleged intelligence agent Richard Doty

223

New Mexico's Kirtland Air Force Base (Kirtland was associated with the green fireball sightings—see Chapter Four). Bennewitz had also designed a means of eavesdropping on the base's secure radio system. He later began to scan the entire radio spectrum for extraterrestrial signals and he pestered government officials with his theories.

As Moore and Doty continued to exchange information, Doty began asking Moore for favors. One favor was that Moore supply Bennewitz with misinformation about UFOs and extraterrestrials, which Moore agreed to do. The plan was to use the misinformation to distract Bennewitz from his monitoring of activity at Kirtland; in addition, it was hoped that Bennewitz would repeat the fictitious information and be discredited. Moore fed Bennewitz certain false documents. Perhaps because of the contents of the documents, Bennewitz's behavior became increasingly bizarre and eventually he suffered a nervous breakdown. Moore's actions were later condemned by his colleagues as highly unethical and having become an outcast, Moore eventually withdrew from the field of UFOlogy. Thus Doty, acting on behalf of the US government, was doubly effective: Bennewitz's credibility was ruined and Moore (the first to bring Roswell to public attention) became a pariah who withdrew from UFOlogy.

* * *

Before withdrawing from UFOlogy, however, Moore became a key player in the Majestic 12 affair. "Majestic 12" is an alleged code name for a secret committee of scientists, military leaders and government officials, which was supposedly formed in 1947 by order of President Harry S Truman, to investigate UFO evidence in the aftermath of the Roswell incident. This group has also been called MJ 12, MJ XII, Majority 12, Majic 12, Majestic Trust, M12 and similar names.

The earliest known use of the term "MJ-12" was as part of the Doty-Moore plan to discredit Bennewitz. Doty created a fraudulent Air Force Teletype to be given to Bennewitz by Moore. The Teletype mentioned Project Aquarius—supposedly a government venture related to UFOs—and said access to information about this and similar projects was controlled by "MJ-12." The Teletype was dated November 17, 1980; not long thereafter, the Majestic 12 board and the MJ-12 documents would become the subject of controversy and conspiracy theories.

The initial MJ-12 documents purported to include a classified order from President Harry Truman asking that a board be assembled to study the Roswell crash. Increasing amounts of paperwork emerged related to this board and eventually the MJ-12 documents seemed to represent a treasure trove of material for UFOlogists. But although the documents are well known today, they have never been verified.[91] Indeed, most UFO researchers now think they are fake. However, the historical accuracy of some of the contents and the huge volume of MJ-12 material, are evidence of an enormous amount of work that went into this hoax—assuming it is, in fact, a hoax.

According to the MJ-12 documents, in 1947 President Truman issued a classified order to Secretary of Defense James Forrestal. This order authorized Forrestal, after consultation with nuclear scientist Vannevar Bush, Ph.D., to establish a board of high-ranking experts to investigate the Roswell crash. This board, called Majestic 12, would eventually include the following: researchers from institutions such as Harvard University and the Carnegie Institute; high-ranking military personnel from the Air Force, Army and Navy, such as the Secretary of the Navy and the Chairman of the Joint Chiefs of Staff; and intelligence and security experts, such as individuals associated with the CIA.[92] Also supposedly involved with this board were such celebrated scientists and leaders as Robert Oppenheimer, Albert Einstein, Karl Compton, Edward Teller, John von Neumann, Werner von Braun, Ronald Reagan and Dwight Eisenhower. Some MJ-12 documents suggest that certain individuals on or involved with the board led double lives as skeptics while involved with UFO studies.

The first individuals to report the existence of the MJ-12 documents included Moore, UFOlogist and nuclear physicist Stanton Friedman and television documentary producer Jamie Shandera. Moore had become friends with Shandera and the two were collaborating on a project in 1984 when the first evidence of MJ-12 emerged: a roll of film that appeared in Shandera's mailbox.[93] Moore sub-sequently received from Doty some documents that mentioned Majestic 12 and Moore showed these papers to fellow UFO researchers Brad Sparks and Kal Korff.

Friedman later asked Moore and Shandera to examine newly declassified Air Force documents at the National Archives (NARA)

UFO researcher Brad Sparks

repository. In the archives, Shandera and Moore discovered a document, dated July 14, 1954, in which Robert Cutler (National Security Council Executive Secretary and Eisenhower's National Security Advisor) told Nathan Twining (Air Force Chief of Staff) of a change of plans for a scheduled Majestic 12 briefing. However, this document, called the Cutler-Twining memo, lacked a distinctive catalog number and this fact has led many to suspect it was forged and planted in the archives.

Meanwhile Moore engaged in behaviors that later called his credibility into question, such as the duping of Bennewitz. In 1982 Moore approached UFOlogist and former *National Enquirer* reporter Bob Pratt and asked him to collaborate on a novel to be called *MAJIK-12*. Pratt thought the MJ-12 papers were an outgrowth of this proposed novel. Moore also concocted a plan to create counterfeit government UFO documents as a way to induce former military officers to reveal UFO information; in 1983 Moore sought UFOlogist Brad Sparks's help with this plan, but Sparks refused and advised Moore not to move forward. Moore also approached Friedman about creating bogus Roswell documents, again with the idea of drawing in witnesses.

Moore denied creating the MJ-12 papers and he came to think the person who had created them had set him up. Like the hoax associated with Arnold that some think it was set up specifically to discredit him because of his importance to the UFO subject, this might have been implemented to discredit Moore for the same reason. Possibly something like this happened to Albert Bender also.

Pratt always thought the documents were a hoax perpetrated either by Moore himself, or by the Air Force Office of Special Investigations (AFOSI) with Doty using Moore as a conduit. Friedman, however, investigated the historical and technical details in the MJ-12 documents and concluded there were no grounds for dismissing the authenticity of some of them. In addition, copies of some MJ-12 documents were mailed anonymously to British researcher Timothy Good in 1987; Good reproduced them in his 1989 book, *Above Top Secret*, but he later decided the documents were fraudulent.

At the 2007 MUFON Symposium, Brad Sparks presented a paper describing the MJ-12 documents as a part of the disinformation campaign by Moore, Doty and other AFOSI personnel; he based this theory on files from 1981 that Pratt gave to MUFON.

Various additional references have been made to a secret government investigatory group having an MJ-12 type of function. For example, according to Michael Wolf, Ph.D., a group calling itself the Majestic 12 Special Studies Group was meeting at Battelle in the 1990s. General Exon referred to a secretive UFO controlling committee of high-ranking officers and civilians called "The Unholy

Major Donald Keyhoe – courtesy Rick Hilberg

Thirteen," which some think referred to Majestic-12. Canadian radio engineer Wilbert B. Smith had the Canadian embassy arrange contact with US officials and was briefed by Robert Sarbacher, Ph.D., a physicist working for the Defense Department Research and Development Board. This board may have been the department that cleared Major Donald Keyhoe (a former Marine, a Charles Lindbergh aide and one of the country's earliest and most respected UFOlogists) to publish some articles. Some of Smith's material indicated that a committee of high-ranking people, headed by Vannevar Bush, existed.

Many UFOlogists now think the MJ-12 documents were part of an intentional disinformation campaign by individuals associated with the US military or government, although it leaves one to wonder why they expended so much research and effort if there was no evidence for UFO phenomena.

Regardless of their authenticity, Majestic 12 and the MJ-12 documents have become a significant part of the popular culture that surrounds UFOs. For example, such authors as Stanton Friedman and Whitley Strieber have written books about Majestic 12 and it has been mentioned in TV shows such as *The X-Files* and *Dark Skies*, as well as in video games.

* * *

Jones and I had some direct experience with the Aviary thrown in our face, when we undertook an additional investigation of MJ-12 and related issues. We interviewed the other principal member of the Aviary Bob Collins (who was operative "Condor") without knowing it. We also interviewed investigators such as Stanton Friedman and gained insight into organizations related to government cover-ups.[94]

In April 1993 while stationed on-base at WPAFB, I placed an advertisement in the *Skywriter*, the base newspaper, requesting government informants with UFO information to contact our local UFO organization or myself. Robert M. Collins answered the ad.[95] Jones and I did not know it then, but Collins was a chief member of the Aviary code-named "Condor." (Timothy Good has identified Collins as

"Condor" and Doty as "Falcon.") Although I don't know who, but several Battelle people must have suspected something, for Jones said that some had warned him not to go.

Collins claimed to have inside information about many subjects, including Doty, Bennewitz, Moore and other key MJ-12 figures. (We don't know why he contacted us and are unable to judge how much of what he said is information and how much is disinformation; thus, we simply relate his account here.)

We arranged to meet Collins at a restaurant he chose. We arrived early and waited, but Collins failed to show. As we stood up to leave, however, he suddenly appeared. He knew who we were and walked right up to us. This led us to think he'd been there for some time watching and maybe even listening to us. He also knew things about us that we didn't recall telling him during the telephone calls that preceded the interview and this caused us to think he or someone else had investigated us prior to the meeting.

One of Collins's first remarks was that he had received harassing phone calls and threats that he thought were coming from space aliens. (This harassment may explain why he was careful about meeting us.) He went on to claim he knew the types of aliens that visited earth, knew where they were from and he knew secrets about WPAFB and another well-known area associated with UFO phenomena, Nevada's Groom Lake (also known as Area 51). He said that in 1986, President Reagan instituted a study of UFOs and alien abductions and that as a result, our government realized it does not know how to protect people from an alien agenda, whatever that agenda may be. Collins said aliens have made a big intrusion into the human genetic code, but that this intrusion is subtle, not overt; we interpreted this to mean aliens have manipulated the human genome. He asserted that aliens were behind the cattle mutilations sometimes seen in rural UFO cases (see Chapter Eight).

Collins claimed the truth about the Bennewitz affair was that government authorities had asked Bennewitz, an expert on UFOs, to cooperate with them. When he refused, the government retaliated by trying to drive him crazy. Collins claimed the government had done this to others, as well. He said Moore became involved with Bennewitz because Moore was working on a report about him.

Collins acknowledged that the American government actively disseminates disinformation and that di-sinformers give both true and false information. Thus there always may be some credibility to the material. Disinformation is spread about many topics other than UFOs, he said. Moreover, he claimed extraterrestrials are ultimately behind these disinformation campaigns: aliens support government disinformation about their activities because it enables them to do whatever they want while the government covers for them.

Collins said those aware of the alien presence are careful about sharing this knowledge. He said President Jimmy Carter, for example, did not learn about the alien presence until six months into his presidency. Collins claimed that while serving as governor of Georgia, Carter reported seeing a UFO and that Carter repeatedly said he'd release all available UFO information if he became president. After the election, however, he reneged on this promise. Collins also said while serving as vice president under Ronald Reagan, the senior George Bush chaired that era's version of Majestic 12.

Collins went on to say the vault system under WPAFB is being studied by outside investigators, who use engineers and NASA overflights to examine the placement of the vaults on the base. Many of these vaults and tunnels were built during World War II, he said, because of the threat of a Japanese attack. Some cover areas as large as 1000 square feet. Others, he claimed, contain examining rooms and cryogenic storage facilities. Collins thought alien bodies were once kept in these vaults. He said he'd seen a tunnel on a blueprint drawing and that the tunnel entrance was through a bathroom. The vaults were located in an area that stretched inward from Buildings 620 (the Avionics Laboratories) and 739, he claimed and there may have been vaults near Buildings 167, 189, 640 and 653. A large underground tunnel was attached to Buildings 739 and 620. Near Building 653, he said, was an underground structure as large as a hangar.

Alien bodies had been kept in a vault at WPAFB as late as 1982, Collins said and then they were moved to Los Alamos, New Mexico. He claimed the government has artifacts from a number of crashes, not just from Roswell. He denied that a crash had taken place at Aztec, New Mexico. He said a well-known informant, Bob Lazar (who claimed to have worked as a physicist near Groom Lake, Nevada and in Area 51 and to have had access to secret government information), had actually worked at the Los Alamos salvage yard. Collins said although Lazar may have had a secret clearance, he did not have the access he claimed, he was not a scientist and he did not have an advanced academic degree. (I think it would be very easy to get an approximate idea of whether Lazar is who he says he is–just give him a physics test such as the GRE.)

Collins added that Richard Doty had deliberately disinformed Linda Moulton Howe, who was a UFO author, director of the film *A Strange Harvest* about cattle mutilations and an expert on cattle mutilations and government cover-ups.[96]

Collins said some aliens were in close contact with and cooperated with our government. He reported that a military colonel had allowed space aliens to live with him in his home for three years, from around 1949 to 1952 and that films exist of these aliens in the colonel's home. He said the Russians have a cooperative program with the aliens similar to one the US operates at Los Alamos and Groom Lake, but not much is known about it.

He showed us computer drawings of "gray-type" aliens. ("Gray-type" aliens or "grays" are presented as grayish in color, short, with large heads, black "wrap-around" eyes, slits for mouths and small noses or no noses.) The aliens' eyes had several inner eyelids and their heads resembled the popular archetype of an alien head. The aliens were about three feet tall, had a small amount of webbing between their fingers and each one's lungs and heart were composed of one organ, as were their kidneys and bladder. These drawings were used on the TV show *UFO Cover-Up: Live!*

The drawings we saw had numbers and letters in the upper corners that Collins said did not show up on TV. (Collins may have wished to imply that these marks were classified government identifiers.) At the top left, one drawing had writing that looked like it read "FTD-SYD, Veh Type WHDDD4," and another had what looked like "FTD YP" and "28 8100." He also showed us photos with numbers at the top. We asked several people, including Ashcroft, if they recognized these letters and numbers, but none did. (However, I recall that the WPAFB US Air Force National Air Intelligence Center was formerly the Foreign Technology Division, FTD. SYD is the three-letter abbreviation for the office responsible for FTD graphics (the office was reported to be under the Directorate of Systems at the Space Systems Division within FTD).

Perhaps the acronym is an older one and perhaps the photos actually came from this office–possibly as a theoretic alien model, or maybe a graphic of an actual alien.

Collins claimed that Brigadier General Exon, who became commander of WPAFB in August 1964, was fearful about certain alien activities of which he had become aware. Collins claimed Exon admitted the government possessed alien material other than that from Roswell. When asked, Collins said human mutilations do not exist and he knew of no crashes in Ohio.

Collins disclosed his own feelings about extraterrestrials. He said the material he'd become aware of during his years of study amazed him. He thought most people would have a hard time believing the truth, but that the truth would eventually come out.

* * *

After the interview, Jones and I tried to verify some of Collin's information and at least some of it is compatible with our other findings and with government material. For example, we confirmed some of his details about the underground tunnels. All the buildings Collins mentioned are located in Area B of WPAFB, near the Avionics Laboratory (Building 620) in a secured area surrounded by a chain link fence.[97] Jones and I have driven through this secured area.

On one occasion, we photographed digging activity: large excavation machines and high piles of dirt, some of which seemed to follow tunnels extending to the north of Building 620. For security reasons, I didn't leave the car to see how deep the digging was or what it uncovered. Area B is on a hill overlooking the prairie area of the base. Building 620 had a large liquid nitrogen tank by it and huge entrance doors, large enough for trucks.

Further evidence of the existence of such facilities as Collins described was contained in a document I came across when working at the Ohio Department of Health. This document, *Tritium Consolidation Comparison Study: Risk Analysis,* DOE/DP/00248-H1, December 1992, described the T-Building at the Mound Nuclear Plant at Dayton, Ohio, (near WPAFB) as follows:

> [It is an] underground, massive, reinforced concrete structure containing two functional floors. The exterior, reinforced concrete walls of the building are a minimum of 16 feet 7 inches thick. The 30-foot thick ceiling and 8-foot thick basement also are constructed of reinforced concrete.... the interior dimensions are approximately 151 ft. wide, 345 ft. long and 30 ft. high. Entrances to the building include two large doors in the south wall at each end of the upper operations floor that permit vehicles to enter the building. (5)

This building was constructed according to certain specifications: it was designed to comply with the Uniform Building Code current when it was constructed and it is a moderate hazard facility as defined in Department of Energy (DOE) Order 6430.1A.UCRL-15910, which requires that it be designed for 0.15 g design basis earthquake (DBE). The DOE order also says that if a facility is to be classified as a high-hazard facility, design for a DBE of 0.23 g is required. This would fit the descriptions of the underground buildings at WPAFB. And if the Mound building is an example of a moderate-hazard facility, imagine what the design for an extreme-hazard facility, such as might be found at WPAFB, could be like.

I also have work-related diagrams for the contaminated areas at WPAFB, known as the "Wright-Patt Superfund Site," in Fairborn, Ohio. Although the area is highly contaminated, the map shows only surface contamination, suggesting the deeper areas are secured.

Such information suggests that the stories about huge underground chambers and their location may, in general, be true.

As was the case with Schmitt and Bragalia, Collins is a chief architect of some of today's disinformation, lies and hoax campaigns. He became widely-known in 1988, when actor Mike Farrell hosted *UFO Cover-Up?: Live!*, a two-hour prime-time syndicated television special broadcast in North America and elsewhere. Moore, Shandera and others appeared and discussed the acquisition of the MJ-12 documents. They introduced their sources, Falcon and Condor, as high-level government intelligence officials (I saw no evidence of this, but Collins may have worked at WPAFB and obviously read the base paper). Interviewed in shadow, Falcon and Condor (Richard Doty and Collins) disclosed information about the US government's involvement in UFOs and aliens.

This show was widely broadcast and sponsored by mainstream American corporations including AT&T. Because of this sponsorship and fanfare, many accepted this as authentic information on UFOs. Meanwhile through TV shows he's been involved with, through his 2005 book *Exempt from Disclosure* and through his numerous Internet postings, Collins continues to be highly influential. Majestic 12 has been featured in numerous books and television presentations.

Although some of Collins' material may include real facts because disinformation can include both true and untrue information, their effort can also do much damage to serious UFO investigation. Collins is one of the main mouthpieces for UFO scammers. He and Doty have continued to work together and to spread disinformation about the UFO subject in general, many aspects of the MJ-12 documents and purvey false information to honest investigators, such as Linda Moulton Howe to make them look bad. Such activities cause people to view the UFO phenomena with ridicule, rather than a complex phenomenon in need of study.

* * *

Their broadcast also included the first known public mention of the now well-known Area 51. Although some say Area 51 is fictional, I am sure it exists because my husband John Scott worked there. After we married, we moved to Nevada. He said the work there was highly classified. Most of the work took place in underground chambers. The area contained craft and equipment. However, these were covered and workers often were not allowed to even look at them. He sometimes traveled to different areas in the Nevada Proving Grounds and other portions of the site by by Department of Defense busses from Mercury, Nevada. He had also been among the people who watched the atomic bomb explosions. He had an Atomic Energy Commission Q clearance and his Air Force release papers showed that he worked in an Area 51 squadron.

* * *

Additional incidents involved materials study in the late 1940s and early 1950s. Obviously, such projects as Stork and WPAFB's FTD group were assigned to investigate the developments of foreign countries. But there were a number on instances suggestive of possible UFO debris study. The following events happened before most people had heard of Roswell.

Not long after the Roswell event, some researchers at the Bridgeport, Pennsylvania, plant of Vanadium Corporation of America (now Shield Alloy), were asked to investigate a strange metal material. In 2009, I interviewed Robert Orndoff, Ph.D., whose father, Robert Orndoff, was a metallurgical supervisor at Vanadium. The younger Orndoff's uncle, Richard Calender, was a supervisor at US Steel across the Monongahela River from Vanadium. When the younger Orndoff was a child in the late 1940s or early 1950s, his father told him he was involved in the metallurgical analysis of a special shipment of an unknown metal. The researchers, who refused to work on the metal unless they knew its history, were told it came from space and was found after a crash in New Mexico; it was the resulting debris, they were told, after the crash of either a meteor or an alien spacecraft.[98]

Orndoff's father described the material as a shovelful of metal pieces and dirt. The metal was burned and carbonized and it looked like the burned cinders from a powerful explosion. The researchers initially speculated that the metal was from a meteorite and they were surprised to find that it did not have the composition expected of a meteorite. Orndoff thinks his father told him the metal contained silicon, magnesium, cobalt, chromium, aluminum, steel, nickel, vanadium and titanium. The researchers felt the metal had been manufactured and they thought it was from an alien spacecraft. Orndoff said his father, his uncle and several others later discussed the material. Orndoff thought that his uncle, who also might have received a sample to analyze, thought the metal was crystalline. Orndoff recalled quite a bit of conversation about the metal among his family and their associates, but eventually the talk died down. Orndoff pointed out to me that because these people hadn't heard of Roswell and weren't aware of any UFO crashes, they lacked today's perspective for interpreting the facts.[99]

The younger Robert Orndoff has been knowledgeable about technology and metallurgy from an early age. He holds a Ph.D. from the University of California at Berkeley, was a post-doctoral clinical fellow at Johns Hopkins University School of Medicine and Hospital, served as a professor at Long Island University in New York and at Muskingum College in Ohio and was director and owner of a full-service mental health clinic in Cambridge, Ohio.[100]

Alien abduction researcher and author, Dr John Mack

* * *

As another example, in the mid-1990s, Jones and I investigated a connection between possible alien debris and the Timken Roller Bearing Company in Canton, Ohio. Timken had one of the hottest furnaces in the country in the 1940s and it is a global business today. We traveled to Canton, interviewed several people there and did research in the company's library.

In August or September 1947, Ralph A. Multer, an A-class truck driver for Timken, was asked to help bring loads from a nearby railroad yard back to the plant. Upon his arrival at the rail yard, Multer and two other drivers were given three flatbed trucks to drive to the plant. The trailer on each truck had a load covered with a canvas tarpaulin. The load on Multer's truck was the largest. It covered the entire width of the trailer and part of its length. The convoy was escorted, but Multer never said who these escorts were.

When the drivers arrived at the plant, several men who identified themselves as FBI agents met them. Multer asked one of them what the loads were. The agent replied that they were parts of a "flying saucer" that had been recovered in New Mexico and that the new Timken furnace was going to be used to try to melt the

234

material. Multer had a security clearance as part of his job, so this revelation was made within that context. As his wife remembers the story, he was told not to discuss the matter with anyone. The agent climbed up on a truck bed and pulled back the tarp, partially exposing the load. From what Multer could see, it was a metallic object, the color of "brushed aluminum," that appeared to have been blackened in places as if someone had used a torch to cut off pieces. He did not see the loads on the other trucks.

A week or two later he asked two furnace operators what had happened to the material. They replied that the furnace "couldn't touch it"—the furnace couldn't break or melt it. He never learned what became of the material after that. However, word got around the plant about the "flying saucer," and people joked about it.

In the years that followed, Multer's wife noticed that the experience changed him; without elaboration, she said the experience "never left his mind from then on." She always believed his story, noting, "He had no reason to make it up." Multer passed away a number of years ago.

This event occurred in August or September 1947, only a month or two after the Roswell crash. Jones and I tried to validate Multer's story by contacting retired Timken employees who'd worked at the plant at that time. MORA contacted six retired management and plant-engineering employees, including George L. Deal, a 35-year employee who served for many years as Timken's Vice President of Finance. None of the six admitted having heard anything about Multer's story, but as one noted, "Timken could keep a secret."

In July 2010, Ed Balint of *The Repositor* (a Canton, Ohio, newspaper) contacted me after coming across our information about the Timken connection on the Internet.[101] Balint was investigating the story and had found a Timken retiree, 84-year-old Dominick T. Rex, who recalled hearing about Multer. Rex had worked at Timken from 1946 in the roller bearings plant. He said he'd heard some kind of rumor about a truck driver and he thought this referred to Multer. But the elderly man didn't remember hearing about a crashed UFO. Balint also interviewed Multer's daughter, who recalled that Multer had repeated his story several times, always in the same form.

Balint's article was published a month after he first contacted me. It elicited several responses from the public, including from a caller who said his uncle had worked for the Air Force and had seen four alien bodies from the Roswell crash. Two were dead, one was injured and a fourth told the military how to care for the injured alien, the caller said.

*　*　*

An additional account comes from Kevin Meggs, who in 1982 was attending Wright State University and taking a course in statics and dynamics. One night while discussing UFO phenomena, an older classmate said that as a young engineer in the late 1940s or early 1950s, he and fellow WPAFB researchers were asked to test an unusual piece of material, the origin of which was never revealed.[102] The material was foil-like, very thin and about three feet square. It wouldn't crease or bend. In one test, they fired projectiles at the material and it absorbed the projectiles and the energy they carried, dropping the projectiles to the floor of the test chamber. The material wasn't penetrated. The classmate said engineers were told the tests were classified and that they should never discuss them with anyone. During this conversation Meggs asked about Hangar 18 (see Chapter Two). His classmate said he'd heard that a building at WPAFB contained items retrieved from a flying saucer. He added that the building contained a test chamber where the temperature could be varied. The classmate knew little about the building or what went on inside, but he thought it had a three-digit number.

Jones and I investigated additional reports about the examination of Roswell debris in Ohio, including one involving the North American Aviation Company in Columbus. We interviewed the daughters of North American Aviation employee Roy Beck (who'd described an earlier UFO incident at the Ohio Penitentiary—see Chapter Five). In 1963, Beck showed his daughters black-and-white photographs of alien bodies that he said were from a crashed flying saucer. He said he borrowed the pictures from a file there. The alien looked like what we call a "grey" today. Beck said he had photographs and the information about them through his work at the North American Aviation Company in Columbus, Ohio, where he and others had been asked to determine what the material from the flying saucer was made of and how it worked. Beck told his daughter they couldn't even scratch the material. She believes his work at North American on the flying-saucer parts—many of which were quite large, he said—took place in 1953 or 1954. She remembers her father saying at least one very large truck was used to move the parts out of the plant and back to WPAFB.

Jones and I investigated additional reports about the examination of Roswell debris, included one involving the Monsanto Research Corporation near Dayton, Ohio. The Monsanto report included stories about government contracts with WPAFB for reverse-engineering studies of gravity waves.

It might seem odd that so many stories about crash debris come from Ohio, however as mentioned, Ohio has been one of the nation's leading industrial and technological states and is the home of WPAFB, thus, it's not surprising that if alien debris existed, it might find its way to Ohio. Moreover before Roswell, people were not yet aware of UFO debris stories and had no reason to associate strange substances with UFOs, but many early stories exist.

* * *

UFOs, extraterrestrials and government cover-ups are today among the most frequently viewed subjects on the Internet. For example, the YouTube site contains millions of videos on the subject of UFOs and some of these have been viewed millions of times. Moreover, such subjects are no longer the province of nonconformists; they are now part of conventional American society. The concepts of government cover-ups, secret government-related societies and underground facilities have become part of popular culture, providing story lines not only for *The X-Files* and *Dark Skies*, but also for a wide variety of today's bestselling fiction, including Dan Brown's books and the Harry Potter series.

We have uncovered several smoking gun leads including where and when investigation may have and still be taking place. As noted above, Battelle's John Center, a chemical engineer, reported that he had studied "parts" from a "flying saucer." As further evidence supporting this, Brigadier General Arthur Exon, commander of WPAFB, spoke of the Roswell material as having undergone chemical analysis (as reported by Carey and Schmitt in *Witness to Roswell*).

This research may be taking place today, for example at Battelle some of Project Stork's research was reportedly housed in rooms on the fourth floor of Building 10 and this area may still be secured. Attached to its windows are special fixtures allegedly designed to prevent vibrations so spies can't use electronic techniques to listen to conversations going on inside the building. For example, when I recently (August, 2016) photographed these fixtures, a guard immediately came up and told me to stop because I wasn't allowed to do this. Several informants said that this area might still house research similar to or the same as that carried on under Stork. The families of the Battelle researchers that were involved may also offer evidence. And there is very strong "grapevine" evidence of such research at both Battelle and WPAFB.

UFO research may also take place at Wright Patterson, particularly in the NASIC centers–where satellite photography is monitored–in Area 51 and comparable desert bases; in the Cheyenne Mountain Complex, home of NORAD; and similar places. In addition, it likely is conducted by offices in Washington DC.

My DIA experience would suggest that one of the mysterious government offices that examines UFO reports is connected with the CIA. It may be in a part of the organization where information from satellite and about flying craft is processed.

However, even though I worked in the office whose mission was to identify all flying objects over an important area, my section received no briefing about UFO phenomena. And when my section dutifully reported an Unidentified Flying Object, it appeared that we were harassed rather than having such a potentially significant report addressed in a professional manner. This suggests that cover-up exists at high levels of the government.

Our recently uncovered documents provide smoking-gun evidence suggesting that organizations such as WPAFB and Battelle made a more intensive study of UFOs than was previously disclosed and that they covered up this information. The fact that some such cover-ups took place suggests that, however much government authorities deny it, they took UFOs very seriously—and likely continue to do so.

CHAPTER TEN

Are UFOs Real?

ENOUGH evidence has been presented here to indicate that some UFO phenomena are real. Rigorous scientific studies completely compatible with today's scientific methodology, such as those done by Rutledge and those sponsored by the government for Battelle's *SR-14*, support this.[103] During this investigation, we have discovered such smoking gun evidence, as John Center's information the he worked with UFO material at Battelle and Joe Wilson's on air comments that he had just called WPAFB and material was on its way from Roswell. My examination of the October 11, 1973, sound that covered a large area of the Eastern US, has been published in the peer-reviewed scientific literature. Many studies also support the idea that UFO phenomena can be much more complex than imagined.

People's attitudes about UFOs have changed such that the public is more open to the idea that a portion of UFO phenomena is real as shown by recent

UFO researcher and author, Dr Bruce Maccabee

Alien abduction researcher and author, Dr David Jacobs

US alien abduction researcher, John Carpenter

surveys. One reason for this is that UFO phenomena are often associated with the idea of extraterrestrial life and the idea that aliens may be visiting earth. Recent discoveries about our universe have provided many reasons for this new acceptance. For example, although only a few years ago it was thought earth was the only life-supporting planet, today it has been estimated that there could be more than a billion earthlike planets in our galaxy alone and some are within the habitable zones of our type of life. Moreover, conditions on nearby planets, such as the newly discovered water on Mars, make it believable that life could exist elsewhere. In addition, since the 1960s scientists have recognized that earth life can exist in all sorts of unlikely places. For example, recently discovered bacteria called extremophiles, can live under extreme temperatures and pressures, in environments having no sunlight and under conditions of extreme radiation. Thus, life may exist in a much broader range of habitats and forms than previously recognized.

Attitudes also are broadening about what UFOs might be. People are becoming

Folklorist, author and alien abduction researcher, Dr Thomas E. Bullard

UFO researcher, Paul Sturrock

more open to the idea that life-forms may differ greatly from us. People no longer expect a UFO to land and a humanoid occupant to walk out and say, "Take me to your leader." [104] And the idea that UFOs are associated with extraterrestrial life is only one theory of what UFO phenomenon might represent.

Crucial new studies provide support for accounts of the strange behaviors of UFOs. [105] For example, Rutledge was reluctant to publish his findings that when a UFO came within range of measurement it would move, change course, or halt. He was loath to report observer-dependent characteristics, or the ability of UFO phenomena to control photographic results, because such characteristics are the opposite of what a physicist expects. Rutledge did, however, have the courage to publish his findings, which are in stark contrast to the billiard-ball paradigms, often viewed as "hard science," of much of today's physics.

However, research into quantum mechanics presents such concepts as observer-dependent phenomena, the observer-created universe, Schrödinger's equation, wormholes, faster-than-light interaction (such as entangled particles), coincidence and the questioning the idea of cause and effect. Study of how energy and matter are related ($E=MC^2$) and can be interconverted are also important. Such ideas could be highly relevant to UFO phenomena with its reports of objects going through walls, balls of light that appear to transform into humanoid shapes and many other accounts that contradict our common sense "nuts and bolts" ideas of reality. The results of some of these experiments suggest that our ideas of time and space and even the framework of what we view as reality should be questioned.

For example, observer-dependent phenomena are characteristic representations of the weird world of quantum relationships. [106] Thus, today's physics could allow one to postulate ways for such mechanisms to occur.[107] For example by the 1940s general nuts and bolts view of the universe, it would be impossible for anything to pass through walls, thus, such observations were ridiculed. However, such processes as quantum tunneling, when a particle passes through a barrier that it seemingly shouldn't be able to, would allow this (although with more finesse than we've developed). Also, the idea of remotely stopping cars once seemed impossible but today's devices can do this. And having something appear when we stare at open space might be some aspect of the quantum idea of "consciousness creates reality," such as shown in double-slit optical system experiments and still under study.

Because the Rutledge researchers had outstanding scientific credentials and used scientific methodology and measurements, the team's observations are highly credible. And the data indicates a need for new study methods to examine occurrences such as interactive phenomena, a need for new techniques embodying new physics paradigms and a need for more complex models to provide testable hypotheses and to explain reality. For example, although the controlled experiment is the foundation of today's science, new paradigms for studying phenomena that is not under human control are needed.

Rather than space ships, some UFOs may also represent drones, robots, or some sort of artificial force fields created by non-humans. Other portions of UFO phenomena may represent unknown natural events. As discussed in the Skinwalker study, a part of UFO phenomenon may also represent some form of tunnel or wormhole into other dimensions and worlds. In addition, what one sees may depend upon their interpretation. For example, if one sees a floating orb or a humanoid, one might view it as form of ghost. But if one sees the same type of phenomena, but it looks a floating craft, one would then interpret it as a UFO or space ship.

Moreover, we are now living in a "Spielberg Era" of cultural change: we've seen space flights and watched a possible future unfold in films such as *Star Wars* and *Star Trek*. UFOs continue to invade our consciousness with endless streams of books, films, TV shows, cartoons, toys, greeting cards and other media. Gallup polls rank UFOs near the top of the list of subjects of widespread recognition. For example, even a 1973 survey found that 95 percent of the public had heard of UFOs. (Possibly their intent is to influence culture, rather than make direct contact.) For example, I was told that one of Dr. Hynek's theories is that the phenomena is interrelating with the government in ways to gradually introduce us to the idea of other life forms in non-threatening ways. However even if the cover-up is done to protect us from knowing about something that could be horrible, we actually have more chance of addressing it if we know about it in advance.

Attitudes are also changing about why, if extraterrestrial life exists, why hasn't it directly communicated with us. We now have answers to this quandary; for example, extraterrestrials might have their own version of the *Star Trek* "Prime Directive," which dictates no interference with alien civilizations. It is also possible that other life forms wish simply to observe us without interacting with us. Indeed looking at the situation from the extraterrestrial point of view, if any space alien group can build large optical telescopes, it undoubtedly knows we are here, because the earth is blue, which indicates that our planet likely has liquid water and a life-supporting environment. Because it has been blue for around four billion years and we have a sun that can produce that type of planet, anyone with much advancement in a many billions of light years sphere around earth would know that this planet is capable of supporting our form of life. This suggests that many alien groups may be observing us.

Another way that attitudes have changed is that previously, instead of being discussed in terms of fact, situating the subject in the realm of science, UFOs have often been presented in terms of belief, relegating them to the realm of religion. UFOlogy has been plagued with the fallacious assumption that only "believers"—oddballs or the mentally disturbed—see UFOs. However, recent studies show that UFO witnesses and abductees range from normal to above average in psychological and intellectual parameters and they are well situated within mainstream society. For example, in her Ph.D. studies, Brenda Denzler found that the average MUFON Symposium attendee is a married, white, male Protestant, between 46 and 60 years old, with above average yearly earnings and education. John Carpenter, who has studied abductions for many years, told me that psychological studies of abductees, published in scientific periodicals such *Journal of Abnormal Psychology*, show that abducted individuals tend to be psychologically normal.[108] This is hardly the fringe.

Many of those who research and write about UFO witnesses and abductees have top credentials. These writers and researchers include Harvard Medical School professor and psychiatrist, John Edward Mack M.D., a psychiatrist, author of over 150 scientific articles and winner of the Pulitzer Prize for his biography of T. E. Lawrence. He became interested in UFO phenomenon in the late 1980s when he interviewed numerous witnesses and he eventually wrote two UFO books. Mack viewed the majority of abductees as ordinary people who were not deluded, lying, self-dramatizing, or suffering from mental illnesses. Among many academic and scientific researchers are: Bruce Maccabee, Ph.D., a physicist listed in *Who's Who in Technology Today* and *American Men and Women of Science*; Michael D. Swords, Ph.D., a professor of natural sciences at Western Michigan University; David Michael Jacobs, Ph.D., an American historian and associate professor of history at Temple University; physicist James McDonald, Ph.D.; psychologists John Wilson,

M.D.; and Rima Laibow, M.D.; psychotherapist David Gotlieb, M.D.; American folklorist Thomas E. Bullard, Ph.D.; and astronomer J. Allen Hynek, Ph.D.

UFO study is being accepted in the scientific literature and as a science; for example, a 1976 poll of the American Astronomical Society by Peter Sturrock, Ph.D., showed that 80 percent of members thought that UFO phenomenon deserved scientific attention. (Although skeptics groups present themselves as scientists, many are writers and media people. There may be more scientists among the UFOlogists than in skeptic's societies.)

Prominent people such as US presidents and astronauts have expressed interest or concern about UFO phenomena. These include Clyde Tombaugh, discoverer of Pluto. Astronauts—such as Edgar Mitchell, Gordon Cooper, Edwin "Buzz" Aldrin, Donald Kent "Deke" Slayton and John Glenn—have made reports indicative of seeing UFOs or have suggested that the US government is covering up UFO information. For example, former astronaut Story Musgrave was the keynote speaker for the 2011 MUFON Symposium. Presidents such as Jimmy Carter, Gerald Ford, Ronald Reagan and George Bush have spoken out about UFO phenomena.

As the scientific community becomes more open-minded regarding the possibility of extraterrestrial life, serious books are appearing about the subject. For example, university presses have published such books as David Jacobs's 1975 *The UFO Controversy in America*, as well as Brenda Denzler's *The Lure of the Edge: Scientific Passions, Religious Beliefs and the Pursuit of UFOs*. College classes about UFOs are offered at institutions such as such as Indiana University-Purdue University at Fort Wayne. Numerous universities have had UFO speakers and conferences; these include the Massachusetts Institute of Technology and many others.

In addition, UFO papers are appearing in conventional scientific literature; for example, I've published five papers containing UFO material in peer-reviewed scientific journals.[109] Acceptance by the scientific world is greatly expanding the possibilities of UFO studies and many scientists today have an interest in UFO phenomena, such as Walt Mitchell, Ph.D., an Astronomy Department professor at OSU.[110]

And most importantly, rigorous scientific study has not only shown that the phenomena is real, it appears to have shown that it is interactive. It is vastly more complex than any traditional "Nuts and Bolts" concept. ARE

Although we are molecular, this doesn't mean UFO phenomena is. It consists of many credible empirical observations that don't fit our Newtonian physics paradigms. It can encompass balls of light that can change to different forms;

objects that appear and disappear, go through walls, merge and separate; groups of lights that come together to form humanoid appearing things; and objects of incredible size and speed. It can include poltergeist-like activity, large and small UFOs, magnetic and radiation effects, abduction phenomena, thought control and telepathy, for a few. Because of this, it doesn't fit the profile of pilots and space ships, but of something vastly different from us. Such observations suggest that this data should be investigated not only with our nuts and bolts ideas of space ships, but with additional paradigms, such as with quantum mechanical or other ideas. UFO phenomenon may be like some kind of a force field that can interact with people, such that we experience and see it in different ways.

New ways and various paradigms of science are needed to study it.

Such changes may aid not only the scientific study of the phenomena, but of all human knowledge.

* * *

This book will end not with a reiteration, but with a challenge:

1. Scientists should continue to develop ways to collect and analyze high-quality UFO data, through studies such as those proposed by Cross and partially implemented by Rutledge and Bigelow.

2. Highly trained statisticians should scrutinize existing data, looking for patterns and developing new methods for data collection and analysis. Repeater phenomena should be intensively studied, such as by statistical comparison of those who might be predicted to be repeaters (for example, people who spend substantial time outdoors) and those who actually report repeat sightings.

3. Professional and amateur astronomers should set up dedicated UFO observation platforms with telescopes and radar technology.

4. UFOlogists should continue to submit petitions and FOIA requests to government agencies requesting the release of UFO documents and photography. Information is especially needed about the cover-up–who or what is doing it, why, what exactly are they are covering up and could it control them? People need to be cognizant of such complex aspects as that of mind control and to study it not only in terms of simple individual interactions, but of masses of people, their leaders and their scientists.

246

5. UFOlogists should strive to gain scientific acceptance of existing UFO data and they should increase their efforts to publish in scientific journals. Effort should be made to encourage and even energize scientists to step out of their often-confining establishment systems and study UFO phenomena with innovative theories and methods, as Hynek, Rutledge and Cross did.

6. Through activities such as devising methods to study quantum interactions, researchers should develop new scientific models and should use these models to examine UFO data.

7. Because a portion of UFO phenomena might represent life, but not the molecular form of which we are conscious, researchers should be open-minded about scientific and cultural paradigms.

8. Although we are looking for dramatic "smoking guns," perhaps the best smoking guns we have are studies such as *SR-14* and Rutledge's work.

9. And most important, although more data collection is needed, it may not be the solution to understanding the phenomena. Perhaps additional study of physics paradigms, such as of entangled particles, faster than light events, Schrodinger's cat paradox and many others, including mind control, may be the best way to understand this. Researchers also need to develop scientific methods to examine a phenomenon that may not be under human control.

As Rutledge told me:

Obviously, private groups lack funding to purchase sophisticated equipment to study UFOs. Obviously, the government does not. Obviously, most scientists do not want government funds channeled into UFO research. Recall the radio astronomer in Sagan's novel. Would NASA be as important in space if UFOs were acknowledged and accepted as extraterrestrial? Would the US Air Force, whose primary mission is to protect our airspace, be content to be regarded as the second best air force in the world . . . and the Russian's third?[111]

It may be fruitless to rely upon the government for activities such as those I've suggested here. The American government is probably not the answer to gaining public acceptance of UFOs. Instead, the answer may lie in highly dedicated individuals. Copernicus, not his government, proposed that the earth was not the center of the universe. Two poorly educated bicycle mechanics—the Wright Brothers—developed flight. Thomas Edison, holder of 1093 patents, invented the phonograph, modern electrical power, the light bulb and the motion picture.

Dr. Hynek and others were convinced the American government was actually abusing the scientific process in its public pronouncements about UFOs. And the role of the government in UFO cover-ups and debunking—as well as in more nefarious activity, such as the tragic case of Paul Bennewitz—is well established.

A related part of the cover-up is skepticism, where people just don't believe the reports instead of exploring the information in depth. Although this is generally presented as simply natural doubt, there is abundant evidence that the government has deliberately created some of it. Observations of UFO phenomena are presented as "unscientific," although good science should encompass good empirical observation and if it doesn't fit a theory, then the theory might need alteration. Not only does the government cover up, but it appears to use brainwashing techniques that produce skepticism rather than scientific examination. As mentioned, there is some evidence that in even the very earliest reports some form of cover-up may have been active. The government has manipulated the results of scientific studies, such as the one done by Battelle, to show that they found noting when in fact they did. In other cases, it has set up panels that purported to examine the subject "scientifically," but instead used them to debunk the phenomena, such as those of Robertson and Condon. It has actively set up debunking campaigns to plant outlandish UFO claims in the media to make UFO reports sound ridiculous. The Condon Report summary cautioned teachers to discourage any interest of pupils in UFOs, because such study would be harmful to their development. So if UFOs do not exist, how would an interest in them harm pupils and why should young people be brainwashed? Such activities might not help people, but they would certainly benefit the UFO phenomena by causing people to not take it seriously, thus helping it to hide its activities.

In addition, because UFO phenomena may be quite complex, one even wonders exactly what governments are covering up. And if the observed phenomenon seems to contradict standard paradigms, such as that of controlled experimentation, then science should accept that it doesn't control the universe and develop methods to explore events that may not be under human control. The is important because the idea of controlled experimentation might even turn out to be a fatal flaw of science.

Finally, it appears from intensive investigation from the inside of three of the most important agencies involved in UFO investigation, that some smoking gun evidence exists that UFO phenomena is real. Moreover, a government cover-up is definitely real and may have been in place since the beginning studies. If the UFO phenomena did not exist, why would the government expend so much time and effort in a cover-up and why wouldn't its efforts cause the phenomena to disappear? Why even do a cover-up, when it is not very effective? Why not release the information and allow everyone including the world's geniuses to examine it?

* * *

In conclusion, as we move forward into our second millennium, we are entering new worlds of thought. Our previous methodology involved using "nuts and bolts," hard science to prove or disprove the existence of UFO phenomena, but this methodology is becoming outdated. Indeed, the new information found here shows that even from its 1947 beginning, modern UFO activity has been much more complex than thought and this has resulted in much miscomprehension of the phenomena throughout its existence. Intensive investigation as done in the Skinwalker and Rutledge studies has shown the phenomena as elusive and difficult to even comprehend let alone study, however, such findings have been suppressed. This government cover-up has greatly impeded any form of exploration and possibly the future growth of humanity. But now besides actively exploring the universe for other life forms, we've begun, through studies such those as of quantum relationships, to question the very framework of our reality. We may be cognizant that our scientific paradigms of controlled experimentation may need revision. We may now have the equipment and knowledge to do the required additional exploration—which may uncover both the most important of all problems and our very reason for being. In undertaking these explorations, we position ourselves to finally not only examine UFO phenomena and to explore communication with other life-forms, but also to better know ourselves.

References

"15 Sightings of UFOs Reported Near Dayton," *Columbus Dispatch* October 11, 1973: 13A.

Alberta UFO Study Group. "Summaries of Some Recent Opinion Polls on UFOs." *Extraterrestrial Contact.* 2011. <http://www.ufoevidence.org/documents/doc999.htm>.

Aldrich, Jan. Project 1947: A Preliminary Report. *UFO Research Coalition.* 1997.

Allen, William. "The Branch Office." *Reader's Digest* January, 1985: 157-162.

Andrus, Walter and Irena Scott, eds. *The Fiftieth Anniversary of UFOlogy.* MUFON 1997 International UFO Symposium Proceedings: Mutual UFO Network Inc., 1997.

___. *UFOs in the New Millennium.* MUFON 2000 International UFO Symposium Proceedings: Mutual UFO Network Inc., 2000.

Arnold, Kenneth and Ray Palmer. *The Coming of the Saucers.* Boise, ID and Amherst, WI: Kenneth Arnold and Ray Palmer, 1952.

Balint, Ed. "Canton's Close Encounter," *The Repository* August 22, 2010: A1, A6.

Barker, Gray. *MIB: The Secret Terror among Us.* Jane Lew, WV: New Age Books, 1983.

___. *The Silver Bridge.* Clarksburg, WV: Saucerian Books, 1970.

___. *They Knew Too Much about Flying Saucers.* New York: University Books, 1956.

Beckley, Timothy Green. *MJ-12 and the Riddle of Hangar 18: The New Evidence.* New Brunswick, NJ: Inner Light—Global Communications, 2003.

Bender, Albert K. *Flying Saucers and the Three Men.* New York: Paperback Library, 1968.

Berlitz, Charles and William L. Moore. *The Roswell Incident.* New York: Grosset & Dunlap, 1980.

Bragalia, Anthony. "The Final Secrets of Roswell's Memory Metal Revealed." *The UFO Iconoclast(s).* June 7, 2009. <http://ufocon.blogspot.com/2009/06/final-secrets-of-roswells-memory-metal.html>.

___. "Roswell Alcoholics: The Alien Anguish." *The UFO Iconoclast(s).* March 14, 2010. <http://ufocon.blogspot.com/2010/03/roswell-alcoholics-alien-anguish-by.html>.

___. "Roswell, Battelle & Memory Metal: The New Revelations." Posted by Maria Luisa de Vasconcellos. *Light Eye: Tribute to an UFO Watcher.* August 8, 2010. <http://fgportugal.blogspot.com/2010_08_01_archive.html>.

___. "Roswell Debris Confirmed as Extraterrestrial: Lab Located, Scientists Named." *The UFO Iconoclast(s).* May 26, 2009. <http://ufocon.blogspot.com/2009/05/roswell-debris-confirmed-as.html>.

___. "Roswell Debris Inspired Memory Metal Nitinol; Lab Located. Scientists Named." *MUFON UFO Journal* (July, 2009): 3-10.

___. "Roswell Metal Scientist: The Curious Dr. Cross." *The UFO Iconoclast(s).* May 21, 2009. <http://ufocon.blogspot.com/2009/05/roswell-metal-scientist-curious-dr.html>.

___. "Scientist Admits to Study of Roswell Crash Debris." *The UFO Iconoclast(s)*. August 16, 2009. <http://ufocon.blogspot.com/2009/08/scientist-admits-to-study-of-roswell.html>.

"Brilliant Fireball Flashes across Midwest," *Columbus Dispatch* December 10, 1965: 1A.

Brown, Dan. *The Lost Symbol*. New York: Doubleday Books, 2009.

Burrafato, Kim. "Redfern Sheds Light on the Real 'Men in Black.'" *MUFON UFO Journal* (August, 2011): 3 and 19.

Burrell, Paul and Paul Althouse. "Ross and Pike Counties, Ohio April/May 1996." *Ohio UFO Notebook* 12 (1996): 8-10.

Burrell, Paul, Delbert Anderson, William E. Jones and Irena Scott. "Dancing Red Lights, Logan, Ohio, October/November, 1995." *MUFON of Ohio Newsletter* (November, 2009): 4-5.

Carey, Thomas J. and Donald R. Schmitt. *Witness to Roswell: Unmasking the Government's Biggest Cover-Up*. Franklin Lakes, NJ: New Page Books, 2009.

Chamberlain, Von Del and David Krause. "The Fireball of December 9, 1965, Part I: Calculation of the Trajectory and Orbit by Photographic Triangulation of the Train." *Journal of the Royal Astronomical Society of Canada* (August, 1967): 184-90.

"City Couples, Ohio Police Chase UFO," *New Castle News* April 18, 1966: 1.

Clark, Jerome. *The UFO Book*. Detroit: Visible Ink Press, 1998.

___. *Unexplained! 347 Strange Sightings, Incredible Occurrences and Puzzling Physical Phenomena*. Detroit: Visible Ink Press, 1993.

Coleman, Ted. *Jack Northrop and the Flying Wing*. New York: Paragon House, 1988.

Collins, Robert M., Richard C. Doty and Timothy S. Cooper. *Exempt from Disclosure*. Vandalia, OH: Peregrine Communications, 2005.

Condon, Edward U. *Scientific Study of Unidentified Flying Objects*. Boston: E.P. Dutton, 1969.

Denzler, Brenda. *The Lure of the Edge: Scientific Passions, Religious Beliefs and the Pursuit of UFOs*. Berkeley: University of California Press, 2003.

___. "Who Are We?" *MUFON UFO Journal* (May, 1977): 9-14.

Desguin, Lillian Crowner. *UFOs: Fact or Fiction?* Laguna Hills, CA: Aegean Park Press, 1992.

Dolan, Richard. *UFOs and the National Security State: An Unclassified History, Volume 1: 1941-1973*. New York: Keyhole Publishing, 2000.

Fawcett, Lawrence and Barry J. Greenwood. *Clear Intent: The Government Cover-Up of the UFO Experience*. Englewood Cliffs, NJ: Prentice-Hall, 1984.

___. *The UFO Cover-Up: What the Government Won't Say*. Old Tappan, NJ: Fireside, 1990.

"Fireballs Are Blamed in Elyria Grass Blazes," *The Plain Dealer* December 10, 1965: A1.

"'Fireball' Slams into County from Lake Erie to Eaton," *The Chronicle-Telegram* December 10, 1965: 1, 3.

Fowler, Raymond E. *UFOs: Interplanetary Visitors*. Bloomington, IN: iUniverse, 2001.

___. *The Watchers: The Secret Design behind UFO Abduction*. New York: Bantam, 1991.

Friedman, Stanton. "Arsenic and (the Same) Old Story: Media Fascination with Aliens Is Misguided." *MUFON UFO Journal* (January, 2011): 8-9.

___. "More 'why' questions." *MUFON UFO Journal* (October, 2016): 6-7.

___. "A Scientific Approach to Flying Saucer Behavior." In *Thesis Antithesis: Proceedings of a Symposium Sponsored by A IAA and World Future Society* (Los Angeles, CA, September, 1975): 22-36.

"From Albert Rosales' 'World of Strangeness,' 2008—# 83." *Truth Seeker Forum.* March 18, 2009. <http://truthseekerforum.com/?s=elk+county+pa>.

Fuller, John. *Interrupted Journey: Two Lost Hours aboard a Flying Saucer.* New York: Dial Press, 1966.

Good, Timothy. *Above Top Secret: The Worldwide UFO Cover-Up.* New York: Quill Publishing, 1989.

___. *Need to Know: UFOs, the Military and Intelligence.* New York: Pegasus Books, 2007.

Hall, Richard. *The UFO Evidence.* New York: Barnes & Noble, 1997.

___. *Uninvited Guests: A Documented History of UFO Sightings, Alien Encounters and Cover-Ups.* Santa Fe, NM: Aurora Press, 1988.

"Have We Ever Had a Piece of a Flying Disk?" *The Big Study.* December 18, 2009. <http://thebiggeststudy.blogspot.com/2009/12/have-we-ever-had-piece-of-flying-disk.html>.

Hesemann, Michael and Philip Mantle. *Beyond Roswell: The Alien Autopsy Film, Area 51, & the U.S. Government Cover-Up of UFOs.* New York: Marlowe & Company, 1998.

Hilkevitch, Jon. "In the Sky! A Bird? A Plane? A . . . UFO?," *Chicago Tribune* January 1, 2007: 1.1.

Holt, Turner Hamilton. *Life's Convictions.* New York: Vantage Press, 1956.

Hopkins, Budd. *Intruders: The Incredible Visitations at Copley Woods.* New York: Random House, 1987.

___. *Missing Time.* New York: Berkley, 1983.

Hynek, J. Allen. *The UFO Experience: A Scientific Inquiry.* Chicago: Henry Regnery Company, 1972.

Jacobs, David. *UFOs and Abductions: Challenging the Borders of Knowledge.* Lawrence, KS: University Press of Kansas, 2000.

___. *The UFO Controversy in America.* Bloomington, IN: Indiana University Press, 1975.

Jacobsen, Annie. *Area 51: An Uncensored History of America's Top Secret Military Base.* New York: Little, Brown and Company, 2011.

Jones, William E. "Another MJ-12 Document." *Ohio UFO Notebook* 11 (1996): 11-14.

___. "Books and Articles of Note." *Ohio UFO Notebook* 10 (1995): 14-18.

___. "Confirmation of UFOlogy's Darker Side." *Ohio UFO Notebook* (July, 1993): 4-7.

___. "Confirmation That J. Allen Hynek Communicated with Neil Armstrong." *MUFON of Ohio Newsletter* (Spring, 2008): 7-8.

___. "Darlington, Ohio, October, 1953: A Case That Can't Be Documented." *Ohio UFO Notebook* 1 (August, 1991): 15-17.

___. "Historical Notes: Thomas Mantell." *MUFON UFO Journal* (April, 1990): 18-19.

___. "Human Mutilations Again." *Ohio UFO Notebook* 6 and 7 (July, 1993): 13-14.

___. "Information, Disinformation, Hints, or Lies?" *Ohio UFO Notebook* 11 (1996): 24-25.

___. "Neil Armstrong and Len Stringfield." *Ohio UFO Notebook* 9 (1995): 20-21.

___. "Point Pleasant, West Virginia Moth Man Follow Up." *Ohio UFO Notebook* 1 (August, 1991): 12.

___. "Project Grudge/Bluebook Special Report 13." *Ohio UFO Notebook* 15 (1997): 1-2.

Jones, William E. and Irena Scott. "June 20-23, 1985, Columbus." *Ohio UFO Notebook* 12 (1996): 19-22.

___. "Laurie, Missouri." *Ohio UFO Notebook* 12 (1996): 26-27.

___. "North American Aviation, Columbus, Ohio, Test Site for UFO Materials?" *Ohio UFO Notebook* 12 (1996): 35-37.

___. "The Spaur Case—Reporting a UFO Can Be Hazardous to Your Health." *Ohio UFO Notebook* 14 (1997): 36-40.

___. "U.S. Navy Support of UFO Research." *Ohio UFO Notebook* 11 (1996): 5-6.

Jones, William E. and Eloise G. Watson. "Pre-World War II 'Creature' Retrieval?" *International UFO Reporter* (Winter, 2001-2002): 6-30.

Keel, John. *The Mothman Prophecies*. New York: Saturday Review Press, 1975.

Kelleher, Colm A. and George Knapp. *Hunt for the Skinwalker: Science Confronts the Unexplained at a Remote Ranch in Utah*. New York: Paraview Pocket Books, 2005.

Keyhoe, Donald. *The Flying Saucers Are Real* (reprint). New York: Cosimo Classics, 2004.

Klass, Philip J. "CIA Mission." *MUFON UFO Journal* (February, 1993): 20.

Lang, Richard. "The SIP Project—Star Team Report." *MUFON UFO Journal* (July, 2009): 7.

___. "Woman and Dog Observe Multiple Lights, Orbs." *MUFON UFO Journal* (August, 2009): 9-10.

LIFE_Magazine_Trent_Photoshoot_1950 - Roswell Proof . "1950 LIFE Magazine Trent UFO photoshoot." http://www.roswellproof.com/LIFE_Magazine_Trent_Photoshoot_1950.html

Maccabee, Bruce S. *Historical Introduction to* Project Blue Book Special Report No. 14. Evanston, IL: Center for UFO Studies, 1979.

Maccabee, Bruce S. *The FBI CIA UFO Connection*. New York: Richard Dolan Press, 2014.

McAndrew, James. *The Roswell Report: Case Closed*. Washington, DC: Headquarters, United States Air Force, 1997.

Morrell, David. *The Shimmer*. New York: Vanguard Press, 2009.

Moseley, James. *UFO Crash Secrets at Wright-Patterson Air Force Base*. Wilmington, DE: Abelard Productions, 1991.

"No Reports UFO Seen in County," *Albany Times Union* April 18, 1966: n.p. Newspaper clipping. Irena Scott Private Collection, Lewis Center, OH.

Oberg, James. "French 'Flap' a Flop?" *MUFON UFO Journal* (September, 1992): 21.

"Photos Taken of 4 UFOs," *Columbus Dispatch* October 18, 1973: 1A.

Project Blue Book Special Report No. 14 (Analysis of Reports of Unidentified Flying Objects). Wright-Patterson Air Force Base, OH: Air Technical Intelligence Center, 1955.

Project-1947 – Air Intelligence Report 100-203-79, "Analysis of Flying Object Incidents in the U.S." Headquarters United States Air Force Directorate of Intelligence, Washington, D.C., 1949.

"RAAF Captures Flying Saucer on Ranch in Roswell Region," *Roswell Daily Record* July 8, 1947: 1.

Randle, Kevin D. *A History of UFO Crashes*. New York: Avon Books, 1995.

___. *The UFO Casebook*. New York: Warner Books, 1989.

Randle, Kevin D. and Donald R. Schmitt. "Roswell and the Flying Wing." *International UFO Reporter* (July/August, 1995): 10-12.

___. *The Truth about the UFO Crash at Roswell.* New York: M. Evans and Company, Inc., 1994.

___. *The UFO Dossier: 100 Years of Government Secrets, Conspiracies and Cover-Ups.* Detroit: Visible Ink Press, 2015.

___. *UFO Crash at Roswell.* New York: Avon, 1991.

Randles, Jenny. *The Truth Behind Men in Black: Government Agents -- or Visitors from Beyond.* New York: St. Martin's Paperbacks; St. Martin's, 1997.

___. *The UFO Conspiracy: The First Forty Years.* New York: Barnes & Noble, 1987.

___. *UFO Retrievals: The Recovery of Alien Spacecraft.* London: Blandford Press, 1995.

Reams, Frank B. "Troy, Ohio, July 1, 1991." *Ohio UFO Notebook* (December, 1991): 44-45.

___. "TV Show Encourages UFO Reports." *Ohio UFO Notebook* 9 (1995): 22-23.

Reams, Frank B. and Barbara Spellerberg. "Columbus, Ohio, Late Fall 1966 Ohio Penitentiary Sighting— Preliminary Report." *Ohio UFO Notebook* 1 (August, 1991): 7-9.

Reddit UFOs/CaerBannog. "Kevin Randle Distances Himself from Schmitt, Carey, Bragalia & Dew's "Roswell Slides."

https://www.reddit.com/r/UFOs/comments/2xntee/kevin_randle_distances_himself_from_schmitt_carey/

Richelson, Jeffrey T. *America's Secret Eyes in Space: The U.S. Keyhole Satellite Program.* New York: HarperCollins, 1990.

Ridge, Francis. *Regional Encounters.* Mt.Vernon, IN: UFO Filter Center, 1994.

Ring, Kenneth. *The Omega Project: Near-Death Experiences, UFO Encounters and Mind at Large.* New York: William Morrow & Co., 1992.

Rondinone, Peter. "Antimatter." *OMNI Magazine* May, 1982: 114.

Rosales, Albert. "1935-1939 Humanoid Reports." *UFOInfo.* 2011. <http://www.ufoinfo.com/humanoid/humanoid1935.shtml>.

Ruppelt, Edward J. *The Report on Unidentified Flying Objects.* New York: Doubleday, 1956.

Rutledge, Harley D. *Project Identification: The First Scientific Field Study of UFO Phenomena.* Englewood Cliffs, NJ: Prentice-Hall, 1981.

The (St Mary's) Evening Leader, "Big Blast, UFO's Shake People Over Wide Area," October 12, 1973.

Schuessler, John F. *The Cash-Landrum UFO Incident.* La Porte, TX: Geo Graphics, 1998.

Scott, Irena. "A Photograph and its aftermath" *International UFO Reporter* (Septeber/October, 1990): 12-14.

___. "Bedroom Light" *International UFO Reporter* (March/April, 1988): 14-15.

___. "Additional Information Wright-Patterson AFB (WPAFB)." *Ohio UFO Notebook* (January, 1994): 23-24.

___. "CIA, UFO Photography and Tunnels." *Ohio UFO Notebook* (July, 1993): 34-40.

___. "Crisman, Military Intelligence and Roswell." *Ohio UFO Notebook* (May, 1992): 27-32.

___. "DCSC Update." *Ohio UFO Notebook* (January, 1994): 34.

___. "Description of an Aerial Anomaly Viewed over Columbus, Ohio." *Ohio Journal of Science* 88.2 (1988): 23.

___. "Examination of Social and Environmental Factors in Relation to Unidentified Aerial Phenomena." In *American Association for the Advancement of Science Abstracts of Papers 153rd National Meeting* (Chicago, IL, February 14-18, 1987): 93.

___. "Fear and ambiguity in Massachusetts" *International UFO Reporter* (July/August, 1988): 14-17.

___. "Informants." *Ohio UFO Notebook* (January, 1994): 24.

___. "Interview with Budd Hopkins." *Ohio UFO Notebook* (January, 1994): 23.

___. "Interview with an Informant." *Ohio UFO Notebook* (July, 1993): 19-23.

___. "Investigation of a Sound Heard over a Wide Area." *Ohio Journal of Science* 87.2 (1987): 11.

___. "Is MORA under Surveillance?" *Ohio UFO Notebook* (July, 1993): 32-34.

___. "More Cattle Mutilation Information." *Ohio UFO Notebook* (January, 1994): 35.

___. "Observation of an Alien Figure." *International UFO Reporter* (January/February, 1987): 20-25.

___. "Ohio UFOlogists." *Ohio UFO Notebook* (January, 1994): 27.

___. *Ohio UFOs (and Many Others)*. Columbus, OH: Greyden Press, 1997.

___. "Ohioans in Aerospace Exploration." *Ohio UFO Notebook* (January, 1994): 31.

___. "Photogrammetric Analysis of a Photograph of an Aerial Anomaly." In *American Association for the Advancement of Science Abstracts of Papers 154th National Meeting* (Boston, MA, February 11-15, 1988): 86.

___. "A Power Failure." *Ohio UFO Notebook* (January, 1994): 34.

___. "Rectangular UFOs." *Ohio UFO Notebook* 12 (1996): 14-18.

___. "Scientists should look closely at the Big Bang, 1973's great wave of UFOs," *MUFON UFO Journal* (March, 2011): 6-7.

___. "SR-71 explanation for the Big Bang of 1973 poses some thorny problems," *MUFON UFO Journal* (May, 2011): 8-9.

___. "Survey of Unidentified Aerial Phenomenon Reports in Delaware County, Ohio." *Ohio Journal of Science* 87.1 (1987): 24-26.

___. "The Ohio UFO Crash Connection and Other Stories." *Ohio UFO Notebook* (Summer, 1994): 19-20.

___. "Tracking Traces." *MUFON UFO Journal* (September, 1991): 8-9.

___. "UFO Activity over Ohio." *MUFON UFO Journal* (May, 1986): 4-5.

___. "UFO Reports from the North Columbus Area, Report 1." *Ohio UFO Notebook* (July, 1993): 24.

___. "UFO Reports from the North Columbus Area, Report 2." *Ohio UFO Notebook* (July, 1993): 24-25.

___. *UFOs and the Millennium*. Columbus, OH: Greyden Press, 1999.

___. "Wright Patterson Air Force Base." *Ohio UFO Notebook* 6 and 7 (July, 1993): 35-40.

Scott, Irena and Pete Hartinger. "Defense Construction and Supply Center (DCSC)." *Ohio UFO Notebook* (July, 1993): 27-29.

Scott, Irena and William Jones. "Aircraft Missing, South Dakota, Summer 1957." *Ohio UFO Notebook* 13 (1997): 10-11.

___. "Bruce Ashcroft." *Ohio UFO Notebook* 10 (1995): 2-4.

___. "The Little Green Men of Wright-Patt." *Ohio UFO Notebook* 10 (1995): 1-2.

___. "The Ohio UFO Crash Connection and Other Stories." *Ohio UFO Notebook* (Summer, 1994): 19-20.

___. "An Original Crash Story Remembered." *Ohio UFO Notebook* 9 (1995): 1-6.

___. "Roswell, the B-29 and the FUGO Balloons." *Ohio UFO Notebook* 6 and 7 (July, 1993): 30.

___. "Telephone Conversation with Len Stringfield." *Ohio UFO Notebook* (Summer, 1994): 31.

___. "UFO Sighted over Missile Base in Southern Indiana." *MUFON UFO Journal* (December, 1999): 10-11

___. "Wright-Patterson Air Force Base Historian Investigates the Roswell, New Mexico Flying Saucer Crash Story." *Ohio UFO Notebook* 9 (1995): 1-3.

Shawcross, Tim. *The Roswell Files*. Osceola, FL: Motorbooks International, 1997.

Sider, Jean. "Results and Reasons for the Roswell Crash." *Ohio UFO Notebook* (1995): 7-11.

Sider, Jean and Irena Scott. "French Flap Goes Largely Unnoticed." *MUFON UFO Journal* (May, 1992): 6-7.

___. "Roswell and Its Possible Consequences on American Policy." *MUFON UFO Journal* (December, 1992): 10-11.

Simmons, C. W., C.T. Greenidge, C.M. Craighead and others. "Second Progress Report Covering the Period September 1 to October 21, 1949 on Research and Development on Titanium Alloys Contract No. 33 (038)-3736." Columbus, OH: Battelle Memorial Institute, 1949.

Spearing, Robert. "New witness surfaces in Pantex Plant case." *MUFON UFO Journal* (December 2016): 12-15.

Story, Ronald D. *The Encyclopedia of UFOs*. Garden City, NY: Doubleday, 1980.

Stringfield, Leonard H. *Situation Red. The UFO Siege!* Garden City, NY: Doubleday, 1977.

Sunlite. "Confessions of a sinister, stalking, lying Skeptic!" http://home.comcast.net/~tprinty/UFO/SUNlite1_4.pdf

Swords, Michael D. "The Portage County (Ravenna), Ohio, Police Car Chase, April 17, 1966." Historical Document Series No. 4. Chicago: The J. Allen Hynek Center for UFO Studies, October, 1992.

___. Swords, Michael D. "Project Sign and the Estimate of the Situation," *Journal of UFO Studies, New Series*, Vol. 7, (2000): 27-64.

Tester, Joseph. "Efidence shows SR-71 Blackbird may have caused the Big Bang of 1973." *MUFON UFO Journal* (April, 2011): 4-5.

"Technical Report No. F-TR-2274-IA Unidentified Aerial Objects Project 'Sign' AMC Wright-Patterson Air Force Base. (B1 UFO 1947)." Wright-Patterson Air Force Base, OH: Air Mobility Command, 1947.

Thompson, Richard. *Alien Identities: Ancient Insights into Modern UFO Phenomena*. Alachua, FL: Govardhan Hill Publishing, 1995.

"Tritium Consolidation Comparison Study: Risk Analysis, DOE/DP/00248-H1." Wright-Patterson Air Force Base, OH: December 1992.

UFO Cover-Up?: Live! By Barry Taff and Tracy Tormé. Dir. Martin Pasetta. Host Mick Farrell. LBS and Seligman Productions. KTLA, Los Angeles. October 14, 1988.

"UFOs A to Z: Cooke, Charles, Lt. Col." *UFOS at Close Sight.* November 17, 2010. <http://wiki.razing.net/ufologie.net/htm/c.htm#cooke>.

Vallée, Jacques. *Forbidden Science.* Berkeley, CA: North Atlantic Books, 1992.

Von Keviczky, Colman. "The 1973 UFO Invasion, Parts I-IV." *Official UFO* (Collector's Edition) Fall, 1976: 10-20.

Webb, Walter, *Encounter at Buff Ledge,* Chicago, Il: CUFOS, 1994.

Weitzel, William B. "The Portage County Sighting." *National Investigations Committee on Aerial Phenomena (NICAP) Report.* Washington, DC: NICAP, April 8, 1967.

Wilkins, Harold. *Flying Saucers on the Attack.* New York: Ace, 1954.

Young, Kenny. "The Lebanon Correctional Institute, April 8, 1993." *Ohio UFO Notebook* 12 (1996): 27-28.

___. "The Monsanto Research Complex and the 'Seeding' of America." *Ohio UFO Notebook* 15 (1997): 9-12.

___. "The Wrong Liberty, Ohio—How Ohio Police React to UFO Incidents." *Ohio UFO Notebook* 13 (1997): 1-8.

Zeidman, Jennie. *Helicopter-UFO Encounter over Ohio.* Evanston, IL: Center for UFO Studies, 1979.

WPAFB. "National Air And Space Intelligence Center History." http://www.wpafb.af.mil/library/factsheets/factsheet.asp?id=21928

___. "I Remember Blue Book." *International UFO Reporter* (March/April, 1991): 7-23.

___. "Internal Lighting." *International UFO Reporter* (July/August, 1988): 21.

___. "Investigating UFOs—Lessons from a Teacher and Mentor." *Ohio UFO Notebook* 21 (Summer, 2000): 1-7.

___. "J. Allen Hynek—A 'Rocket Man.'" *Ohio UFO Notebook* (Summer, 1999): 2-5.

Notes

(Endnotes)

1   William Jones, email to the author, December 10, 2010.

2   Walter Andrus and Irena Scott, eds, *The Fiftieth Anniversary of UFOlogy*.

3   Walter Andrus and Irena Scott, eds, *The Fiftieth Anniversary of UFOlogy*.

4   These individuals included Air Force intelligence officers Lieutenant Frank Brown and Captain William Davidson.

5   Julia Shuster, interview with the author, March 9, 2012.

6   The results of research by Donald R. Schmitt and Kevin D. Randle ("Roswell and the Flying Wing," in *International UFO Reporter*) and of my own research at WPAFB, support the idea that the UFOs Arnold saw cannot be explained by any known airplanes from any country.

Using resources at WPAFB, I also investigated foreign aircraft and supersonic planes. The Germans had jet aircraft before the US and some of their planes—such as the Messerschmitt, the Lippisch and the Horten Brothers' Ho 229—had a flying wing design. There is limited evidence that a German aircraft broke the sound barrier before US planes did so, but this evidence does not extend beyond newspaper accounts. In addition, there's no evidence that nine flying wing airplanes from any country were present at the time and place of Arnold's sighting.

7   Investigators with little knowledge of Roswell have also noted an apparent change in the behavior of government representatives after Arnold's sighting. See Harold Wilkins, *Flying Saucers on the Attack*; Edward Ruppelt, *The Report on Unidentified Flying Objects*; Donald Keyhoe, *The Flying Saucers Are Real*; and David Jacobs, *UFOs and Abductions: Challenging the Borders of Knowledge.*

8   Dahl's colleague Crisman may have been an intelligence agent. See Irena Scott, "Crisman, Military Intelligence and Roswell," in *Ohio UFO Notebook.*

9   See Bruce Maccabee's analysis in Walter Andrus and Irena Scott, eds., *The Fiftieth Anniversary of UFOlogy.*

10   International UFO Museum and Research Center, Roswell, New Mexico, archives.

11   Walter Andrus and Irena Scott, eds, *The Fiftieth Anniversary of UFOlogy.*

12   Anonymous, interview with the author, June 4, 1993.

13   Anonymous, interview with the author, June 4, 1993.

14   Stringfield was publisher of the newsletter, "ORBIT"; and was a board member of MUFON. See Irena Scott, "Ohio UFOlogists," in *Ohio UFO Notebook.*

15   William E. Jones, "Neil Armstrong and Len Stringfield," from an article that first appeared in the July/August 1994 issue of the Roundtown UFO Society Newsletter, P.O. Box 52, Circleville, Ohio 43113.

16   Anonymous, interview with the author, July 3, 1997.

17   Hynek was involved in all aspects of UFO study and was scientific adviser to UFO studies undertaken by the U.S. Air Force under three consecutive names: Project Sign (1947-1949), Project Grudge (1949-1952) and Project Blue Book (1952-1969). He worked on these projects at Battelle, WPAFB and Ohio State University. He founded the concept of scientific analysis of UFO evidence.

His credentials as a scientist are impeccable. He received his Ph.D. in astrophysics from Yerkes Observatory. As an astronomer with the Smithsonian Astrophysical Observatory, he was responsible for tracking the earth's first artificial satellite, Sputnik. At Ohio State University, he was Professor of Astronomy, Director of McMillin Observatory and Assistant Dean of the Graduate School. At Johns Hopkins Applied Physics Laboratory, he helped to develop the US Navy's radio proximity fuse.

He was Chairman of the Northwestern University Astronomy Department, Director of its Lindheimer Astronomical Research Center and Visiting Lecturer at Harvard University. He conducted pioneering work on image orthicon astronomy, which the National Science Foundation proposed as the most significant astronomical advance since photography and on rocket research for such projects as the V-2, where he was considered one of the nation's leading rocket researchers.

As an author, he wrote an astronomy textbook and his articles appeared in numerous periodicals, including an astronomy column for *Science Digest* and a column called "Scanning the Skies" for the *Columbus Dispatch*. He wrote five enormously successful books and many articles published in popular magazines. He went against the establishment and founded the Center for UFO Studies (CUFOS). In his *The UFO Experience: A Scientific Inquiry*, he famously presented three classes of "close encounters." Director Stephen Spielberg used *Close Encounters of the Third Kind* as the title of his film about UFOs.

18   Kevin Randle, *The UFO Dossier: 100 Years of Government Secrets, Conspiracies and Cover-Ups*, 228.

19   Anonymous, interview with the author, June 4, 1993.

20   Maccabee, who is listed in *Who's Who in Technology Today* and in *American Men and Women of Science*, has worked on optical data processing, lasers and the Ballistic Missile Defense (BMD).

21   Dan Brown, *The Lost Symbol*.

22   Linda Wallace, email to the author, September 26, 2009 and subsequent interviews.

23   Linda Wallace, email to the author, October 5, 2009.

24   Anonymous, interview with the author, January 17, 2013.

25   See the December 2016 MUFON, UFO JOURNAL.

26   Information in this chapter about this incident comes from the following sources: Michael D. Swords, "The Portage County (Ravenna), Ohio, Police Car Chase, April 17, 1966," in Historical Document Series No. 4, which contains the original case reports, notes, documentation and newspaper clippings; William B. Weitzel, "The Portage County Sighting," in *National Investigations Committee on Aerial Phenomena (NICAP) Report*; William E. Jones and Irena Scott, "The Spaur Case—Reporting a UFO Can be Hazardous to Your Health," in *Ohio UFO Notebook*; Ronald Story, *The Encyclopedia Of UFOs*; and Jerome Clark, *The UFO Book*.

27   DeSimone sent me additional material about sightings in that area.

28   The material in this section is from Diana DeSimone's and Raymond Fowler's material, which DeSimone sent to me.

29   Leo Sprinkle, letter to the author, January 9, 1985.

30   Irena Scott, "A Photograph and its aftermath" *International UFO Reporter* (Septeber/October, 1990): 12-14.

31 Scott, Irena and Phyllis Budinger, MUFON of Ohio Newsletter, "Uncommon Commonalities: A Personal Experience Comparison to Buff Ledge and Other Events," July, 2016, p. 6-9.

32 In the 1990s I viewed the inside of the north prison wall from the high-rise Rhodes Tower in downtown Columbus. I could, indeed, see a large darkened area, but now that the prison has been destroyed, there's no way to determine if this was a carbon-like streak such as that reported by H. White.

33 Budd Hopkins, interview with Bill Jones and the author at the Triad Conference in Indianapolis, November 20, 1993.

34 Sam's father later gave UFO researchers some information about his military experience as background, but he did not want this information published.

35 http://www.thedailybeast.com/articles/2015/08/12/the-spy-satellite-secrets-in-hillary-s-emails.html

36 I recall seeing at least three pictures—probably two pictures from one mission and one from another.

37 See my "Investigation of a Sound Heard over a Wide Area." Ohio Journal of Science 87.2 (1987): 11.

38 See my description and references in UFOs and the Millennium. Columbus, OH: Greyden Press, 1999.

39 Described in numerous newspaper articles, such as The (St Mary's) Evening Leader, "Big Blast, UFO's Shake People Over Wide Area," October 12, 1973.

40 See MUFON Report 79592 (The great UFO wave of 1973 for additional references

41 https://ufomg.com/2016/10/04/ufo-sighting-in-lewis-center-ohio-on-1973-10-11-210100-loud-boom/

42 See piece by Joseph Tester in 2011 MUFON, UFO JOURNAL

43 See my write-ups about the Big Bang in two 2011 MUFON, UFO JOURNAL.

44 See Jennie Zeidman, Helicopter-UFO Encounter over Ohio; and Irena Scott, "A Power Failure," in Ohio UFO Notebook.

45 Robert Dixon, interview with the author, August 7, 1993.

46 Robert Dixon and Jerry Ehman, email to the author, May 21, 2007.

47 Robert Dixon, email to the author, December 10, 2010.

48 Rutledge's research could also answer the question of whether UFOlogy is a real science. Because the phenomena being studied is not under human control, controlled experimentation, standard in science, is difficult. Thus, as discussed in Jacobs's UFOs and Abductions: Challenging the Borders of Knowledge, some claim UFOlogy is not a true science. For example, sociobiologist Edward O. Wilson, Ph.D., has noted that UFOlogy lacks both repeatability and measurement. However, in Rutledge's data, there is real-time repeatability and measurement.

49 Harley Rutledge, letter to the author, May 17, 1986.

50 J. Allen Hynek, letter to the author, February 4, 1986.

51 Budd Hopkins, interview with Jennie Zeidman and the author, October 27, 1985.

52 James Diuguid (of the Formulation Laboratory of the Ohio Department of Agriculture), letter to the author, December 20, 1984.

53   Bryan Thompson, interview with author, September 18, 1990.

54   See Irena Scott, "Survey of Unidentified Aerial Phenomenon Reports in Delaware County, Ohio," in *Ohio Journal of Science* and "UFO Activity over Ohio," in *MUFON UFO Journal*.

55   The information about these sightings was provided by Beverly Trout, MUFON State Director for Iowa and was prepared by the Actaeon Group. See William Jones and Irena Scott, "Laurie, Missouri," in *Ohio UFO Notebook*.

56   The first reported livestock mutilation might have been "Skippy," a horse found in Colorado in 1967.

57   Kenneth Ring, letter to the author, February 23, 1989.

58   To protect the identities of informants, certain aspects of informant information have been changed here.

59   Beverly Trout, email to the author, August 20, 2011.

60   Stanton Friedman, email to the author, September 16, 2011.

61   UFOlogists and others generally accept the idea that Roswell crash debris was shipped to WPAFB. Anthony Bragalia notes this theory is supported by a verified FBI memo from Special Agent Percy Wyly; the memo suggests WPAFB was the base to which the Roswell debris was flown. See Anthony Bragalia, "Roswell Metal Scientist: The Curious Dr. Cross," in *The UFO Iconoclast(s)*.

62   Scott and Jones, "The Ohio UFO Crash Connection and Other Stories." *Ohio UFO Notebook* (Summer, 1994): 19-20.

63   Reddit UFOs/CaerBannog. "Kevin Randle Distances Himself from Schmitt, Carey, Bragalia & Dew's "Roswell Slides." https://www.reddit.com/r/UFOs/comments/2xntee/kevin_randle_distances_himself_from_schmitt_carey/

64   LIFE_Magazine_Trent_Photoshoot_1950 - Roswell Proof . "1950 LIFE Magazine Trent UFO photoshoot." http://www.roswellproof.com/LIFE_Magazine_Trent_Photoshoot_1950.html

65   These discussions, conducted via telephone and email between 2009 and 2011, include email messages dated April 15, 2009.

66   Anthony Bragalia, email to the author, July 5, 2010.

67   Anthony Bragalia, "Roswell Alcoholics: The Alien Anguish."

68   This government-funded scientific research occurred under ventures such as Project Sign, Project Grudge and Project Blue Book. (The American government had been studying UFOs even before the Roswell crash and it is known that authorities initially called UFOs "unidentified aerial objects." The names of these pre-Roswell research undertakings are unknown, however.) A fourth endeavor was called Project Stork. Subsequently the government used two-word names for these projects, such as White Stork and Have Stork. An informant told me that yet another UFO project was called something like Gold Eagle. Some information from Stork, White Stork, Have Stork, et al., supported the findings of Projects Sign, Grudge and Blue Book and some contradicted these findings.

69   According to archived records of the former UFO study group National Investigations Committee on Aerial Phenomena (NICAP), on December 12, 1952, Cross and Project Blue Book were visited by H. Marshall Chadwell, Ph.D. (head of the CIA's Office of Special Investigations), Howard Percy Robertson (of the Robertson Panel) and Frederick C. Durant, Ph.D. (a missile expert and Robertson Panel member).

70   This information comes from a list of Project Blue Book UFOs that have never been identified. Don Berliner of the Fund for UFO Research posted this list on the Internet for UFO research.

71   I also searched for evidence that Cross had published research about nitinol and I found none. Cross's co-authors in work on titanium (other than Simmons, Greenidge, Craighead) included L. C. Page, J. W. Freemen, L. W. Hodge, J. A. VanEcho and C. H. Lorig. I also looked for information about the authors of the "Second Progress Report": Simmons, Greenidge, Craighead and the others. I found no articles by Greenidge or Simmons. Some of VanEcho's research included work with "superalloys," also called high-performance alloys. Cross, Craighead, Eastwood, Hodge and Lorig had worked with boron.

72   Jennie Zeidman, interview with the author, September 29, 2009.

73   In addition, there is no proof Cross knew that physical evidence of UFO debris existed. But even if he did not, the fact that he was a metallurgist studying UFO phenomena under a government contract suggests that someone at Battelle or WPAFB may have had knowledge of UFO debris. If the individual who was assigning scientists to the UFO project was aware that UFO debris was involved, this individual would probably have appointed researchers with credentials appropriate to the study.

74   Anonymous interview with a Battelle worker the author, September 24, 2009.

75   They likely included investigations of Soviet inventions, Soviet metallurgy and Soviet aerospace development. Some Stork projects in the 1950s focused on Soviet and Chinese technology. One Battelle employee told me that Stork had originally been housed at the National Electric Coil Company across the Olentangy River from Battelle. It was highly secured then and its relocation to Battelle included flashing patrol cars and secured containers. Later it was housed on the fourth floor of Battelle Building 10. An important early project was to design a system using 5" x 8" cards to index technical information (prior to computers). Only later was Stork identified with the UFO projects.

76   Jennie Zeidman, interview with the author, September 29, 2009 and September 30, 2016; and October 6, 2016, e-mail message.

77   Bill Jones, interview with the author, June 9, 2011.

78   Information about Simpson was provided to me by a Battelle employee who knew him.

79   Co-authorship by Simpson with Cross, Center, Craighead, or Eastwood would link Simpson to government UFO studies, but I found no such co-authored papers

80   Anthony Bragalia, email to the author, July 5, 2010.

81   Have Any Materials Been Recovered from ETs/UFOs? (http://rigorousintuition.ca/board2/viewtopic.php?t=28942&p=352146)

82   WPAFB. "National Air And Space Intelligence Center History." http://www.wpafb.af.mil/library/factsheets/factsheet.asp?id=21928

83   Because some people interviewed are currently employed by Battelle or have only recently retired, I haven't divulged information herein that might identify some informants.

84   During my communications with Jennie Zeidman, she noted that the original mission of Stork was to ascertain the capability of the Soviet Union to engage in technological warfare. Thus, the Stork projects were not necessarily tied to Battelle UFO work.

85   In the 1950s and 1960s Battelle was under a long-term Air Force contract to evaluate Soviet and Chinese aerospace technologies in conjunction with the ATIC.

86   This information suggests that in addition to nitinol and titanium, boron was an element of interest in Battelle's metal studies during the period of the studies.

87   Although either Battelle or Hynek used it once, the "special report" designation was not otherwise used again by the Air Force until *SR-14*.

88   William Jones, email to the author, July 12, 2010.

89   Panel members included scientists and military personnel who were skeptical of UFO reports such as: physicist, radar expert and later Nobel Prize winner Luis Alvarez, Ph.D.;

missile expert Frederick C. Durant, Ph.D.; Brookhaven National Laboratories nuclear physicist Samuel A. Goudsmit, Ph.D.; astrophysicist, radar expert and deputy director of the Johns Hopkins University's Operations Research Office Thornton Page, Ph.D.; physicist Lloyd Berkner, Ph.D.; and Hynek.

90   At the July 1, 1989, annual MUFON Symposium in Las Vegas, Nevada, William Moore, in his talk "The Status of the UFO Situation in 1989," described the campaign to discredit Bennewitz.

91   A verified document is one that either has been issued by a known and acknowledged source or has been authenticated by such a source.

92   Members of the board are said to have included the following: Vannevar Bush, Ph.D., president of Washington's Carnegie Institute; Rear Admiral Roscoe H. Hillenkoetter, the first CIA director; James Forrestal, Secretary of the Navy and the first Secretary of Defense; General Nathan Twining, Air Force Chief of Staff, Chairman of the Joint Chiefs of Staff and head of Air Materiel Command at WPAFB; General Hoyt Vandenberg, Air Force Chief of Staff who directed the Central Intelligence Group; General Robert M. Montague, commander of Fort Bliss who headed the nuclear Armed Forces Special Weapons Center; Rear Admiral Sidney Souers, first director of the Central Intelligence Group and first executive secretary of the National Security Council; Gordon Gray, Secretary of the Army and intelligence and national security expert; Donald Menzel, Ph.D., Harvard astronomer and cryptologist; Detlev Bronk, Ph.D., who chaired the National Academy of Sciences; and Lloyd Berkner, Ph.D., executive secretary of the Joint Research and Development Board.

93   In 1978 some Canadian documents from 1950 and 1951 appeared; these mentioned a secret US government UFO study group operating via the Pentagon's Research and Development Board and headed by Vannevar Bush, Ph.D.

94   I interviewed Stanton Friedman on September 17, 1994, on the general subject of government cover-ups. He showed me numerous documents, such as ones classified as top-secret in which one could read only a few words because the rest of the information had been blacked (or whited) out. He has a large collection of such documents, released from several agencies, including pre-1980 code word National Security Agency (NSA) UFO documents and CIA UFO documents. Such documents provide physical evidence of government cover-up.

95   Because this was the base newspaper, Collins's reply suggested that he either worked there or had on-base connections.

96   Collins may have been referring to a document Doty gave to Howe. This document detailed UFO crashes and recoveries, including one in which an alien was supposedly alive and in the care of the US government at Los Alamos Laboratory until it died.

97   Building 653 is the Materials Laboratory and 640 is the Air Force Graduate School of Engineering.

98   A meteorite was reported in New Mexico circa November 1947. Lincoln LaPaz, Ph.D. and *Life* photographer Allen Grant, who had just photographed the flight of the Spruce Goose, were among the searchers, but this meteorite was never found.

99   At Battelle, however, a different situation might have existed: some people likely knew through the grapevine that work on UFOs was going on there and employees would thus have been more attuned to the significance of the studies.

100 Robert Orndoff, email to the author, September 26, 2009 and additional interviews.

101 Ed Balint, email to the author, August 5, 2010 and telephone conversation with the author, August 5, 2010.

102 Some informants who worked at WPAFB have said it was routine to show a strange material to scientists and to allow them to experiment on it and make reports of its properties.

103 The reality of UFOs was refuted by the *Condon Report's* summary, but it was supported by the report's data.

104 One compilation of alien-encounter reports focuses on cases that took place before the UFO concept became widespread. Compiled by Albert Rosales, the "1935-1939 Humanoid Sighting Reports" mentions a high proportion of "glowing" entities. Current notions of what aliens look like, such as the "grey" or "reptilian" stereotype, would not have influenced the 1930s reports and this fact suggests that some of today's reports may be biased.

105 Quantum mechanics involve such concepts as observer-dependent phenomena, the observer-created universe, Schrödinger's equation, wormholes, faster-than-light signaling and questioning the idea of cause and effect.

106 Moreover, the chief known way for information to be transferred by faster-than-light mechanisms is through quantum interactions, such as those shown in "entangled pair" studies.

107 For example, the fundamentals of physics are based on conservation laws, such as the conservation of momentum. One might hypothesize a new fundamental law of physics: that everything is composed of a field of potential values, a quantum field, or Q-Field. Under this law, what is conserved is not actual properties, such as momentum or particles, but the quantum values of which our universe is composed. One might further propose that these quantum values to which humans are sensitive are points in a range of values and that any specific point, such as the energy of an electron, is dependant on everything else in its Q-Field (as I proposed on pages 245 through 267 of *UFOs and the Millennium*). This theory would allow one to exchange the billiard-ball concept of today's physics with the idea of a Q-Field potential. And perhaps a quantum is actually a form of gateway into a more complex physics than we understand.

108 John Carpenter, interview with the author, November 21, 1993.

109 See Irena Scott, "Description of an Aerial Anomaly Viewed over Columbus, Ohio," "Investigation of a Sound Heard over a Wide Area," and "Survey of Unidentified Aerial Phenomenon Reports in Delaware County, Ohio," all in *Ohio Journal of Science*; "Examination of Social and Environmental Factors in Relation to Unidentified Aerial Phenomena," in *American Association for the Advancement of Science Abstracts of Papers 153rd National Meeting*; and "Photogrammetric Analysis of a Photograph of an Aerial Anomaly," in *American Association for the Advancement of Science Abstracts of Papers 154th National Meeting*.

110 Walt Mitchell, letter to the author, February 18, 1988.

111 Harley Rutledge, letter to the author, June 17, 1988.

http://flyingdiskpress.blogspot.co.uk

UFOs OVER POLAND

THE LAND OF HIGH STRANGENESS

Piotr Cielebiaś

UFOs OVER ROMANIA

Fürce Hoffe auf den
Herrn P. 130. 7.

DAN D. FARCAS PH.D.

WWW.CLOTHESENCOUNTERS.CO.UK

RECOMMENDED READING
www.hauntedskies.co.uk

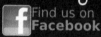

Lightning Source UK Ltd.
Milton Keynes UK
UKOW06f0931210717
305775UK00008BA/104/P